THE
FRANCISCAN SISTERS

Outlines of History and Spirituality

THE
FRANCISCAN SISTERS

Outlines of History and Spirituality

Raffaele Pazzelli, T.O.R.

Translated from the Italian by Aidan Mullaney, T.O.R.

Franciscan University Press
Franciscan University of Steubenville
Steubenville, Ohio 43952

Cover photograph is used with permission and is taken from p. 10, **Quel Bambino della Madonna di Foligno**, a commemorative book published by the monastery of Saint Ann in Foligno, on the occasion of the fifth centenary (1385-1985) of the foundation of the motherhouse of the Regular Franciscan Tertiary Sisters of Blessed Angelina. The photograph reproduces a seventeenth century portrait in the Monastery of Saint Ann of Blessed Angelina along with a representation of a contemporary of the same monastery. So many communities sprang directly or indirectly from this foundation that Angelina is regarded as the foundress of the Third Order Regular for women.[1]

[1]See Damien Isabell, O.F.M., *Workbook for Franciscan Studies*, Chicago, 1979, p. 140.

Cover design: Dan Gallio

Originally published as *Le Suore Francescane*,
©1989 Prov. Pad. F.M.C. Editrice
Grafiche Messaggero di S. Antonio

Published by:
Franciscan University Press
Franciscan University of Steubenville
Steubenville, Ohio 43952

Printed in the United States of America

Library of Congress Cataloging in Publication Data
    Pazzelli, Raffaele.
        (Suore francescane. English)
        The Franciscan Sisters: outlines of history and spirituality/by
    Raffaele Pazzelli; translated by Aidan Mullaney.
            p.   cm.
        Includes bibliographical references (p. 221-226) and index.
        ISBN 0-940535-52-1 (pbk.)
            1. Poor Clares–History. 2. Poor Clares–Spiritual life.
    I. Title.
    BX4362.P3813 1992   92-38686
        271'.973–dc20   CIP

ISBN: 0-940535-52-1

CONTENTS

Translator's Preface.. X

Foreword.. XI

Introduction to the Italian Edition........................ XV

Signs and Abbreviations.. XVII

Introduction: 1
   1. Who are the Franciscan sisters? 1
   2. Is it possible to have a history of the
       Franciscan sisters?... 3
   3. An overview 5

Chapter I: Common Life in the Twelfth and Thirteenth
Centuries 6
   1. A phenomenon characteristic of the age............ 6
   2. The beguines and the beghards 7
   3. The organization of the beguines...................... 10
   4. Penitential groups in the thirteenth century...... 11

Chapter II: Beginnings of "Religious" Life in the
Order of Penance.. 16
   1. Factors which promoted "religious" life 16
   2. Saint Elizabeth of Hungary (or of Thuringia) 18

Chapter III: The Second Half of the
Thirteenth Century 22
   1. Franciscan and non-Franciscan elements 22
   2. Further development of the female Third
       Order Regular.. 25
   3. The Rule of Nicholas IV and its problematic 27
   4. Saint Clare of Montefalco 30
   5. Was Clare of Montefalco a Franciscan
       Tertiary?... 32

Chapter IV: First Serious Conflicts at the Beginning
of the Thirteenth Century....................................... 38
   1. Official papal favor? 38
   2. The cloister.. 39

3. Further difficulties 41
4. Heterodox beguines and beghards 42
5. The defense of the Tertiary sisters.................... 44
6. The bull "Etsi Apostolicae sedis" 48

Chapter V: The First Congregations 52
1. Tendencies and federations............................. 52
2. The Elizabethan sisters.................................... 52
3. From beguine sisters to Franciscan sisters........ 54
4. The Grey Sisters (or Hospital Sisters) 55
5. The bull "Personas vacantes,"
   August 26, 1413... 56
6. Further development of the Grey Sisters 58

**Chapter VI: The Congregation of Blessed Angelina of
Montegiove** 63
1. Angelina of Montegiove 63
2. The bull "Sacrae religionis,"
   (August 19, 1428) 67
3. Evaluation of the importance of "Licet inter
   coetera" (December 9, 1428) 68
4. The appearance of Regular Tertiary friars.......... 72
5. The bull of Eugene IV "Ad apostolicae
   dignitatis," (November 15, 1431) 73
6. After the death of Blessed Angelina 74
7. The bull "Apostolicae Sedis providentia,"
   (May 2, 1440)... 75
8. Events occurring in the male Third Order
   Regular.. 78

**Chapter VII: Questions About Cloister and
Jurisdiction** 81
1. The bull "Ordinis tui," (February 5, 1447) 81
2. The bull of Pius II "Ut tollatur discursus,"
   (December 3, 1461)... 83
3. Questions concerning jurisdiction..................... 84
4. The action of Sixtus IV (1471-1484) 86
5. Solemn vows and the cloister........................... 89

**Chapter VIII: Franciscan Sisters in the Sixteenth
Century** 93
1. The Rule of Leo X, 1521 93

2. The Council of Trent and the cloister 98
3. Particular prescriptions of Pius V concerning
   the cloister.. 99
4. The question concerning jurisdiction 102

Chapter IX: Franciscan Sisters in the Seventeenth and Eighteenth Centuries 109

1. Events following the Council of Trent 109
2. Franciscan sisters in the cloister....................... 115
   a) The "Reform of Limbourg" (Holland) 116
   b) The Franciscan Sisters of the Sorrowful
      Mother, Mexico.. 117
3. The spread of charitable communities in the
   seventeenth century... 118
4. The very first of the "new congregations" 120
   a) The English Dames of Mary Ward
      (1609-1610) 121
   b) The Daughters of Saint Francis of Assisi
      (Pisa, Italy, 1611) 123
   c) The Elizabethans of Aachen, Germany
      (1623) 123
   d) The Franciscans of the Immaculate
      Conception, Sebenik (1673)........................ 124
5. The conservatory and the houses of mercy........ 125
6. The eighteenth century characteristics of the
   new institutes... 126
7. The new congregations.................................... 129
   a) The Franciscan Missionaries of Assisi,
      (formally called "del Giglio," 1702) 129
   b) The Franciscan Tertiary Sisters of
      Bressanone (1700) 130

Chapter X: The End of the Eighteenth Century, the Era of Napoleon and the "Restoration" 133

1. The Enlightenment 133
2. A typical example: The Franciscan Teaching
   Sisters of Hallein (1723)................................... 135
3. The French Revolution..................................... 136
4. Napoleon Bonaparte 138
5. The Restoration 139
6. Franciscan sisters congregations 142
7. Franciscan Elizabethans of Padua, 1828........... 144

Chapter XI: Principal Events of the Nineteenth Century 146

  1. The evolution of juridical status 146

  2. Some congregations founded in the middle of the nineteenth century 149

    a) The Franciscan Sisters of Oldenburg, Indiana (1851) 149

    b) The Poor Daughters of the Holy Stigmata of Saint Francis (The Franciscan Stigmatines, 1855) 150

    c) The Sisters of Saint Francis of Philadelphia (1855) 151

    d) The Franciscan Sisters of Allegany (1859).... 154

    e) The Franciscan Missionaries of the Immaculate Heart of Mary (called "of Egypt," 1868) 155

    f) The Franciscan Teaching Sisters of Christ the King (1869) 157

  3. The Storm in the Middle of the Century 158

  4. New congregations by subdivision 160

  5. Some more important congregations of the second half of the nineteenth century 161

    a) The Franciscan Alcantarines (1869)............. 161

    b) The Franciscan Sisters of Mary (1872)......... 164

    c) The Franciscan Missionaries of Mary (1877) 166

    d) The Franciscan Sisters of Rochester (1877) 168

    e) The Franciscan Missionaries of the Infant Jesus (1879) 170

    f) The Capuchin Sisters of the Holy Family (1885) 171

    g) The Franciscan Sisters of the Heart of Jesus (Franciscan Sisters of Malta, 1886).............. 171

Chapter XII: Further Developments in the Twentieth Century 173

  1. Evolution of legislation: the constitution *"Conditae a Christo"* 173

  2. Some congregations at the beginning of this century 176

    a) The resurgence of the Franciscan Tertiary Sisters of Blessed Angelina 176

b) The Franciscan Sisters of Christ the King
of Venice (1907) 177
c) The Daughters of Mercy of the Franciscan
Third Order (1919) 178
3. The Rule of Pius XI (1927) 179
4. Sorrowful events 181
5. Towards a new Rule 183
a) The Assisi Assemblies 1976, 1979 184
b) The meeting at Grottaferrata,
March 8-10, 1980 186
c) The Reute Draft, 1980; the Brussels Draft,
1981 189
d) Towards the General Assembly 190
6. The International Franciscan Conference (CFI),
1985 193
7. The activity of the Franciscan International
Conference, 1986-1988 196
8. Corollary: Aggregation 197

**Chapter XIII: The Spirituality of Franciscan
Sisters** 200
1. The main components of penitential
spirituality 202
2. Explanation of these concepts 203
a) The life of penance 203
b) The life of active charity 206
3. The voice of history 207
a) The life of penance 207
b) The works of mercy or active charity 208
4. Two elements in the Rules 210
5. Corollary: How penance became a characteristic
of the "Brothers and Sisters of Penance" 212

Pontifical Documents 217

Bibliography 221

Index of Persons and Places 227

TRANSLATOR'S PREFACE

Readers who are familiar with the Italian edition of *Le Suore Francescane, Lineamenti di storia e spiritualità* will note changes made in this English edition. In Chapter Eleven some typical American congregations have been added by choice of the author to take the place of some that were included in the original Italian edition. Some footnotes have been added to this and other chapters for the sake of clarity.

The Italian edition also included addresses of the various sisters' congregations which have membership in the International Franciscan Conference. The English edition omits this list. An updated list of these congregations can be obtained on request from the International Franciscan Conference, Piazza di Risorgimento n. 14, 00192 Roma, Italia.

Many persons have generously given their time and talent to assist the appearance of the English version of this work; without their help the work would not have been published. Among these persons must be included the author, Fr. Raffaele Pazzelli, T.O.R. Special thanks are due to Sister Margaret Carney, O.S.F. for her encouragement and counsel; to Fr. Thomas Edwards, T.O.R. for his expert reading and correcting the English text; I am grateful to Sister Katherine Caldwell, T.O.R., Sister Atilia Todaro, H. R., Laraine Hofmann, Sister Mary Rose Bratlien, T.O.R., for their assistance; and to Mr. Sterling Spears, Director of Franciscan University Press for his unfailing kindness and assistance. Finally, gratitude is offered to the President of Franciscan University of Steubenville, Rev. Michael Scanlan, T.O.R. for making it possible in many ways to bring this work to completion.

AIDAN MULLANEY, T.O.R.

FOREWORD

Between 1976 and 1979 members of Franciscan congregations of the Third Order Regular found themselves facing their first experience of world-wide communication as they tried to re-draft their Rule and Life document. Natural challenges arising from cultural differences, language barriers, and varied degrees of agreement about what constituted core values for such a project seemed, at times, to present insurmountable obstacles. Faced with these difficulties leaders in the various countries and regions succeeded, little by little, in identifying reasons why so many institutes who professed the same rule and claimed the same heritage found consensus so difficult. It was increasingly apparent that the lack of an historical overview of the Third Order Regular's development was a significant handicap for the participants.

Many congregations come to assemblies and consultations with clear values articulated out of their own specific history, but a variety of founding experiences spanning the centuries back to Francis and Clare had marked the development of the Third Order Regular in subtle and profound ways. Still, the story of these venerable prototypes of contemporary congregations and the spirituality they espoused were lost to us. The task of preserving an authentic line of development that spanned seven centuries was made more difficult by the absence of historical descriptions that could instruct twentieth century seekers.

Experts, consultants, and major superiors themselves offered countless hours in committees trying to trace the core values and assure the preservation of the life-line of Third Order Regular tradition in the dissemination of a new Rule. Pierre Péano, O.F.M. addressed one of these early assemblies with a presentation entitled *Sisters of the Franciscan Order, Origins, History and Constant Values.* This essay was a brief history of early Franciscan Third Order women's groups. It was circulated as part of the proceedings and published in Brazil as part of the Rule publication managed by CEFEPAL in 1983.

Another consultant, Raffaele Pazzelli, T.O.R., had lectured widely on the history and spirituality of the Third

Order Regular and finally committed his work to publication in Italy in 1982. (The Franciscan Herald Press published this book in English in 1989 with the title, *St. Francis and the Third Order*).

No sooner was this general history completed in its Italian language edition, than Pazzelli set to work to address the lack of an historical overview of the development of Third Order women's congregations. Pazzelli has accompanied the many phases of the development of the Rule text. He served as consultant to the International Franciscan Bureau during the years of the Rule Project. His knowledge of the English language had allowed him to engage in many educational conferences with a wide variety of feminine congregations. He understood well the intense work done to recover historical sources by each individual congregation. He also knew the frustration of those who recognized that each living congregation owes much to past foundations whose histories are often extraordinarily difficult to decipher.

In 1989 *The Franciscan Sisters: Outlines of History and Spirituality (Le Suore Francescane: Lineamenti di Storia e Spiritualità)* was published by Edizione Messaggero, Padova, Italy. While he was at first reluctant to attempt publication in English, Pazzelli was ultimately persuaded by the entreaties of Margaret Carney, O.S.F. and Nancy Celaschi, O.S.F. to consider such a venture. When Aidan Mullaney, T.O.R., who had served in the General Curia of the Third Order Regular with Pazzelli, offered his services to expedite the project, it was clear that the potential for success in making this important work available was assured. The consequent commitment of the Franciscan Heritage Office of the Franciscan University of Steubenville to serve as publisher and the unflagging efforts of Fr. Aidan and Sr. Katherine Caldwell to manage the publication details has provided a service to us all. They have helped to augment this edition with historical information about a number of foundations native to the United States not found in the original edition.

Readers will quickly perceive that a vast amount of historical research is reflected in Chapters I-XII. Congregations that have often wondered about such early influential women as St. Elizabeth of Hungary, and

Blessed Angelina of Montegiove (Marsciano) will find their curiosity more than satisfied with this material. Congregations struggling with the transformational questions that face us at this point in our history, will no doubt be fascinated to learn of the forms that early pre-Trent groups of Third Order Franciscan women developed. Congregations with strong traditions of cloistered or semi-cloistered life-styles will see how ecclesiastical practice and legislation created some of the norms that have had such important consequences in our life and legislation. Finally, all contemporary congregations will recognize in Chapter XII that we are also writing our page in the history of our beloved Franciscan family as we have worked to reform our Rule and re-found our congregations.

In Chapter XIII, Fr. Pazzelli offers some reflections on the spiritual principles that have emerged in the historical sources. Here he offers a glimpse of the riches of scholarly encounters of the last fifteen years that have plumbed the riches of documentation from the distant ages that form part of our modern spiritual patrimony.

Throughout the work Pazzelli demonstrates his devotion to precise documentation. The ample footnotes and bibliography will permit the willing and able to continue to follow the lines of historical research that Pazzelli shares with us.

All who have had a role in bringing this publication to birth agree that it may serve as a stimulus in other parts of the English-speaking world to encourage transmission of historical material to the International Franciscan Conference in its future efforts to serve as a clearinghouse for this kind of work. Thus, this book can serve as a cornerstone for future research and communication of our incredible story/stories. Those of us who may not be called to such formal study, will nonetheless have the exceptional satisfaction of being able to trace our own "root system" back to its origins even as we peer into the mists of the future and ask, "What will the twenty-first century bring in the way of Franciscan congregational life?"

The Franciscan Federation of the USA has facilitated the participation of many Franciscan sisters in the processes described in Chapter XII. In my service as

President, I am happy to present a word of gratitude to all who have made the book available to us, and a word of encouragement to the thousands of Franciscan Third Order women who share the English language to give this valuable work the study that it so richly deserves.

Sister Madonna Marie Cunningham, OSF
President (1991-1992)
Franciscan Federation of Brothers and
Sisters of the Third Order Regular

INTRODUCTION TO THE ITALIAN EDITION

This work of Raphael Pazzelli is the history of events and attitudes on the part of the Church and civil authorities, attitudes which down through the centuries promoted or hindered the rise and establishment of congregations of Franciscan sisters of the active life.

By the nature of things, the telling of this tale intertwines with the provisions taken by the Church at various times concerning these congregations. These provisions have directly touched every congregation in its own birth and development no matter in what country or in what period of time a particular congregation was started. One of the elements which has greatly influenced and conditioned the rise and establishment of women's congregations of active life was the Church's legislation on the cloister. The author examines this question under the aspect of Church law and under its practical consequences.

When dealing with the actions of civil governments, Pazzelli systematically sets forth what was meant and done in different periods of time, such as the Enlightenment, the French Revolution, the Napoleonic Era, the Restoration, the time of the suppression of religious orders in Italy, etc. Thus the reader is able to better understand how and why one's own congregation, or another of which the reader knows its history, had to pass through particular troubles or difficulties.

Together, with all these questions, the author traces through each epoch "short histories" of particular congregations which generally are the most typical of a determined historical period or the congregation with the largest membership.

The presentation reaches our own day by including the account of the work that resulted in the renewed Rule of the Third Order Regular of 1982 and the establishment of the International Franciscan Conference in 1985. The last chapter is dedicated to a clear exposition of the spirituality more proper to the Sisters of the Third Order Regular of Saint Francis.

The work of Fr. Pazzelli is a further contribution to the knowledge of religious life of women that has flourished in the mainstream of Franciscan spirituality. For this we are grateful to the author and we recommend this volume not only to our Franciscan sisters, but to all those who are called to work together with them for the realization of the Franciscan ideal.

SISTER M. ELETTA BERTOLINI
President
Movimento Religiose Francescane
(Franciscan Sisters Movement, Italy)

SIGNS AND ABBREVIATIONS

AFH   *Archivium Franciscanum Historicum*, Quaracchi, 1908, ff.

AnP   *Anonymous Peruginus*

BF n.s. *Bullarium Franciscanum, Nova Serie*, Quaracchi, 1929, ff.

DIP   *Dizionario degli Istituti di perfezione*, Roma, 1975, ff.

DTC   *Dictionnaire de Théologie Catholique*, Paris, 1903-1954

EC   *Enciclopoedia Cattolica*, Citta del Vaticano, 1949-1954

LM   *Saint Bonaventure, Major Life of Saint Francis*

MEP   *Missions Etrangères de Paris*

OMN   *Omnibus of sources*, Franciscan Herald Press, Chicago, 1973

RNB   *Rule written by Saint Francis in 1221*

TOR   *Third Order Regular of Saint Francis*

1Cel   *First Life of Saint Francis* by Thomas of Celano

3Comp *Legend of the Three Companions*

INTRODUCTION

1. Who are the Franciscan sisters?

Franciscan sisters are religious women belonging to congregations or institutes of active life. They are also called the Sisters of the Third Order Regular because most of them follow the Rule of the Third Order Regular of Saint Francis. They share ideally and spiritually in the charism of Saint Francis, whether or not they are aggregated to one of the male Franciscan families (the three families of the First Order–the Friars Minor, the Capuchins, the Conventuals, and the Third Order Regular).

The history of the Third Order Regular, both male and female branches, shows that the Rule has had its own development. It has not been something static like the Rule of the First Order, the Friars Minor, (the second Rule written by Saint Francis in 1223) or even similar to the Rule of the Second Order, the Poor Clares (the Rule of Saint Clare in 1253 or the Rule of Urban IV in 1263).

The Franciscan Tertiary movement in the lifetime of Saint Francis was known as the "Order of the Penitents" and at the end of that same thirteenth century, the "Third Order of Saint Francis." The first Rule of the Tertiaries was the so-called *Memoriale Propositi*, the Memorial of 1221 that was to last until 1289 when it was reformulated, approved and promulgated by Pope Nicholas IV. Hence, appropriately it was called the Rule of Nicholas IV.

The approval of the Rule of 1289 occurred around the period of time the Order of the Penitents existed with two forms or two branches which will gradually become more and more distinct from one another. The first branch of the Penitents was composed of those who followed the spiritual direction of Francis while they remained in the world. For the most part, they married and worked for their living in various occupations. The second branch was composed of those who had begun to live community life, more or less perfectly, and more or less totally. Immediately after the Rule of Nicholas IV, the Order of Penitents began to call themselves, or were called, the Third Order of Saint Francis. A short time later, these two branches were openly called the Third Order Secular and the Third Order Regular respectively.

In the formula of profession both branches, while clearly distinguished from one another, promised to follow the Rule of the Lord Pope Nicholas IV. However, in 1521 Pope Leo X promulgated a new Rule in a bull explicitly declaring that it was not fitting that persons living in community with vows of religion should follow a Rule intended principally for persons living in the world who were for the most part married. This Rule, which was called after him the Rule of Leo X, was intended to assist congregations of both men and women.

The Rule of Leo X remained in force until 1927 when Pius XI approved and published a new Rule that was to be accepted by all active congregations of men and of women who followed the inspiration of Saint Francis. This Rule was written especially from a viewpoint of being an updating and bringing it into conformity with the revised code of canon law which had been published ten years earlier (in 1917). The Rule of Pius XI directed all Franciscan Congregations until 1982.

During the last half century, and especially from 1972 to 1982, a great amount of work has been done by a vast number of congregations, to prepare a spiritual document or Rule which would be more representative of our Franciscan charism. Soon this work acquired its own history and was synthesized and published by this author in his commentary on the new Rule of 1982.[1]

We said above that the Rule of the Third Order Regular is followed by almost all Franciscan sisters who for this reason are also called Sisters of the Third Order Regular. There are a very few congregations (in Italy there are three) which follow the Rule of Saint Clare, that is, the Rule of the Second Franciscan Order instead of the Rule of the Third Order Regular. According to our judgment, this is an anomaly because the Rule of the Second Order foresees and requires papal cloister and contemplative life. These few congregations of Franciscan sisters cannot be said to belong to the Third Order Regular.

---

[1] This commentary was presented as "A historical introduction" in our "Commento alla Regola e vita dei fratelli e delle sorelle del Terzo ordine regolare di san Francisco," Messaggero, Padova, 1983, pp. 41-53. It will be presented here in Chapter Twelve, p. 173.

After the reformulation of the new Rule and its approval by John Paul II, Franciscan sisters continued their work together to create an International Franciscan Council. While respecting the complete autonomy of each individual congregation, this council should be a means of coordinating and sharing information and a means of extending mutual help to all congregations which follow the "Rule and life of the brothers and sisters of the Third Order Regular of Saint Francis." The establishment of this International Franciscan Council took place during the Second International Franciscan General Assembly which was held in Assisi from October 19th to 26th, 1985.[2]

Therefore, the Franciscan sisters are those in active congregations of women "who proclaim that they are Franciscan," except those who belong to the Second Order or the Poor Clares.[3] The Poor Clares, contemplatives with strict cloister, are more properly called "Franciscan nuns."[4]

2. Is it possible to have a history of the Franciscan sisters?

A. We do not believe that it is possible to talk about a *specific and particularized* history of Franciscan sisters for the reasons given by various authors.[5] In fact:

1) Today congregations of Franciscan sisters number about 400.[6] Each congregation has its own history from its beginning to the present day. The histories of these congregations differ from one another because of the particular circumstances in which each congregation arose and flourished, and according to the country and times in which the congregation began.

2) It is good for us to recall here that male and female congregations in the Franciscan Third Order

---

[2]The First General Assembly took place in 1985. For further information on this assembly see p. 191 *ff* of this present work.

[3]See Pierre Péano, OFM, *LeReligiose francescane, Origini, storia e valori costanti*, Movimento francesco, Roma, 1983, p.3.

[4]See E. Frascadore - G. Odoardi, *Francescane monache*, in DIP, IV col. 174.

[5]See Pierre Péano, OFM, *LeReligiose francescane, Origini, storia e valori costanti*, Movimento francescano, Roma, 1983, p. 3-4.

[6]A first attempt to formulate a listing was presented in our *Regola e Vita*, cited above, pp. 97-140.

Regular movement arose and developed independently from each other within national, and at times regional boundaries according to the political and geographic composition of the area at the time each congregation began. Hence, the "history" of each congregation differs from the other.

B. Still, it is possible to have a history of Franciscan sisters *in a general sense.* We can examine those components which in the course of centuries have been identified as common characteristics. In this way we can single out such common elements as:

1) the attitudes of the Church toward community life in particular historical periods;

2) requirements of the Church such as provisions regarding the cloister;

3) the Rules which have been given by the Church, as we have mentioned.

C. The same concepts can be applied to the spirituality of the Franciscan sisters:

1) There are elements common to all congregations

a) first of all core values or elements common to the Franciscan movement;

b) there is a common and permanent characteristic of the congregations of the Franciscan Third Order, at least in comparison with the Second Order; i.e, the Franciscan Tertiaries' belief in personal sanctification through the practice of works of charity;

2) A spirituality can be present in some particular way in every congregation or in groups or families of congregations. This quality is expressed in the Constitutions which are proper to each congregation. Most early congregations, especially the very few that have come down to our own time with an almost uninterrupted continuity from the *Penitents of blessed Francis,* have more easily preserved the Franciscan element of "penance" through the centuries. These congregations have done this even if at times the element of "penance" was obscured for a certain time or even if the congregations remained unclear about its meaning for a certain period of time.

These *common elements* or essential policies will form the goal of our study. These common elements will give us an outline according to which all congregations which arose during that particular period of time had to conform themselves. The predominant characteristic of a given period has impressed a particular quality on all congregations which arose during that time. For example, the monastic cloister was imposed absolutely by the Council of Trent, 1545-1563. This fact marked the Franciscan sisters of that time with a clear direction towards "cloister." The imposition of cloister made Tertiary congregations, which were in themselves directed towards the active life, assume an obligation to observe the monastic cloister and to live completely independently from one another. It was as if the Franciscan sisters, in the meaning we have discussed above, became nuns of the cloister with the Rule of the Third Order.

3. An overview

In our study we hope to:

A. Identify a common history of the Franciscan sisters, bringing to light a general history or outline in which all the congregations, started in a particular period of history, find a common development. We shall look for those attitudes of the Church, as well as those of civil governments, which created a particularized climate that in turn exercised a marked influence on the start and the life development of congregations of Franciscan sisters in that particular period of time. We shall attempt to do this from the time of Saint Francis to the present.

B. Identify the more common elements of Franciscan spirituality which are found in the movement of the Third Order in contrast with other "currents" of Franciscan spirituality.

CHAPTER I

COMMON LIFE IN THE TWELFTH AND THIRTEENTH CENTURIES

1. A phenomenon characteristic of the age

Almost unanimously historians recall, among those signs characteristic of the twelfth and thirteenth centuries, a remarkable tendency towards associative life. It is this element that we must keep before our eyes for the relationship it bears to the Order of Penance. In the second half of the thirteenth century this phenomenon of common life already has a predominantly Franciscan character. It will become, as we shall see, one of the primary sources leading to the emergence of the Franciscan sisters.

"From the end of the twelfth century, groups of faithful had tried to form confraternities and associations based on mutual help, common life, and collective work. Their purpose was sometimes religious and sometimes economic: thus one could dedicate oneself more completely to God and/or make better provision for one's life support."[1] A classic example of this tendency is the movement or association of the Humiliati which arose among the wool-workers of Lombardy between 1170 and 1178.

"We should keep in mind the number of widows of the Crusaders who had died during the expeditions to the Orient. Common misfortune had brought these women to seek one another's company and friendship, creating in this way a noticeable growth of beguinages and other groups. The common life was also a means for many to defend their rights."[2]

---

[1] Raffaele Pazzelli, *Saint Francis and the Third Order*, Franciscan Herald Press, Chicago, 1989, p. 129.

[2] *Ibid*, p. 129.

2. The beguines and the beghards

The most widespread and well-known movement resulting from this tendency towards associative life was undoubtedly that of the beguines. This movement has particular significance in our history because many houses of beguines accepted at various times the Rule called the Franciscan Rule of Nicholas IV. Thus, from an historical perspective, beguines are seen as the origin of some congregations of Franciscan sisters, for example, the Franciscan Sisters of Dillingen.

The movement of the beguines, generally speaking, is a manifestation of the religious fervor which pervaded the twelfth and thirteenth centuries and gave rise to various forms of ascetical and evangelical life. Besides the beguines, other movements which could be listed among the examples of the beguine way of life are the Waldensians in southern France with their branches such as the "Poor Catholics," and the already mentioned Humiliati of Lombardy. The beguine movement was primarily made up of women: however there were some male communities, the beghards, who also were called the good men (viri boni, boni pueri, etc.) The women, *mulieres religiosae*, religious women, were brought together mostly into local and independent associations which set up a religious life quite different from the life of traditional monastic institutions.

The beguine movement, properly speaking, began and "took form in the east and south of present-day Belgium about the year 1170."[3] The initial motivation for this beginning is related to a decision to gradually suppress the "double monasteries," which were quite common among the monks beginning with the second half of the twelfth century. This decision included the suppression of the "Houses of Penance," "converserie," the places where devout women or converted women (the *mulieres piae* or *conversae*) lived in the shadow of the monasteries for men. A decision was made to deny affiliation even to "the devoted women who lived outside but served the hospitals and other institutes of mercy."[4]

---

[3]Mens, Alcantara, *Beguine e begardi*, in EC, vol. I, col. 1145.

[4]*Ibid.*, col. 1146. See the presentation of Marco Bartoli in *Francescanismo e mondo femminile nel XII secolo* in *Francesco, il*

We must remember that some of the itinerant preachers at the beginning of the twelfth century, among them Robert d'Arbrissel, +1117, had to deal with the enthusiastic movement that they themselves, perhaps unconsciously, stirred up among their followers, men and women who followed after them day and night in a form of quasi-religious life. These preachers established "some double monasteries in which women's communities were dedicated to the contemplative life under the Rule of Saint Benedict and were assisted by a men's community which was located in a small adjacent monastery."[5] When the monks discontinued these forms of community for the *piae mulieres*, these women without the support of an Institute or a monastic Rule, were forced "to form themselves into autonomous associations." From these sets of circumstances the beguine movement was born. It was not from the start due to the initiative of a founder, although we can recall famous names associated with their origins:[6] rather the beginning of the movement was due to the combined action of many circumstances. Principally these factors were religious in nature and due to the spirit of the Gregorian reform which still permeated the Church. Other tendencies were due to the influence of the eremitical movement whose penitential thrust was among the more constant and remarkable aspects of reform down through the centuries.[7] These tendencies were very much alive at the time of Saint Francis and continued right up to the close of the fourteenth century. Secondarily, there were

---

Francescanesimo e la cultura della nuova Europa, Istituto dell'Enciclopedia Italiana, Roma, 1986, pp. 167-180.

[5]See R. Mainka, *I movimenti per la chiesa povera nel XII secolo*, in AA.VV., *La povertà religiosa*, Clarentianum, Roma, 1975, p. 147.

[6]Among these must be mentioned the priest reformer Lambert of Liege who organized some communities of beguines in that city in 1170 and the Blessed Ivette di Huy from the province of Liege who established another community in the city of the same name. This community "was composed of an arrangement of cottages around a small church and a hospital. In this compound virgins and widows lived separately on one side, religious men (later called beghards,) lived on the other." A. Mens, *op. cit.*, col. 1146. These facts lead us to think that the "first beguines" did nothing more on their part than, independently of monastic direction, continue the same kind of life they had previously led in the double monastaries or in the shadow of monastic institutions.

[7]See Pazzelli, *op. cit.*, pp. 32-33.

the social and economic factors which we have already mentioned, "among them the demographic situation of the surplus number of women, increased by the vast participation by the Brabant nobility in the crusades and other military expeditions."[8]

With respect to the relationships between groups of beguines and ecclesiastical authority, we must admit that from the beginning the Church maintained an attitude of mistrust and aversion. The basis for such an attitude can be found in similar relationships between ecclesiastical authority and the semi-religious groups who followed the itinerant preachers at the beginning of the twelfth century. The Church desired that religious life, even semi-religious life, should be lived under a juridically approved Rule of life. The itinerant preachers established new orders, but under the Rule either of Saint Benedict or Saint Augustine. With the closing of the double monasteries and the appearance of the first beguinages, these new entities were considered not to be in conformity with the norms of canon law because they were living a quasi-cloistered community life without the necessary affiliation with an approved monastic order. In effect, they were living the religious life without a Rule recognized by the Church. This official position of the Church was reaffirmed by the Fourth Lateran Council of 1215. This Council forbade in canon 13 of its decrees the establishment of new religious groups or orders which had not accepted an approved Rule. But in 1216 while staying at Perugia, Cardinal Jacques de Vitry, by his insistence before the court of the just elected Pope Honorius III, obtained verbal approval of the primitive associations of beguines in Belgium, an approval which was later extended to those beguinages of France and Germany. Even if a papal bull had not been written at this time, this implicit approval "favored the spread of the new institute in west and central Europe."[9] Groups of beguines which had arisen here and there, seeking to save their own institution condemned by the Fourth Lateran Council, adopted the approved program of

---

[8]Mens, *op. cit.*, col. 1146.

[9]Mens, col. 1147. See Andrea Boni, *Gli Istituti religiosi e la loro potestà di governo* (c. 607, c. 596) Antonianum, Roma, 1989, p. 238.

the beguines of the Low Countries, and with this program they also adopted the name, the organization and the mystical doctrines (the Flemish school) of these devout women."[10]

3. The Organization of the beguines

Groups of beguines lived in beguinages which, more than monasteries, were something like a small religious city immersed in the world. The beguinage was generally surrounded by a canal (as at Bruges) or a wall (as at Louvain) and was equipped with one great entry gate. "It had its streets, its squares, and its houses, small buildings generally uniform in style with low roofs covered with red tiles."[11] Frequently the beguinage had the style of a huge courtyard with plants and flowers surrounding the cottages of the beguines. The cottages were joined to one another and so formed a closed circle with the great entrance door as the only opening, as the beguinage today at Bruges. On line with the little houses were the Church, halls for community work, administrative offices, and offices for dispensing charity. The only inhabitants were women. "Besides the individual cottages where the beguines found shelter alone or with another sister and went about their work, there was one *conventen*, sometimes more than one, in which some beguines lived a more monastic form of life and took their meals in common."[12] Every beguinage was autonomous.

The beguine did not make a profession of public or perpetual vows. She obliged herself to make a profession of private vows for the time that she intended to live in the beguinage. There were two vows: obedience and chastity. The beguines were able to have ownership of property but they were obliged to lead a plain and simple life. The habit was uniform, brown-grey in color (in the modern period it became black). The work of the beguine in the middle ages was involved with the manufacture or the finishing process of cloth. The endowments of the beguinage came from the generosity of benefactors as well as from

---

[10]*Ibid.*

[11]A. Mens, *Beguine, begardi, beghinaggi*, in DIP, I. col. 1171.

[12]*Ibid.*

bequests by the beguines themselves. In many beguinages instructions and classes were given to young girls. This was a source of support and also of esteem from the people of the city. The very large beguinages had their own cemetery and their own priest. The spiritual exercises were similar to those of religious communities, properly so called. Among these exercises were the assistance at Mass, the recitation of the office or the rosary every morning, the frequent reception of the sacraments, and the observance of many days of fast and abstinence.[13]

4. Penitential groups in the thirteenth century

It would be good for us here to give a brief description of the development of congregations and penitential movements in the thirteenth century and the pertinent decisions of the Holy See in order that we might better understand how seriously the Church was opposed to the establishment of new religious orders (a policy which had been confirmed by the Fourth Lateran Council) and how difficult it was, at least until the second half of the fourteenth century, for new congregations of the Third Order Regular to come into existence.

In the footsteps of the two first mendicant orders, the Friars Minor and the Friars Preachers (the Dominicans), various eremitical groups developed.

a) *The Carmelite Hermits* had their origins in groups of Latin hermits established at the time of the Crusades "near the springs of Elijah on Mount Carmel and at other holy places." About the year 1209 the Patriarch of Jerusalem gave the Carmelites a brief Rule. "Following the difficulties that resulted from canon 13 of the Fourth Lateran Council, the hermits turned to the Holy See, obtaining from Honorius III in January 1226 permission (with the letter *Ut vivendi normam*) to continue to live according to that Rule."[14] Gregory IX reconfirmed this letter in 1229 as also did Innocent IV in 1245.

Although

> they were already caught up in the currents of
> the apostolic works of the mendicants...the

---

[13]*Ibid.*, col. 1173.

[14]A. Dal Pino, *I Frati Servi di santa Maria dalle origini all`approvazione* (1233ca.-1304), Louvain, 1972, p. 623.

Carmelites also ran up against the difficulties that involved the mendicants in various sectors of the Church and which were put into specific terms by canon 23 (*Religionum diversitatem nimiam*) of the Second Council of Lyons in 1274. While the Minors and the Preachers had come to be accepted once and for all, the Carmelites and the Hermits of Saint Augustine were left in a state of uncertainty, although recognized as institutions that existed before the Fourth Lateran Council (to which canon 13 of Second Lyons refers). "Concerning the Orders of Carmelites and Hermits of Saint Augustine, whose institution is said to have been prior to the General Council, we allow them to remain in their present condition until other provisions shall be made for them."[15]

The Carmelites were later on confirmed by Boniface VIII in 1298.

b) The *Augustinian Hermits* owe their origins to the union of autonomous groups or foundations of "black hermits" whose members included clerics and laymen. At first these hermits formed themselves around the person of an outstanding hermit. Union came in 1256 through the work of Cardinal Richard Annibaldi and Pope Alexander IV first in north central Italy, and then it was extended to other countries in Europe. Well known among these groups were the Hermits of Saint William (who had their origin from Saint William of Malavalle, +1157) in the diocese of Grossetto and the Bretinese and Giambonini hermits.[16]

Canon 23 of the Council of Lyons was applied to these hermits also and their status remained canonically unresolved until they were approved by Boniface VIII in 1298.[17]

c) The *Brothers of Penance of Jesus Christ*. Clearly these brothers arose from the penitential movement, forming a community about 1248 through the preaching of Hugh of

---

[15]See *ibid.*, p. 629

[16]See *ibid.*, p. 632.

[17]*Ibid.*, p. 658.

Digne, a Friar Minor. Hugh was a man faithful to the pristine Franciscan ideal, a friend of John of Parma and a fervent Joachimite. While he was still a law student at Montpellier he had known the Friars Minor and he entered the order before 1230. He was minister provincial probably during the years 1239-1242. "What we know about Hugh of Digne (+1255ca.)," writes Dal Pino,

> and about the groups who followed his preaching, about the brothers and sisters, about the sister of Hugh, Douceline (+1274) who founded the beguinage at Heyères, permits us to establish a connection between the Brothers and Sisters of Penance of Jesus Christ and the entire lay penitential movement which had developed in Italy. It is also related to the foundation of beguinages (a movement characterized by a somewhat secluded life that was poor and directed towards the works of mercy.) Thus, the Brothers of Penance of Jesus Christ as well as the two groups of Servants of Mary can be considered as projections of the penitential movement into the more specialized area of religious life.[18]

Innocent IV in the year 1251 entrusted to the Bishops of Marseilles and Toulon the task of giving the Rule of Saint Augustine to these Brothers.[19] In the same manner, Alexander IV repeatedly showed himself interested in these brothers and granted them various privileges. Their expansion was rapid. In the official year of their formation, 1251, they had thirteen houses listed and by the year 1274 their houses numbered about 110 in France, England and Italy.

"Even though the expansion was joined to a strong spirituality that shines through their legislative texts...they did not escape the condemnation of canon 23, *Religionum diversitatem nimiam* of the Second Council of Lyons. These Brothers were its most outstanding victim."[20]

---

[18]*Ibid.*, p. 663.

[19]*Ibid.*, p. 664

[20]*Ibid.*, p. 670.

They were considered to be among the "unnamed" mendicants which, according to the above canon, were to be denied the faculty of admitting novices to profession, acquiring new houses and selling existing houses without permission of the Holy See, even though they had been approved by the Holy See before the Council. From the year 1274 on the community began to die, year after year, house after house.

d) Another institute condemned but not listed by name was the *Servants of the Mother of Christ of Marseilles.* These servants began around the year 1257 as a "group of lay people who had withdrawn from the world to lead a penitential life in community" near the little church of Arenc, a suburb of Marseilles. The bishop of that city, in accord with the decree of Alexander IV, had given these lay people the Rule of Saint Augustine. The institute spread moderately. There were about fourteen houses in 1274. Then this institute fell before the decree of the Council of Lyons and very soon they disappeared.

e) The *Servites of Mary or the Servites* began as a community having an evangelical-penitential orientation. They were instituted at Mount Sonoro (later called Senario) in the diocese of Florence about the year 1233. Cardinal Raniero approved this community in 1249. At the end of the Pontificate of Innocent IV and the beginning of the Pontificate of Alexander IV (1254-1256) the canonical status of the Servites suffered from the last disciplinary measures decreed by Innocent IV. Innocent had granted many privileges to various orders or groups of mendicants. Among these privileges were faculties given to these religious to hear confessions in their own churches and to bury people in their own cemeteries. In 1253, Innocent IV reserved to himself (through the promulgation of the papal bull *Excelsi dextera*) the dispute between the Mendicants and Secular Masters of the School of Theology at Paris. In the year following, the pope restricted the rights of the Mendicants on the points that were in controversy (*Etsi animarum*). Alexander IV, on the other hand, showed a very favorable attitude toward the Mendicants, and the Servites too became the beneficiaries of this papal favor. In

---

[20]*Ibid.*, p. 670.

1259 the pope recognized a prior general of the Servites and decreed that the Servites could bury in their own cemeteries people who asked for this.[21] In this way the Servites came to be listed along with other mendicant orders.

The Council of Lyons, while it named the two orders which had received final approval, the Friars Minor and the Dominicans, also named the orders which for the moment were excluded from condemnation, the Hermits of Saint Augustine and the Carmelites. However, the Council did not clearly say which other mendicant orders were condemned to slow extinction. However, it was clear that among these were included the Brothers of Penance of Jesus Christ, who were very well established in France where the Council of Lyons was held. Other orders were implicitly condemned but not listed by name. These orders used the very fact of procrastination by the Holy See as an anchor of salvation. This is what happened to the Servites. After some concessions from Honorius IV (1275-1286) and some protective decrees promulgated by Nicholas IV, Benedict XI gave the Servites final approval with the bull *Dum levamus*, dated February 11, 1304.[22]

---

[21]See *ibid.*, p. 914
[22]See *ibid.*, p. 1291.

CHAPTER II

THE BEGINNINGS OF "RELIGIOUS" LIFE IN THE ORDER OF PENANCE

1. Factors which promoted "religious" life

We have noted that in the penitential movement which received the spiritual direction of Saint Francis, a tendency towards life in community appeared from earliest times. This tendency was in full agreement with the general tendency of the age towards associative life that we have already mentioned.

Even during the lifetime of Saint Francis *hermits* and *recluses* were received into the Order of Penance. According to the ecclesiastical practice of that time, these persons were considered true *religious*. Some of these people were admitted to the Order of Penance by Saint Francis, e.g. Blessed Verdiana of Castle Fiorentino, the noble lady Praxedes of Rome and Gerard of Villamagna near Florence. We even have information that Bartholomew Baro's *community of penitents* was directly received as such by Saint Francis.[1] From this it is clear that when Saint Francis was still alive, there already existed in the Order of Penance the beginning of religious life, properly so called, in the form of eremitical and community life.

As we have remarked many times, the Order of Penance during the thirteenth century did have remarkable development and good organization. Also from the beginning "regular religious life" had to keep pace with this develop-

---

[1]See the whole treatment of this matter in R. Pazzelli, *Il Terz'Ordine Regolare di San Francesco attraverso i secoli*, Roma, 1958, pp. 42-59. On Bartolomeo Baro see latest presentation of most recent research by Gabriele Andreozzi, *Il Bartolomeo Baro nelle fonti storiche e nella tradizione*, in AA.VV. *Prime manifestazioni di vita comunitaria, maschile e femminile, nel movimento francescano della Penitenza (1215-1247)*, Roma, 1982, pp. 507-541.

ment. Knowledge of the fact that Saint Francis had received *hermits* and *recluses* and even established a *community of penitents* must have had a remarkable influence on the spread of this kind of life. The very nature of the Order of Penitents favored the intensification of community life. This is in fact what the Order of Penance was from the beginning, not some kind of sodality, but a true "order" with its Rule, habit, novitiate, profession and privileges granted to it by the decrees of the Church. The institute had a natural affinity for development towards the "regular" religious state.

> The Memorial of 1221 the first Rule of the Order of Penance, did not speak of life in common under the same roof, but listed conditions for fraternal life e.g. meetings, religious offices, subscriptions, and the internal organization of government for each group since the members resided in their own homes. These prescriptions could set up an attractive model for a more perfect life for those who found themselves free from worldly ties and responsibilities and who desired to make an even more complete offering of themselves. In any case, fraternities sprang up in both large and small cities, first in Italy and later on in other countries where the sons of Saint Francis had established regular provinces. This development was especially remarkable when towards the end of that century these local fraternities in some regions grouped themselves into provinces and even held General Chapters. The participants in these Chapters were always the men.[2]

Another reason for this development was the climate of open benevolence and protection given by the Holy See to the Friars Minor, beginning with Pope Gregory IX, as we have mentioned in another place.[3] This very same benevolence was given also to the Order of Penance. On November 21, 1234 Gregory IX sent a letter, *Ut cum maiori*, to all the bishops of Italy and this letter is witness

---

[2]Péano, *Le Religiose francescane*, p. 11.

[3]See Pazzelli, *Saint Francis and the Third Order*, pp. 142-144.

to the extension of this kindly attitude to the Order of Penance. Gregory ordered the bishops, each in his own diocese, to exercise the office of visitator and corrector of the fraternities. The bishops were to show themselves clearly benevolent to the penitents by reason of the reverence that is due to the Holy See and to the pope himself. "Having recommended these (Penitents) because of reverence due to the Holy See and to us," the bishops were not to disturb the Penitents and they were not to allow them to be unduly troubled by others.[4]

So it was almost natural that from the beginning there were instances of eremitical life, community life and works of mercy which promoted community life among the followers of Saint Francis who lived under the Third Rule.

2. Saint Elizabeth of Hungary (or of Thuringia)

At the beginning of this development towards the religious state there is a shining example of a woman we cannot fail to mention. She has become, through chance or through thoughtful choice, the inspiration of many endeavors to live community life in various countries of Europe, endeavors which fully matured in the establishment of congregations of Franciscan sisters. This person is *Saint Elizabeth of Hungary, Landgravine of Thuringia.*

Elizabeth was born in the year 1207, daughter of Andrew II, King of Hungary. She was engaged to be married to Louis IV, Landgrave of Thuringia, at the tender age of four, in accord with the custom of the time among princely or royal families. She was educated at the Castle of Wartburg in Eisenach. In 1221 she was married to Louis and they had three children. From her youngest years, Elizabeth lived an ascetical life and gave herself to the practice of works of mercy. Her first spiritual director and confessor, about the year 1223, was the Franciscan Friar Rudiger and then, about 1226, Conrad of Marburg, the official preacher of the Crusades in Germany, who today is considered to have been a Premonstatentian.

Thuringia was politically dependent on the principality of Magonza, which in its turn was ruled by its Prince-Archbishop. The relationship between Thuringia and

---

[4] BF, n. 149, pp. 141-142.

Magonza for some time had been rather tense. In May of 1233 a message of Pope Honorius III was sent to the Landgrave of Thuringia, husband of Elizabeth, inviting him to take up the sign of the cross "ut signum crucis assumat," i.e. take an active part in the Fifth Crusade (1217-1229). This *taking of the cross* would have included the privilege of exemption from the jurisdiction of the Prince-Archbishop. Louis IV "took the Cross" (official oath of the Crusader) in June of 1224 and participated actively in the preparations for the Fifth Crusade. In 1226 Louis was in Ravenna seeking to establish peace among the princes of Germany. However, he died at Otranto (Lecce) on September 12, 1227 when he was just about ready to embark with the army of Frederick II.

During the absence of her husband, in the midst of a great famine in the country, Elizabeth, against the wishes of some of the nobility, supported many hundreds of poor people with public funds. Upon receiving the news of her husband's death, Elizabeth had to leave Wartburg Castle. She wandered for some time leading a life of extreme poverty, but one rich in works of charity. Conrad of Marburg forbade her to renounce her dowry as she had at this time desired to do. Later on Elizabeth used the dowry for the construction of a hospital at Marburg in which she gathered poor and abandoned sick people, and with humble service provided for their needs herself. Desiring greater perfection, "ad summam tendens perfectionem," as Conrad would write of her, Elizabeth on Good Friday, March 24, 1228, placing her hands on the bare altar of the Franciscan church in Eisenach, renounced her own will. She rejected the honors of this world "and gave herself to the matters the Savior had counseled in the gospel." She dedicated the chapel of the hospital to Saint Francis just after Francis had been canonized. Twice a day Elizabeth visited the poor in the hospital, serving them personally. She sold all her belongings, even "all her costly garments," and distributed the proceeds as alms for the poor.

Elizabeth died at the age of twenty-four, on November 17, 1231. She was buried in the Cathedral of Marburg. "Very soon many miracles occurred" near her tomb. "The first list of these miracles compiled very early after her death...informs us of those miracles which occurred starting on November 20, 1231."[5] It was Conrad of Marburg himself who asked Pope Gregory IX to canonize Elizabeth, and she was canonized on July 1, 1235.

The sources that enable us to know something about Elizabeth's spirituality are two: the *Summa vitae* or the exposition of her life which Conrad of Marburg sent to the pope on November 16, 1232, and the testimony of Elizabeth's four maidservants that was given at the time of the process for canonization.[6] The portrait which Conrad gives of Elizabeth is a personification of compassionate charity to the poor and the sick. After the death of her husband, Elizabeth was no longer content with such works of mercy; she wanted to be poor herself so that she could go begging from door to door. Her director, Conrad, would not permit her to do this, and even contrary to his direction, she made her vow of total renunciation of her goods in the Franciscan church.

Although we cannot affirm in the modern historical sense, that Elizabeth belonged to the Franciscan Third Order, it is only because we do not know with certainty when the Franciscan Third Order received its official constitutions. It is certain that Elizabeth was an integral part of that movement which at the end of the century would be called the Franciscan Third Order. Elizabeth, in fact, did enter the state of the penitents and she did this in a Franciscan context. No one can deny her total dedication to Saint Francis of Assisi. The "irrefutable proofs are her love for poverty, her consideration of begging as a supreme form of perfection, her veneration for the Poor Man of Assisi, and her contacts with Francis' followers."[7] Remembering that her first confessor was a Franciscan, one can trace the path along which Elizabeth walked seeking to know and strive after the Franciscan ideal and way of life.[8]

---

[5]Edith Pasztor, Elisabetta d'Ungheria, Langravia di Turingia, santa, in Bibliotheca Santorum, IV, col. 1112.

[6] This testimony has recently been examined closely and evaluated by Raoul Manselli, Santità principesca e vita quotidiana in Elisabetta d'Ungheria, La testimonianza delle ancelle, in Analecta TOR, vol. XVIII (1985), pp. 23-45.

[7] E. Frascadore, *Elisabetta d'Ungheria, santa*, in DIP, III, col. 1112.

[8]See E. Pasztor, *op. cit.*, col. 1121.

For these reasons and because Franciscans must have felt obliged to make this outstandingly holy woman known wherever they went, congregations of Franciscan sisters have taken her name and consider her as their foundress from earliest times: "they have made their own her ideal of poverty, charity and service to the poor and the sick."[9]

The spirituality of Elizabeth is essentially the spirituality of the penitential movement when this movement was enriched by the Franciscan ideal. Therefore, in the Secular Franciscan Movement or the Third Order, Saint Elizabeth's example of dedication was so great that it demanded something more than that which can be expressed by the words "secular life," understanding this as "life in the world" with its series of daily preoccupations of all kinds which hinder or make more difficult our complete service to God and our brothers and sisters.

This is the situation which repeats itself tens of times, perhaps hundreds of times, at the beginning of new congregations of Franciscan sisters. This situation begins in the very moment when young women become imbued with the ideals of Saint Francis. Very often these ideals are loved and known because they are already enrolled as members of the Secular Franciscan Order. Then, with the help, direction and protection of a bishop, and more often of a priest of the First Order, women will direct those elements towards the birth of the new congregation itself.

---

[9]E. Frascadore, *op. cit.*, col. 1112.

CHAPTER III

THE SECOND HALF OF THE THIRTEENTH CENTURY

1. Franciscan and non-Franciscan elements

There were examples of small groups of women bearing the hallmark of Franciscan life in the second half of the thirteenth century. We can say that from the beginning, on the fringes of the secular fraternities, there were attempts to live community life in the Third Order of Saint Francis. When exactly did this phenomenon start? It is very difficult, as Péano says,

> to make authoritative statements on this matter because well into the middle of the thirteenth century the outlines of the organization of the Order of Penance were not clearly defined, not even within the movement itself. This is so clear that historians are still wondering whether or not such and such a person belonged to the Order of the Penitents or whether such and such a group of individuals should be considered as belonging to its orbit of influence. It seems that individuals, and groups as well, were classified according to their intentions as well as according to their spiritual and temporal needs determined by time and place.[1]

The first cause of our uncertainty in fixing an exact date is due to the lack of original documents coming down from the time of the first foundations. Given the simplicity of life and the absence of any external organization and time continuity with the past, this situation is quite understandable. Nevertheless we do have some external witnesses worthy of trust. Says Péano:

---

[1]Péano, Le Religiose Francescane, p. 16.

We read in the life of Saint Rose of Viterbo, 1234-1253, that she gathered around herself some young women intending to live the religious life under the Rule of the Order of Penance. A short time later in Tuscany, Saint Margaret of Cortona, 1247-1297, who was admitted to the Third Order in 1277, gathered together some devout young women who were called the Poor Little Sisters (the Poverelle). In the following year Margaret founded a "House of Saint Mary of Mercy" for the care of the sick. In the same way, Saint Angela of Foligno, 1248-1309, gathered under her direction a group of brothers and sisters who cared for the lepers in the district hospital. All these centers of spirituality, and many others whose existence is unknown to us, show the vitality of the works of Francis of Assisi in the thirteenth century. These "cenacles" were informal in their style, of course, but they were also the fruit of an inspiration that led to a life more fully consecrated to God and to the works of charity.[2]

We must admit, however, that in the second half of the thirteenth century not everything was always Franciscan. For the male branch, we know that besides the Order of Penance which followed the spiritual direction of Francis, there were other organizations which could also be considered projections of the lay penitential movement in the thirteenth century. An example of this projection is the Order of the Servites of Mary, already mentioned above.[3] The same may be said for the feminine branch of this family: "In the second half of the thirteenth century," writes Langeli Bartoli, "central Italy was teeming with communities of devout women, who were called the 'incarcerated' or the 'recluses' because of the strict rule of cloister, and who could not be described as belonging to any religious order."[4] Given the time and place, we might presume that there was a heavy contribution of Franciscan direction,

[2]Péano, op. cit., p. 17

[3]See Pazzelli, Saint Francis and the Third Order, p. 141

[4]Attilio Langeli Bartoli, I Penitenti a Spoleto nel Duocento in L'Ordine

but we do not have any explicit evidence of it. However, it is certain that these "devout women were not disposed to embrace the lifestyle that prevailed at San Damiano nor that of other communities guided by the Hugoline Constitutions.

And there are examples of women's monasteries whose circumstances of origin and spiritual assistance would indicate a Franciscan inspiration; yet they still received the Rule of Saint Augustine from episcopal authority. "We are dealing," says Nessi, "with some fundamental stages in the progress of some of the religious houses of women in the Spoleto area. These houses, during this same time and in a similar manner as the monastery at Montefalco, passed through the same phases of development and the phases of becoming 'regular.'"[5]

These groups in the valley of Spoleto which have been mentioned and others, notes Bartoli Langeli,

> show a historical development and a substantial character that are alike on many points.... It is not being arbitrary to say that we consider them as manifestations of a single monastic peniten-tial movement of great vitality. The Cistercian

---

della penitenza di san Francesco d'Assisi nel secolo XIII, a cura di O. Schmucki, Roma, 1973, p. 303.

[5]Silvestro Nessi, *Santa Chiara de Montefalco e il Francescanesimo*, in MISCELLANEA FRANCESCANA 69 (1969) p. 405. We quote here these examples given by Nessi: "On September 8, 1278 Roland, Bishop of Spoleto, granted the monastery of Santa Caterina 'del Floré permission to observe the Rule of Saint Augustine... In 1293 on February 28, Bishop Gerard granted a certain Elena di Paolo of Spoleto and her companions living in the house of the "Carcere" of Colpetroso, the Rule of Saint Augustine and the faculty of establishing an oratory dedicated to Saint Clare of Assisi. But he declared that these persons would remain directly dependent on the ordinary. This same bishop on December 2, 1294, granted Sister Mattea of the Order of Penitents, the faculty of building a church at the foot of Mount Monteluco (of Spoleto) near the house in which she and her companions were living. This exceptional concession relating to the first certainly documented family of female Franciscan Tertiaries organized in monastic communities was due to the special intercession of Cardinal Giacomo Colona. The Franciscan monastery of Saint Clare of Assisi was the one involved. Francis, the bishop, on August 10, 1297, granted forty days indulgence to those who would make a visit to the monastery of Saint Mary of Mercy on the feast days of Saint Francis, Saint Anthony, Saint Clare of Assisi and the Blessed Mother. Nothing was said about which Rule they were observing, but it is clear that we are dealing with a monastery of Franciscan Tertiary women."

model (of the beguines in the Brabant) is substituted in our case by a happy joining of the great eremitical and ascetical tradition, for which Monteluco is famous,[6] and Franciscan spirituality. This Franciscan influence is clearly visible in the intensity of the personal relationships with the Friars Minor; in the lively participation in the troubled happenings in the order at the time; in devotional attitudes; and in general, in the ideal of life that was pursued.[7]

Now when these communities of women, who were almost certainly inspired by the Franciscan ideal, asked for a Rule, why were they not given the Rule of Nicholas IV, which had been approved? Why instead were they given the Rule of Saint Augustine? This is a problem we must deal with.

2. The further development of the female Third Order Regular

The expansion of the feminine branch of the Third Order Regular has been better documented for the city of Strasbourg and the district belonging to the Franciscan Province of "Upper Germany," that is, Alsace, the Palatinate, part of Hess, Franconia, Swabia, Bavaria and German Switzerland, thanks to the research of Father Michael Bihl, O.F.M.[8] The first foundation of Franciscan sisters in Strasbourg seems to have been made in 1286. By means of a bill of sale to a certain Brother Conrad of Tubigen, former provincial and at that time Bishop of Toul, a certain benefactress handed over the residence she owned in the city. Thereupon, the bishop offered the building to the Poor Clares so that they could

---

[6]On this point, Bartoli Langeli notes how M. Gatti (in his study *Le Carceri di San Francesco del Subasio, Assisi*, 1960, p. 24) puts "in relationship to Monteluco the eremitical flowering of Subasio which was influenced by Saint Francis, among others." *op. cit.*, p. 307, note 20.

[7]Bartoli Langeli, *op cit.*, pp. 306-307.

[8]Michael Bihl, O.F.M., *De Tertio ordine Sancti Francisci in provincia Germaniae Superioris, sive Argentinensis syntagma*, in AFH 14 (1921).

house "twenty-six beguines without cost and in perpetuity." In 1294 still another house was given to the Poor Clares for sixteen more "poor beguines" but with the stipulation that permitted the guardian of the friars' convent to intervene in case of discord among the beguines over the substitution for a deceased sister, or for one who had been expelled for grave fault.

The following year saw two more foundations: the first was near a friary of the Franciscans. It was a house for twelve sisters with the clause that all should be subject to the correction of the Franciscan Superior of the Friars Minor. The second foundation could take care of twenty sisters. Other foundations of beguines were made in the city in the years that followed. The historian quoted concludes his research affirming that at least twenty-five houses of these Regular Tertiaries were dependent on the Friars Minor during the fourteenth and fifteenth centuries.

In other parts of this vast Province the same kind of activity took place. Ingolstadt seems to have been the first to have a house of this kind in 1276. Before the end of the century, Munich had two houses: one from the year 1284 near the convent of the Friars Minor, and another in 1295 in a suburb of that city. The sisters of this convent were under obligation, stressed by their founder, to pray for the faithful departed. At Worms a house was donated in 1288 for "twenty sisters or beguines whose duty it would be to prepare in their kitchens food which would be served by the superior (the *ministra*) and two companions to the sick in a hospital located near the New Gate." This expansion continued in the following years and the convents of the beguines prospered right up to the end of the fifteenth century. Thus, the Provincial Chapter of Spire, held by the Friars Minor in 1319, took up the task of regulating the powers and establishing the duties of the visitator of the Order of Penance, who had been designated to care for the spiritual welfare of both Secular Tertiaries and the beguines.[9]

Taking all these matters into consideration, it does not seem exaggerated to say that we do have enough documentation to show how community life in the female branch of the Order of Penance had already experienced more than enough development towards the end of the thirteenth century, even before the Rule of Nicholas IV.

3. The Rule of Nicholas IV and its problematic

We would like now to consider some of the problems which we see are connected with the rise of the first communities of women in the Third Order Regular. We would like to pay special attention to those problems which revolve about the exceptional event of the promulgation of the Rule of Nicholas IV.

This Rule, as you know, was promulgated in 1289.[10]

For some time now it was commonly said that the new edition of the Rule contributed to giving a vigorous thrust towards life in community, and among the Franciscan penitents, a life that was religious in the strict sense of the word.[11] "The changes which were made," affirms Frascadore, "were not so much in the text, which substantially remained that of the primitive *Memorial* of 1221-1228; rather they were more in the spirit and in the canonical and legislative arrangement of the various ordinances. The changes showed the preoccupation of the pope that the Rule conform more with the religious state."[12] It is historical fact that about the year of the promulgation of this Rule, 1289, and especially immediately after the promulgation, "the practice of living in community and making the profession of the three vows by Tertiaries very quickly developed."[13]

Was this due to the circumstance–as attested by

---

[9]Péano, *op. cit.*, pp. 18-19.

[10]See the circumstances surrounding its composition and its promulgation in Pazzelli, *Saint Francis and the Third Order*, pp. 150-152.

[11]R. Pazzelli, *Il Terz´ordine regolare di san Francesco attraverso i secoli*, Roma, 1958, p. 64; E. Frascadore, *Francescane, suore, op. cit.*, col. 196.

[12]Frascadore, *Francescane, op. cit.*, col. 196.

[13]Péano, *op. cit.*, p. 16

authors of the seventeenth century[14]–that it was the Tertiaries already living community life in the city of Toulouse who, together with the Secular Tertiaries of Italy, presented fervent requests to the just elected Pope Nicholas IV asking that he would deign to proceed with official approbation of the Rule of the Penitents? Even admitting these circumstances, we are no longer able to attribute such a notable influence as to say: "The pope in drawing up the new Rule must certainly have kept in mind, as a good lawgiver, the new conditions of many of the tertiaries, that is, the community life that so many had embraced."[15]

It has also been said that the communities of tertiaries

> did not limit themselves to simply asking the pope for definitive approval of the Rule, but they were even asking for permission to make public profession of the three vows of obedience, poverty and chastity, as this was already taking place in other non-Franciscan branches of Penitents who, in hermitages or near special hospices, lived in community. Even before the Franciscan movement began, these hermits frequently made their profession of the three essential vows in the hands of the bishop or the Benedictine abbot in whose territory the community had arisen... Nicholas IV, as more than one early author has affirmed... besides approving the Rule also gave permission for the profession of the three religious vows.[16]

We do not have strong enough documentation today to affirm one side or the other, i.e. that a request like that was made or that permission was granted by the pope for the profession of religious vows.

The certain fact is that a more critical study of this text

---

[14]See Pazzelli, *Il Terz'ordine regolare, op. cit.*, p. 65. Father Elzear de Dombes affirms in 1664 that the original bull *Supra Montem* was preserved in the convent of Our Lady of Peace in Toulouse by the regular tertiaries "because it had been requested by the religious of that same house who had established themselves in community in that aforementioned city some years before the above mentioned request."

[15]*Ibid.*, p. 66.

[16]Frascadore, *Francescane, op. cit.*, col. 196.

shows the Rule of Nicholas IV did not consider life in community either explicitly or implicitly. Much less did Nicholas consider profession of religious vows by those who professed that Rule.[17] This Rule, then, was not intended nor approved for "women living in community." This lack of intention, writes Nessi, "could explain the reasons which motivated the Bishop of Spoleto to give the Rule of Saint Augustine to so many communities that had arisen among lay women almost certainly Franciscan tertiaries."[18]

The phraseology used in the documents which record the conferral and approbation of the Rule of Saint Augustine casts some light on our question. The Bishops of Spoleto were asked explicitly by three of the groups living in community, and almost certainly drawing their inspiration from Franciscan sources, to give them "a safe Rule which was suitable for persons living the Regular life 'under a Rule.'"[19] The documents involved in this matter bear the dates 1290, 1293, and 1300 and so were issued after the Rule of Nicholas IV. The phraseology would seem to indicate that the Rule of Nicholas IV, which had not been explicitly requested, had not been proposed or granted by the bishop because it had not been considered *certa* that is "safe and suitable" for community life *in loco regulato*, that is, in a monastery which had to live under an approved Rule. In this context, the Rule of Nicholas IV would be seen as contrary to the decree of the Fourth Lateran Council, that decree being reconfirmed by the Second Council of Lyons. Furthermore, it would have been seen as contrary to the decree *Periculoso* of Pope Boniface VIII in 1298 on matters concerning the cloister. To each of these three communities, the "Rule of Saint Augustine was given as a Rule believed to be more suitable particularly for women."[20]

---

[17]See various authors, AA.VV., *La "supra Montem" di Niccolò IV (1289): genesi e diffusione di una Regola*, Acts of the Congress of Franciscan Studies (Ascoli Piceno, October 26-27, 1987), edited by R. Pazzelli and L. Temperini, ANALECTA TOR, Roma, 1988.

[18]Nessi, *op. cit.*, p. 407.

[19]"Certam regulam et alia que *loco regulato* conveniunt." See Bartoli Langeli, *op. cit.*, p. 306, note 16.

[20]Nessi, *op. cit.*, p. 407.

In our opinion, this interpretation offers the most plausible argument for explaining the whole situation.

4. Saint Clare of Montefalco

The silence in the Rule of Nicholas IV as to whether or not this Rule had been intended for those living religious life in community, caused difficulties in the following centuries for those men and women tertiaries who had already begun, or who were about to begin, living the religious life properly so called. This happened right away in the cases of well-known Regular Tertiaries who had to adopt the Rule of Saint Augustine. The first, and perhaps the most well known of these tertiaries was Clare of Montefalco.

Clare was born in 1268 in Montefalco, a city in Umbria a short distance from Foligno in the Province of Perugia. She was barely seven years old when she wanted to follow her sister, Joan Frances, to the Monastery. Joan had established and directed a house of women Franciscan Penitent Tertiaries. When Joan died there in 1291, Clare was elected Abbess, even though she was very young.

> She received from God special mystical graces, ecstasies and visions, and a profusion of supernatural gifts that made her aware of what was going on outside the monastery. To Clare's prompt action a particular heretical movement among the begards called "the Spirit of Freedom," that had already begun to spread the errors of quietism throughout Umbria, was discovered and eliminated.[21]

Clare died in her monastery of the Holy Cross in Montefalco on August 17, 1308. She was immediately venerated as a saint. "She had a special devotion to the Passion of the Lord. Even the sight of a crucifix was enough to urge her to live a more penitential life."[22]

While Clare was still alive, she had many times declared that she was carrying the signs of the Passion of the Lord physically in her heart. "Soon after her death, the nuns of

---

[21]Niccolò Del Re, *Chiara da Montefalco*, santa, in *Bibliotheca Sanctorum*, III, col. 1219-1220.

[22]*Ibid.*, col. 1217-1218.

the monastery opened her body and indeed found in her heart the symbols of the Passion of the Lord: the scourge, the crown of thorns, three nails, the lance, and the sponge. In her gall bladder were found three round stones of the same size, weight and color arranged to form a triangle as a symbol of the Trinity."

Naturally, "the spreading of the news of such matters created excitement among the people, and a public process was held with the participation of the clergy and public authorities."[23] On August 22 a kind of canonical process was inaugurated. The Vicar of Montefalco and the clergy were present as well as the mayor and his officials, the sisters of the monastery and the doctor of the monastery. The doctor and the nuns affirmed that there was no deception or fraud concerning the articles found in her body. Some days later the vicar of the Bishop of Spoleto, whose name was Berengario di S. Africano, went to Montefalco "riding his horse furiously because he supposed a deception." But when he had heard the witnesses and examined the heart of Saint Clare personally, he recognized the reality of these marvelous symbols. Consequently, he changed from inquisitor to defender of the holiness of Clare and became her first and most important biographer.

The fame of these events quickly reached Rome. Cardinals Peter and James Colonna and Napoleon Orsini became greatly interested in this matter. James Colonna personally wished to examine the three spheres that were found in Clare's gall bladder. Present at this inspection were Cardinal Orsini "and many other persons worthy of trust" among whom was Ubertino da Casale, who had met Clare many times at Montefalco and who gave witness at this time that he had been miraculously healed of a hernia from which he had suffered much for many years.[24]

Clare's process of canonization officially began on June 18, 1309, only ten months after her death. It was many times interrupted and commenced again.[25]

---

[23]E. Menestò, *I processi per la canonizzazione di Chiara da Montefalco, a proposito della documentazione trecentesca ritrovata*, Montefalco, 1983, p. 984.

[24]*Ibid.*, p. 987.

[25]See the phases of the process in E. Menestò, *op. cit.*, p. 375.

Clare was solemnly canonized by Leo XIII on December 8, 1881.

5. Was Clare of Montefalco a Franciscan tertiary?

Let us begin by examining the facts about which we are certain.

In 1290 the "devout virgins living in penance" requested *an approved Rule.* The bishop, Gerard of Spoleto, gave them the Rule of Saint Augustine: "Vestrum laudabile propositum in Domino commentantes...beati Augustini Regulam...duximus concendendum."[26]

It seems certain that the monastery of Saint Clare from that day in 1290 on until 1411 lived under the Rule of Saint Augustine. However it is a curious "fact that in the year 1363 Peter di Simone, vicar of the Bishop of Spoleto...wrote of the monastery as ascribed to the Order of Clare of Assisi. The thought comes to mind: was the vicar so ill-informed or did his letter respect a factual situation which had in it some kind of equivocation?"[27]

In 1411 for practical reasons the monastery of Holy Cross was united to the Benedictine monastery of San Benedetto del Poggiolo inside the walls of Montefalco. However, in 1413 the nuns of the ex-monastery of Holy Cross "who had submitted themselves to the Rule of Saint Benedict because they had been interested in this Rule, now saw themselves cheated and began to show signs of discontent, and the desire to return to the primitive observance."[28]

In 1460 the juridical union of the monastery of Montefalco with the monastery of (Santa Maria) *della Stella* of Spoleto which belonged to the Order of Saint Augustine was decreed by the vicar of the Archbishop of Spoleto. However, very soon the nuns of Montefalco "became undecided, some of them wishing to observe a different Rule."[29] In 1478 Sixtus IV, seeking to resolve the

---

[26]Archives of the Monastery of Saint Clare. See Nessi, *op. cit.*, p. 375. "Commending your praiseworthy proposal in the Lord, we are moved to grant the Rule of Blessed Augustine."

[27]Nessi, *op. cit.*, p.404.

[28]Nessi, *op. cit.*, p. 404.

[29]B. Piergili, *Vita della beata Chiara detta della Croce da Montefalco,* Foligno, 1663, p. 245.

quarrel which resulted, dissolved the union of the two monasteries.

As soon as autonomy was realized, the "question of the Rule" again exploded. This happened when the sisters had to decide whether or not to return to the original observance of the past. After so many changes, nobody had a clear idea of what that original observance was. So polemics broke out over the Rule observed by Saint Clare, and by the community of Santa Croce until 1411, and even over the habit to be worn.

Some sisters wanted the Franciscan Rule and habit, others wanted to continue to live under the Rule of Saint Augustine. The Franciscan party prevailed and presented a petition to the pope asking that they might observe the Rule of Saint Clare of Assisi and to pass from the jurisdiction of the Bishop of Spoleto to the jurisdiction of the Fathers of the Friars Minor of the Observance. Innocent VIII granted all they asked for and immediately, unknown to all, the nuns began to wear the Franciscan habit in spite of the fact that three of nuns had dissented and refused their consent to the petition. Immediately, the Bishop and the Augustinian Fathers asked for and obtained a declaration of nullity of the bull on the basis that the petition of the nuns sent in the name of the whole community had not taken into consideration the position of the dissidents.[30]

From that time on there was "a dispute between the Franciscans and the Augustinians, the former saying that Saint Clare was recognized as a Franciscan tertiary and had worn the Franciscan habit."[31]

There is certainly enough documentary evidence to prove the Franciscan origins and spirituality of Saint Clare of Montefalco. On the other hand, it is certain that her monastery, in 1290, received the Rule of Saint Augustine. Why did this happen when the Rule of the Penitents had

---

[30]Nessi, *op. cit.*, p. 372.

[31]*Ibid*, p. 374.

been promulgated the year before on August 18, 1289 by Nicholas IV?

The plausible answer, it seems certain to us, has already been mentioned: the Rule of Nicholas IV did not explicitly envision religious life, properly so called, with the three religious vows.

About the year 1290, in the monastery of the "devout virgin penitents" of Montefalco, the same conditions could indeed be found that existed in the monastery of San Damiano in Assisi with Saint Clare of Assisi and her companions in the year 1216. After the decree of the Fourth Lateran Council in 1215, Saint Clare and her community at San Damiano had to choose an approved Rule and chose the Rule of Saint Benedict. So in 1290 when the Sisters of Montefalco asked Gerard, Bishop of Spoleto, to give them an approved Rule he decided to give them the Rule of Saint Augustine.

All of this does not invalidate the information we have that has led us to believe that the monastery of the "devout virgin penitents" of Montefalco was deeply imbued with Franciscan spirituality.

1) It is historically certain that Saint Clare wore the Franciscan habit, was buried in it, and that "her body was clothed with that habit for a long period of time."

2) In the lifetime of Saint Clare, the Friars Minor were the chaplains and confessors for the monastery and continued in this service for a long time after her death. In the life of Saint Clare "we meet with many Franciscans, the well known and the unknown, priests, lay friars, saints and heretics."[32]

3) When Clare discovered the heretical sect, the "Spirit of Freedom," she denounced it to Friar Andrew of Perugia, the Friar Minor who was the inquisitor for the Province of Umbria, so that he, Andrew, would take care of the matter.

4) The apostolic process for the canonization of Clare was begun September 6, 1318 under the direction of two apostolic commissaries in the Church of the Friars Minor in Montefalco.

5) Remembering the last days of Saint Clare's life, her

---

[32]See the list given by Nessi, *op. cit.*, p. 383.

first biographer Berengario wrote:

> She called out the names of the Blessed Virgin and the saints uttering the words as if she had seen them present and at intervals invoked Saint Francis, saying: "My Saint Francis, how truly beautiful you are.... Saint Francis and all the saints are coming to accompany me because my Lord Jesus Christ wants me to come."[33]

6) At the official inspection of the symbols of the passion of Christ discovered in the heart of Saint Clare, (at a public meeting decreed by the Mayor and the officials of the commune of Montefalco on August 22, 1308), there were many other people present. These included Friar Francis di Damiano, a Friar Minor who was a brother of Clare and who was guardian of the Spoleto region, Franciscan friars Andrew of Fingisone, James di Gonso who was rector of the convent of Bevagna, and John of Mibuccio. *It is strange that there were no Augustinians present,* as much as to say, in effect, that there were no Augustinians associated with Clare during all her life.[34]

7) When the news of finding the symbols in the heart of Clare reached the Roman Curia, Cardinals Orsini and Colonna took care of the entire matter. Everybody knows that these Cardinals were involved with the Franciscan movement. Napoleon Orsini was "closely involved with the Spirituals and with those mystics or penitents who were associated with these events such as Angela of Foligno, Margaret of Cortona, Clare of Rimini and naturally our Clare of Montefalco."[35]

8) The oldest paintings of the saint show Clare in the habit of a Franciscan tertiary. Such an image of Clare was painted in 1333 in the apse of the Church of the Holy Cross in Montefalco because of the decision of the rector of the Duke of Spoleto, then bishop of that city, John d'Amelio (or Jean Amiel).[36] Even after 1411, during the

---

[33]*Ibid.,* p. 393.

[34]Nessi, *op. cit.,* p. 393.

[35]E. Menestò, *op. cit.,* p.986, nota 28.

[36]See Nessi, *op. cit.,* p. 395.

time of the changes, first the Benedictine and later the Augustinian, the Conventual Franciscans had the image of Clare, clothed as a tertiary painted in their Church of Saint Francis in the very same city of Montefalco. This was done in 1452 by the well-known Benozzo Gozzoli and in 1461 by a painter of his school.[37]

To all this we should add the witness of the anonymous author of Montefalco, an author of the seventeenth century who affirms that he transcribed the news related to those things that occurred in his city from the Annals of the first Regular Tertiaries.[38] According to this account, the parents of Saint Clare were so devoted to Saint Francis and Saint Clare of Assisi, that not only had they themselves received the habit of the tertiaries and made profession of that Rule, but they had also given the names (of Francis and Clare) to their own children, the boys as well as the girls: Joan Frances, Francis, Clare, Theodora. The mother of Clare of Montefalco, whose name was Jacopa, entered the new monastery with her daughters after the death of her husband and she died there about the year 1285 as a "regular tertiary sister."[39]

"All this," concludes Oliger, "makes quite credible the fact that Saint Clare had lived originally as a tertiary Franciscan sister, that she wore the Franciscan habit and that she continued to wear it."[40]

There can be no doubt about "the Franciscan formation" of Clare of Montefalco. Francis of Assisi was too near in time and space. The whole Umbrian plain, which lies under the mountain of Montefalco, was imbued with Franciscanism. Clare had to look to Francis in his most interior life and follow him faithfully in his most outstanding characteristics.

> In the hermitage founded by her sister Joan
> Frances, flourished a sense of evangelical
> poverty, and of complete detachment from
> things of earth. Her first biographer, Berengario,

---

[37]See *ibid.*, p. 395.

[38]See Gabriel Andreozzi, *San Rocco in Montefalco, La "Portiuncula" del Terz´ordine regolare*, in ANALECTA TOR, IV (1945-1947), p. 210.

[39]*Ibid*, p. 211.

[40]See Nessi, *op. cit.*, p. 381.

wrote: "In most strict poverty Joan and her companions served the Lord in the hermitage. They had nothing and they asked for nothing but they lived with what was freely offered to them and from alms they did not even ask for."[41]

Let us look at that characteristic which distinguished Clare, just as it had distinguished Francis. It was the contemplation of the Passion of Christ which left in Francis the extraordinary signs in his body. So too did contemplation of the Passion leave extraordinary signs in Clare's body. Berengario wrote:

> From the time of her childhood, Clare was so accustomed to fixing her attention on the consideration of the severity of the Passion of Christ, that whatsoever she apprehended through her senses was always referred to His bitter sufferings.... Through such constant meditation Clare was so moved to compassion for the Sufferings of Christ that, because of the profusion of her grief, her eyes became two fountains of tears.[42]

"It is enough for us to know," concludes Nessi, "that Saint Clare was truly Franciscan in the very innermost part of her spirit and in her clothing. There was a concordance between the interior and the exterior, between the spiritual and the material which has its own value and which therefore merits reaffirmation."[43]

---

[41]See *ibid.*, p. 383.
[42]See *ibid.*, p???.
[43]*Ibid.*, p. 408.

CHAPTER IV

FIRST SERIOUS DIFFICULTIES AT THE BEGINNING OF THE FOURTEENTH CENTURY

1. Official papal favor

The beginning of community life among the "Brothers and Sisters of Penance of Saint Francis" during the years from 1290 to 1300 many times found support and encouragement from Papal documents. But sometimes there were difficulties and delays, and so it is not easy to say, over all, if the beginnings of community life met with favor or opposition. Beginning with the 1300's a number of difficulties appeared.

Among the few factors that favored community life was a letter of Pope Boniface VIII *Cupientes cultum* of July 11, 1295 addressed to the "Brothers and Sisters of the Order of Penance of Saint Francis in Upper Germany."[1] This document stated that these brothers and sisters

> having many houses and places in which they lead the common life under the observance of the Rule of the Penitents of Blessed Francis, devoutly served the Lord of Virtue in many regions of Upper Germany. Since, however, they did not have their own chapels and oratories in these houses, they asked for this privilege. The pope granted them permission to build chapels or oratories where they could celebrate the Divine Office, hear Holy Mass and receive the sacraments of the Church without prejudice to the rights of others.[2]

---

[1]Upper Germany included the provinces of Alsace, the Palatinate, Franconia, Swabia and German Switzerland.

[2]BF IV, n. 22, pp. 356-357

The letter was clearly favorable to common life among the Tertiary men and women. Because of this letter we have documentation about the increase of the number of Tertiary communities in this region of "Upper Germany." For Tertiary convents "of women were quite numerous. It is sufficient to recall here that among them were the convents of Munich in Bavaria, the 'Bittricher' of 1284 and the 'Riedler Regular House' of 1295, named after their founders Henry and Haus Bittrich and Henry Riedler."[3] Also in Swabia, "at the time when Boniface wrote, in addition to the three houses of the brothers, there were twenty-five houses of sisters who were said to be most strictly 'cloistered or enclosed.' "[4]

2. The cloister

The first element which became a serious obstacle to the development of common life among Tertiary women was the cloister. The problem concerning the cloister centered around the point that for some decades, if not for centuries, controversy held back the formation of associations which truly merited the status of being a congregation. It represented a problem that troubled the movement towards community life in the female Third Order Regular for long periods of time causing even the dissolution of congregations of sisters when these congregations had become well established.

We must say something more concerning the problem of the cloister at least in its principal details.[5]

The term "cloister" is understood here as Church legislation (which changed at various times) that dealt with the manner "in which women could enter inside the communities of men, and vice versa." Here we want to speak only about the cloister of women.

Even though the Church was interested in this problem from the very beginning of religious life, from the start there was a certain flexibility since "cloister" was regulated

---

[3]Stefano Ivancic, *Cronologium seu historica monumenta Tertii ordinis regularis de Poenitentia S. Francisci*, Editio Assiensis (a cura di R. Pazzelli), 1957, p. 44.

[4]Ivancic, *op. cit.*, p. 45.

[5]See the word "clausura" in DIP, I, col. 1166-1183, written by various authors.

by conciliar decrees and other laws which were more local in character. "The first explicit witness dealing with the cloister of women is found in the Rule for some virgins written by Saint Caesarius of Arles about the year 513."[6] The Carolingian reform, in the eighth and ninth centuries, favored more precise laws, laws of general import. The political and social anarchy which followed the Carolingian age threw everything into chaos and caused abuses and even scandals in monasteries. The remedies of the Gregorian reform, which endured throughout the entire twelfth century, worked to remove abuses. This was a period in which minute prescriptions concerning the cloister were introduced. They dealt even with walls of monasteries, doors, keys and grills. The concept of monastery was changing. Up to that time the term in use was the "house of consecrated virgins." Changing also in the same period was the concept of monastic life.

It was also a time in which a decidedly pessimistic concept of the nature of woman very quickly developed. The monk Idungo of Prufening summed up the attitudes of his day by saying: "the very frailty of the feminine sex demands a more strict guardianship."[7] Under the influence of similar attitudes, laws concerning the cloister became severe. The cloister was understood to be "a good in itself," a good to which all else must be sacrificed. Thus in a monastery one could not allow absolute poverty because if the nuns could not go out even to beg, the monastery must have possessions to be able to provide for their sustenance. Since 1225 the Poor Clares had been recognized as enclosed nuns. This had required that they remain inside the monastery. Clare had to fight all her life to obtain the *privilege of poverty* (privilegium paupertatis). She obtained this privilege only after the assurance was given that the friars would provide for the monastery by begging for them.

Until the time of Saint Francis, feminine religious life was exclusively monastic in form. The life of the beguines was the first lifestyle not to meet this standard. Consequently, the beguines immediately experienced a

---

[6]Leclercq, *Clausura*, in DIP, I, col. 1168.

[7]*Ibid.*, col. 1170.

cool welcome from the Church, a welcome all too quickly transformed into opposition. The same fate befell the beginnings of community life among the Franciscan Penitent Sisters. The pessimistic concept of women had spread very quickly. Soon the prevailing principle was that "in order to remain virtuous, a woman must have a husband or a wall, *maritum aut murum.*" This was called "the doctrine of the two m's: matrimony or monastery."[8]

The decree *Periculoso ac detestabili* of Boniface VIII in 1298 codified this concept concerning the nature of women in a piece of very restrictive legislation. This decree had both high and low moments of compliance. It would be reinforced by the Council of Trent, which extended its legislation to all religious women without exception.

This constitution or decree required that all, "each and every nun, present and future, in every order whatsoever, must remain under perpetual cloister in their monasteries."[9] Boniface VIII's decree remained the basis of legislation on the cloister for centuries. The Council of Trent renewed those prescriptions and in addition decreed that those who violate the cloister would be excommunicated *ipso facto.* Pope Saint Pius V, during the years 1566-1568, strengthened the importance of the cloister through practical applications of the law.

The entire female religious movement in every future action would have to keep in mind such legislation. For the most part the practical application of this legislation would depend on the interpretation of the local bishops, at least until the Council of Trent. Because of this practice in interpretation, even after the above mentioned decree, some groups of Franciscan sisters were able both to beg and to work more or less freely.

3. Further difficulties

That part of the female penitential movement that had begun to live community and religious life properly so called, was considered equal in all effects to the beguine movement. As a matter of fact there were similarities,

---

[8]See *ibid.*, col. 1170.

[9]See the decree *Periculoso* in AE, Friedberg, *Corpus Iuris Canonici,* II, Graz, 1959, col. 1053-1054.

especially external ones. Both movements were marked by a simple lifestyle, by frequent prayers and by a voluntary dedication to hospitality and the care of the sick.[10]

The first opposition, or at least we could say, the first less than benevolent regard, came from the official Church itself because of the new way of community life. The opposition here dealt with the fact that these associations of community or semi-community life, which were religious or semi-religious in character, did not live under an approved Rule.

When legislation concerning the cloister was made more restrictive, there was an added motive for opposition by the Church. (This period of time corresponds more or less with the time when the new beginnings in religious life were being made.) The female communities of Tertiaries that were being formed did not want to hear anything about a cloister. It is true that the legislation spoke exclusively about *nuns*. Neither the beguines nor the first Franciscan sisters (we are now able to begin using this terminology even if imperfectly) had any intention of becoming *nuns*, neither Benedictine nor Poor Clare nuns. The concept of a religious sister who would not be a nun and who would thus not have to live in a monastic cloister, did not even exist at this time.

4. Heterodox beguines and beghards

A third element must be considered all by itself because it cast great discredit on the new communities and drew the open and active opposition of the Church. Part of the beguine movement became involved with heterodoxy. "Little by little," wrote Vernet, "beguines and beghards allowed themselves to become involved with theories which drew censures of the Church upon themselves"[11] and to such an extent that thereafter the very names beguine and beghard came to mean "followers of heretical doctrines." It is true that many beguines and the overwhelming majority of the Franciscan sisters adhered to orthodox teachings but the external appearances of both

---

[10]Vernet, F., *Béghards, béguines heterodoxes*, I, *Histoire*, II, *Doctrines*, in DTC II/1, col. 528.

[11]Vernet, *op. cit.*, col. 529.

groups were the same. The inquisitions of the Church, which at that time were just beginning, were not known for subtlety. Hurried bishops and prelates did not make many fine distinctions and they struck out indiscriminately against true heretics and those who only externally appeared to be such.

We must note here that the female part of the movement, the beguines, did not start out as an heretical movement. It followed the heretical movement of the beghards. Ordinarily the beghards did not enlist the beguines in their excesses, but at the time of correcting error, the beguines were considered to be on the same level as the beghards.

The heterodox beghards and beguines can be classified into two principal groups. The first group was confused with the Franciscan Spirituals of that era, and were also called the Fraticelli. The second group would be those who had contact with the sect called the "Brothers of the Free Spirit." These last mentioned are "those who are commonly called beghards."[12] They were found mainly in Flanders, in northern France and in Germany.

There were public and clamorous condemnations hurled against both groups. The bulls of John XXII *Sancta romana* of December 30, 1317 and *Gloriosam ecclesiam* of January 23, 1318, were issued against the Fraticelli.[13] The heretical beghards and beguines were condemned in the Council of Vienne in 1311. These condemnations were published under the name "the Clementine Constitutions" by John XXII himself on October 25, 1317. These condemnations also included a listing of their errors. The fundamental idea of the sect the "Free Spirit" was that a man could arrive at such a state of perfection that he could become "one with God and God one with him without any distinction." From the *speculative* viewpoint, the result of this was that man could attain such perfection that the possibility of further progress could not be admitted since "God does not undergo progression." In this state a man not only can enjoy final beatitude, even in this present life

---

[12]*Ibid.*, col. 530.

[13]See the content of these two bulls in R. Pazzelli, *La personalità di Giovanni XXII and the bull "Altissimo in divinis" del 18 november 1323*, in *Prime manifestazione, op. cit.*, pp. 56-59.

but he becomes absolutely faultless. From a practical viewpoint a man could allow his body everything that it desires: fornication itself would not be a sin. There were other errors in the field of philosophy, but the doctrine just mentioned was more than enough for censure.

The Church had taken measures even before the Council of Vienne. In 1290 beghards and beguines were arrested at Bale and Culmar (above Strasbourg). In 1310 the beguine Margaret Porete was burned at the stake in Paris. After the censure of the Council of Vienne, the beghards did not disappear. On the contrary, they increased in their errors, becoming really involved with intellectual and moral aberrations. This is why the Church was so severe even against mere suspects. The beghards became fewer towards the end of the 1300's and were mixed up with other errors until they disappeared completely in the Protestant reformation.[14]

5. The defense of the Tertiary sisters

How did the Tertiary sisters defend themselves during the trials mentioned above?

a) Concerning the accusation that they did not live under an approved Rule, the sisters used more or less the strategy of the beguines. We do know that many beguine associations adopted as their own the Rule of Nicholas IV (1289). They were, at least in some places, able to be recognized as living under an approved Rule. The Tertiary sisters, at least those who desired to remain faithful to their Franciscan orientation and did not adopt other Rules to escape the difficulties (as seems to have happened in the cases of some monasteries in Umbria) these sisters were able to assert that they followed a Rule approved by the pope for an order which the same bull of approval had recognized as having been "instituted by Saint Francis." Even with this strategy, the sisters were not always able to avoid difficulties with ecclesiastical authorities such as bishops and minorite visitators. According to the majority opinion of these dignitaries, the Rule of Nicholas IV had been composed

solely for persons in secular life and this Rule

---

[14]See Vernet, *op. cit.*, col. 530-534.

ought not to be understood as being a norm for religious life, properly so called. Therefore, whoever professed such a Rule, neither could nor should have been able to make a public profession of vows. The religious profession of the Tertiary, affirmed minorite visitators, is contrary to the will of Saint Francis and is not indicated...in the Rule of Nicholas IV.[15]

Unfortunately, even the bull *Sancta romana* of John XXII, directed against the Fraticelli in 1317, later on seemed to support that interpretation. The pope in this document was seeking

> to bring about the full effect of his censure (against the Fraticelli) and he specified and proscribed every possible subterfuge or camouflage already attempted or available to the rebel Spirituals that they could use to disguise themselves and their attempts to free themselves from the censures..."some of them affirming that they belonged to the Third Order of Blessed Francis, called the Order of Penitents. They are seeking to cover over their status and life by hiding under the name of the Third Order of St. Francis. The truth of the matter is that such a manner of life was not granted to the Rule of the Third Order."[16]

Even if it was not the intention of the pope, this last phrase from *Sancta romana* was used by others for more that a century as a weapon against the community—religious life of the friars and sisters of the Third Order Regular.

In 1323 there came a beautiful letter *Altissimo in divinis* addressed by Pope John XXII to the "Brothers of the Order of Penance throughout Italy." This letter seemed to settle the question for once and for all. To the Tertiary friars who were complaining to the pope that they were persecuted because of their profession of vows, John replied: "The practice of making a profession of vows, started by you, is

---

[15]R. Pazzelli, *Il Terz´ordine regolare, op. cit.*, p. 95.

[16]R. Pazzelli, *La personalità di Govanni XXII e la bolla "Altissimo in divinis" del 18 november 1323*, in *Prime manifestazioni, op. cit.*, p. 52

very useful and praiseworthy and in accord with the will of Blessed Francis. We now approve this practice and declare that it is not contrary to the Rule of Nicholas IV. While understanding that this order was instituted by Saint Francis for people living in the world, there is nothing to prohibit a more perfect life to those who wish to enter this Order."[17] This document was then an explicit approval of the regular religious life in the Franciscan Third Order.

Unfortunately, this bull remained largely unknown because very soon traces of it were lost or hidden or forgotten in some Umbrian hermitage and "it would not have any weight in the disputes of those years" and even for centuries to come.[18]

Nevertheless, the Tertiary friars and sisters in the majority of cases continued on their way towards regular religious life and regarded the Rule of Nicholas IV as "their Rule." They continued to appeal to this Rule and to follow it at least until 1521 even if it did not free them from misunderstandings and persecutions. A primitive formula of their profession of vows has been preserved. "This involves the promises of the Secular Tertiaries with the addition at the end of the three vows of religion."[19]

b) The laws of the Church regarding the cloister modified the emergence and development of all congregations of the Franciscan sisters. Generally, the practical application of the cloister depended on the interpretations and decisions and we might say, at times, the conciliatory attitude, of the individual bishops in whose territories the congregations were found. This fact allows us to know how it was possible to have the start of so many associations and how on the other hand it was also possible later on to have the dissolution of some congregations which were already well established. The congregation of Blessed Angelina

---

[17]See the circumstances and details surrounding this bull in Pazzelli, *Il Terz'ordine regolare, op. cit.*, pp. 98-100.

[18]See Pazzelli, *La personalità di Giovanni XXII*, in *op. cit.*, p. 64.

[19]Here is the Latin formula of the profession: "Ego frater N.N. voveo et promitto Deo et B. Mariae Virgini et B. Francisco et omnibus Sanctis et tibi Pater, servare mandata Dei, toto tempore vitae meae, et satisfacere, ut convenit, transgressionibus contra Regulam et vivendi modum Tertii Ordinis de Poenitentia institutum per B. Franciscum, et per D. Nicolaum papam IV confirmatam, cum de hoc interpellatus fuero ad voluntatem Visitatoris nostri, vivendo in obedientia, sine proprio et in castitate."

beguines in the Council of Vienne. Under such a pretext they have attempted and are attempting to oblige the aforementioned "Brothers and Sisters of Penance" under the pain of excommunication and interdict, to abandon their habit and the religious status of their Rule.

Because, then, they have not obeyed in these particulars (the abandon of the habit and rule)— which after all they were not obliged to do—the aforementioned prelates have pronounced sentences of excommunication against them and levied various other grave impositions.

We therefore decree that the above mentioned Constitution of Clement V does not at all refer to the Brothers and Sisters of the Third Order, and we command those to whom this bull is addressed that they are not to interfere with nor permit others to interfere with these brothers and sisters, nor with the Friars Minor with whom they are associated. Anything that has been done to the contrary against these same persons, is now revoked by us.

This bull represents the official judgement of the Church on the movement of the Franciscan Tertiaries after the *Sancta romana* document.

In the first part of this document, besides the judgement above, reasons are presented why the Apostolic See undertook the defense of the order. Expressions of such force, would not be found in a bull if the Holy See had not been aware of the spiritual reality under consideration.

No distinction is made between a lay form of life and a regular religious form of life (community life with vows). Judgement was given on the order as it was. It is for the historians to say whether or not it is possible that in the order, in this period of history, there were in practice two clearly distinct forms of life. The first form would be the life lived "in domibus propriis," and the second form, the life in the hermitages and in community.

There is more. The bull explicitly stated: a) this order was instituted by Saint Francis. It was immediately ("iamdudum") approved and confirmed by the Apostolic

See and was strengthened ("communitus") by the granting of various privileges. b) The Brothers and Sisters of the Third Order have lived and are living in the observance of their Rule ("Vixerint et vivunt in observantia Regulae tertii Ordinis").

Etsi Apostolicae Sedis did not bring about the hoped for effects everywhere. Some bishops and prelates continued to harass the tertiaries. They continued to command them to abandon the habit and status of the Third Order. These prelates excommunicated these tertiaries when they did not obey their orders.

The following year in 1320 (on April 8) John XXII took energetic measures to counteract the disobedience of some bishops and prelates. The bull *Dudum delectis*, addressed to the Archbishop of Besançon and various other local deans and canons, gives evidence of this intent. The pope ordered that the Bishop of Basel, Gerald, and his officialis, Richard, be called to judgement: the pope commands them to recall the decrees they had promulgated which were in contrast to the position of the Holy See in the bull *Etsi Apostolicae*. This new document grants authority to promulgate sentences of excommunication, suspension, and interdict against the bishop and his officialis should they not obey. The bishop had two months with which to comply with this order and the officialis had twenty days from the time of receiving this citation.

It seems that stronger language could not be used to support the Third Order.

The historians do tell us that bishops, prelates and inquisitors here and there did harass the tertiary friars and sisters along with the heretical beghards and beguines, even to the point of closing some of their houses. But now the Franciscan sisters had a document from the Apostolic See that they could invoke in their defense, and little by little, unfounded persecutions began diminishing.

In this fourteenth century "in spite of opposition and mistrust," Péano has written,

> the movement towards regular religious life
> intensified and became more organized. Houses
> seemed to multiply and statutes were worked

out. From the profession of the Rule of the Third Order with a common life there gradually emerges true religious life with the living out of the vows of religion, even if some authorities were unwilling to acknowledge these friars and sisters as authentic religious.[26]

[26]Péano, *op. cit.*, p. 21.

CHAPTER V

THE FIRST CONGREGATIONS

1. Tendencies and federations

The second half of the fourteenth century marks the rise of many communities of Franciscan sisters. This period of history has its distinct characteristics. Each community or monastery has its own beginning within its own region or country. Each remains independent and so is not federated with another.

The phenomenon of individualism tends to become somewhat modified near the end of the same century. It seems there are two reasons for this modification: 1) monasteries which have been successful, that is, those who have a good number of vocations, are forced to make new foundations. It is natural for these new houses to retain ties with the mother house. It is the beginning of a congregation. 2) Even monasteries which had their beginning independently of one another and which had maintained that independence, now began to form confederations with other monasteries which had more or less the same characteristics or purpose. Here we have the beginning of a federation which in time may change itself into a congregation.

2. The Elizabethan sisters

Typical evidence for this phenomenon of individualism which moved towards federation in the very heart of the Franciscan Third Order movement is represented by the case of the Elizabethan sisters. In the earliest history of the Franciscan sisters of this name, we find sisters living in semi-cloistered community; we find individual convents or small groups of houses. Elizabethan sisters began in the thirteenth century and were found in Austria, Germany, and France, where they were better known as

Sisters of Mercy. This group of sisters had dedicated themselves to the care of the sick in hospitals following the example of Saint Elizabeth of Hungary, +1231, whom they often took as the patron saint of their houses.[1]

These communities first began as an association of common life and were gradually transformed into full religious communities as members made their profession of religious vows. Some convents had dependent houses which grouped together and became true congregations. The evolution of the Elizabethan sisters was typical of the transformation of the Third Franciscan Order from secular to regular status. Together with the Grey Sisters, whom we will shortly consider, the Elizabethan sisters had a remarkable influence on religious life in central Europe during the thirteenth and fourteenth centuries. These sisters were the focus of attraction for many penitential groups which had a similar purpose. They followed the Rule of Nicholas IV to which they sometimes added their own statutes. In the middle of the sixteenth century, in spite of pressures from the Protestant Reformation that closed many of their houses, the Elizabethans then still numbered more than 3,800 professed sisters. Some of the earliest communities of these sisters are still in existence as independent houses. Some Elizabethan communities, still existing, have started new institutes which have maintained the special apostolate of the earliest communities and at times have retained the original name. There are also other institutes or congregations of Franciscan sisters today which arose after the Council of Trent, and while these new institutes retain the original name and the original ideals of the earliest Elizabethan sisters, they are not directly associated with them.

Among these newer institutes are found the Elizabethan Sisters of Aachen who were founded in the seventeenth century by Apollonia Radermacher. Founded in the nineteenth century were the Elizabethan Sisters of Padua and the Franciscan Elizabethans, called the Suore Bigie in Italian. The Elizabethans of Padua were founded by Elisabetta Vendramini and the Franciscan Elizabethans were founded by Father Ludovico da Casoria.

---

[1]E. Frascadore, *Elisabettine, Suore*, in DIP, III, col. 1114.

3. From beguine sisters to Franciscan sisters

It is necessary to say a word about the phenomenon of Franciscan orientation that was adopted by some beguinages, especially in Upper Germany. One such community of beguines that became Franciscan was the community of Dilligen-Donau. This group of sisters had its beginning as a beguinage very early, about the year 1241. They had the good fortune to survive and become a Franciscan congregation and to pass unscathed through the religious wars and civil suppressions down to our own time.

The statutes of the beguinage of Dilligen during the years 1302-1307 legislated for the beguines that "in everything that pertains to our spirituality, they must be under the guidance of the respective minister of the Minorites in Germany." The free community of beguines thus became a community having a Franciscan orientation. On the advice of the Bishop of Augusta, Degenhard by name, they adopted in the middle of the fourteenth century the Rule of Nicholas IV. Afterwards, from the time of the Council of Trent until the year 1774 they would be obliged to follow the law of the cloister. At that time, under the direction of Bishop Clement Wenceslao, they adopted the apostolate of education. It was this new apostolate which saved them from civil suppression in 1803. In the second half of the last century, by means of academic organization and hospital work, they expanded rapidly. Today these sisters have about 1970 professed sisters and are the only congregation of Franciscan sisters who can boast of a direct uninterrupted lineage from their community of the thirteenth century.[2]

Among the examples of beguines who adopted the Rule of Nicholas IV and thus became Franciscans, we also remember the case of the community of Kaufbeuren in the diocese of Augusta in Germany. The beguinage of Kaufbeuren received the Rule of the Third Order in 1313 and their spiritual care was entrusted to the Friars Minor. This community lived a contemplative life, and at the

---

[2]G. Rocca, *Francescane*, di Dillingen, in DIP, IV, col. 226-228. The Sisters of Saint Francis of Dillingen, Germany have a province in the United States: The Sisters of Saint Francis of the Immaculate Heart of Mary at Hankinson, North Dakota.

same time worked in the apostolate of caring for the sick and also of needlework.

During the storm of the Protestant Reformation, the majority of the citizens of Kaufbeuren left the Church, while the religious sisters remained faithful under the guidance of their superior, Regina Kirchmayr, 1545. In the year 1703, a remarkable young woman, Anna Hoss known in religion as Crescenzia, 1682-1744, entered this monastery and became its illustrious member. She was beatified by Pope Leo XIII on October 13, 1900.[3]

This monastery remained a single foundation until the nineteenth century when it began to open daughter-houses and was transformed into a congregation. Today this congregation has eight houses and is known as the Franciscan Sisters of Kaufbeuren.

4. The Grey Sisters (or Hospital Sisters)

The first process of federation for which we have certain knowledge is the Congregation of the Grey Sisters. The official date of their recognition as a congregation is the year 1413, given in the bull *Personas vacantes* from the Pisan Pope John XXIII on August 16, 1413.

Their origin as a community, however, goes back much further in time to the first half of the thirteenth century. Their beginning is somewhat the same as that pattern we have seen with the Elizabethan sisters: "Some women who worked in the hospitals of northern France and Flanders experienced the desire to lead a spiritual life in community while at the same time they continued their charitable work.... Many of these communities chose the Rule of the Third Order."[4] Here is something that is very clear, something we need to emphasize as an essential point: It is the motive why these sisters desired the religious life. They desired "to strive for greater perfection"; nevertheless, they did not want to accept the Rule of Saint Clare of Assisi and enter a monastery for the reason that they wanted to

---

[3]G. Rocca, *Francescane di Kaufbeuren*, in DIP, IV, col. 234. See Péano, *op. cit.*, p. 31. Also see notes on their Statutes of 1300 and 1400, in M. Bihl, *De Tertio ordine*, in AFH, 15 (1922), pp. 353 ff.

[4]Péano, *Le Religiose francescana, op. cit.*, p. 27.

continue with their charitable work. This is a fundamental motivating reason for the sisters and also for the friars of the Third Order Regular. This is also the reason why, on this road to the religious state, the last vow that was mutually agreed upon was that of poverty. Men and women in a Franciscan vocation intended to dedicate themselves to external works of mercy. This apostolate demanded that they be able to dispense material resources freely. Most well known among these works of charity were construction and administration of hospitals and hospices of various kinds.

5. The bull *Personas vacantes*, August 26, 1413

The bull *Personas vacantes* is a document which gives us the greatest amount of certain information that we possess about this group of sisters who were called the "Grey Sisters." "The name was given to them," remarks Lemaitre, "because of the light grey color of their habit. It is known also that the color of their habit changed somewhat, and that in certain convents the color became black, as at Saint-Omer. In other convents the color was changed to white or dark blue.... The houses of the Grey Sisters were spread throughout the dioceses of Therouanne, Tournai, Cambrai and Arras."[5] The bull of John XXIII names six of these houses: Bergues St. Winoc, Dixmude, Furnes, Nieuport, Poperinghe and Ypres. The bull speaks of the request of the "Brothers and Sisters of the Third Order of Penance, instituted by Saint Francis," who live in the above mentioned cities. They are asking the pope if he would deign to "add the force of Apostolic confirmation to their particular Statutes." The brothers and sisters observed the Rule of Nicholas IV, lived in separate houses and divided their time between work and prayer.

> Profession could not be made before the age of eighteen and the bull gives the formula for this profession. The Divine Office comprises the praying of the breviary *sine nota*, without notes or *recto tono*, and in accord with the usage of the holy Roman Church for those brothers and sisters who know Latin. For others who have

---

[5]Henri Lemaitre, *Statuts des Religieuses du Tiers ordre franciscain dites Soeurs grise hospitallières (1483)*, in AFH, 5 (1911), p. 714.

less education there was the obligation to pray the Office of the Blessed Virgin Mary, or the psalms for matins and the other hours. Finally, those who knew no Latin at all were to recite the Our Fathers.

This bull informs us that there were two supreme authorities in the congregation: the visitor, *from another religious order*, and the minister of the order itself, who had authority over the friars and sisters. The sisters in their turn would have a *ministra*, elected in the same way as the minister and for the same period of time. "In the absence of the minister, she would have authority over all the sisters just as the minister would have authority over all the friars and sisters." Every house would have a male superior for the friars and a female superior for the sisters elected by all the members of that community. The Statutes established in detail the form and color of the habit. For the sisters, there was a grey tunic with a rough cord and wooden sandals. In the house, the sisters wore a white veil and outside the house they could wear a mantel of the same cloth with something "to cover the head and shield the face." Especially outside the convent, the sisters must avoid wearing clothing opposed to poverty.

> Chapters were to be held separately, to deal with internal matters. Chapters had the authority to reform ancient customs and to replace them with new ones with the consent of the visitor. New statutes would become law after the local ordinary gave his approval. The jurisdiction of the local ordinary also included punishable offenses. Finally, the male Tertiaries were granted the faculty to celebrate solemnly Mass and Divine Office in their chapels, of having the bell-towers extend above the roof tops (ab extra super tectum) and they might have the bell rung "toties quoties" i.e., as often as they pleased, as long as they gave due consideration to the rights of the parish churches and other persons having benefices.[6]

---

[6]Péano, *op. cit.*, p. 47 (English typescript); p. 28 of Italian version. Here is the formula for profession given in the bull *Persona vacantes*: "In nomine Patris et Filii et Spiritus sancti. Ego N. voveo et promitto Deo et

From other sources we know that the Grey Sisters had "as their principal apostolic work the care of the sick. They must do this work without any recompense and without having in mind any other purpose but the love of God and neighbor. They extended this care in their hospitals as well as in private homes."[7] It was for this reason that the Grey Sisters in many places were also called Hospital Sisters.

6. Further development of the Grey Sisters

From Pope Martin V the Grey Sisters received a second bull *Ex Apostolicae Sedis* on June 19, 1430. This document ratified the privileges granted by John XXIII who was, as we mentioned above, a pope of Pisa. Not everyone recognized John XXIII as pope and consequently not everyone accepted his decrees as certainly valid. So Martin V confirmed the earlier privileges and extended them to three other monasteries which in the meantime had been added to the federation: Saint-Omer, Houschoot and Dunkirk.[8]

Saint-Omer soon became one of the most important houses and has remained so down to our time. At the moment of *Ex Apostolicae Sedis* there were two monasteries of sisters in the city of Saint-Omer. The first was the House of Saint Margaret, established about the year 1350 and the second the House of Saint Catherine of Zion, founded in 1324. The religious women of Saint Margaret adopted the grey habit of the Third Order in 1388 and had received special privileges from Pope Martin V in 1427. The Sisters of Saint Catherine were also called the Black Sisters, the Sisters of the Cellar (because they begged), the Sisters of Lombardy (because of the name of the street on which the monastery was located) and the Sisters of the

---

beatae Mariae virgini, beato Francisco et omnibus sanctis et tibi fratri N. omnibus diebus vitae meae esse obediens domino Ioanni papae et suis successoribus canonice intrantibus et vivere in obedientia et paupertate, sine proprio et in castitate, et observare regulam Tertii ordinis beati Francisci secundum declarationem et ordinationem sanctae romanae ecclesiae factam et traditam per praedictum dominum Nicolaum papam, et cetera omnia, quae huic modo vivendi ad salutem animae meae conveniunt, ad discretionem meorum superiorum."

[7]Lemaitre, *op. cit.*, p. 714.
[8]See the bull in BF, VII, n. 1891, p. 376.

Mantel (because of the large mantel they wore outside the convent). They received the Rule of the Third Order in 1377 from Pope Gregory XI.

The Sisters of Saint Margaret had been entrusted with the care of the hospital of Our Lady of the Sun. This work made up the greater part of their activity and almost their identity for some centuries.

Various pontifical documents refer to this house. The *Vestrae devotionis* of Nicholas V in 1447 informs us that among other things the visitator was to be elected by the Tertiary sisters. The bull *Speciali gratia et favore* of Pope Pius II in 1458 entrusted the sisters to the direction of the Observant Visitator of the Province of France and extended the same privilege to other houses founded by the hospital of Our Lady of the Sun. In the years that followed, other houses were founded or were united to this hospital, and they all soon constituted a federation of independent houses, always remaining subject to the Observant Visitator of the Province of France.[9]

In the document *Devotionis et sinceritatis* sent to these sisters September 14, 1465, Pope Paul II confirms the right of the Sisters of Saint-Omer to elect their own visitator. In the meantime, four other hospitals had been united to the Sisters of Saint-Omer in the dioceses of Saint-Omer, Cambrai and Arras, ("Moriensium et Cameracensium et Attrebatensium") and two more were in the process of being associated with the Province of France. This was in accord with the divisions the Friars Minor had made in that territory. Pope Paul said he now extended the same favors and privileges already granted to the congregation, also to the new hospitals and to all persons associated with them.[10] On August 15, 1483 a Chapter was held at Wisbecq in the Diocese of Brugelette, where there were twenty-four superiors or their delegates present from the regions of Artois, Flanders or Hainaut. This Chapter

---

[9]Péano, *op. cit.*, p. 29.

[10]See *Devotionis et sinceritatis*, in F. Bordoni, *Archivium Bullarum Privilegiorum, Instrumentorum et Decretorum Fratrum et Suorum Tertii Ordinis S. Francisci*, Parmae, 1658, pp. 265-269.

accepted the "Statutes and ordinances of the sisters called the Hospital Sisters of the Third Order of Saint Francis in the Province of France." This document of regulations or statutes was drawn up by the Visitator, Brother Jacques Stoetlin, with the approval of the Vicar Provincial of France, who at that time was Brother Jean Crohin. The text was divided into seven chapters and included the following points:

1. On the manner of receiving aspirants into the order and the manner of the instruction of novices and young sisters.
2. On divine worship.
3. On the work of the sisters and the manner of working.
4. On the care of the sick.
5. On deportment outside the convent.
6. On correction and visitation of sisters who have been remiss in their duties.
7. On suffrages and prayers for the dead.

This legislative text interests us because it reveals the spirituality and activities of the Franciscan sisters of this congregation. Their historian concludes:

> These sisters did not confine themselves merely to works of charity inside their own hospitals. We can see that from the beginning of the fifteenth century, the Rule of the Third Franciscan Order, so flexible in practice, had been adapted to the care of the sick of that city and had given the sisters freedom allowing them to live in the world while obliging them at the same time to follow the same exercises of piety of the nuns.[11]

At the chapter of 1518 thirty-three local superiors were present. This seems to indicate the vitality of this federation at the close of the middle ages.[12]

During the Protestant Reformation the civil government arrogated to itself the right of closing monasteries and convents in those regions where the government, usually the prince, had adopted the Reformation. During this time male communities became totally extinct. Many women's communities were able to survive because they

---

[11]Lemaitre, *op. cit.*, p. 713.

[12]Péano, *op. cit.*, pp. 29-30. (Italian version)

were dedicated to the care of the sick, especially in the hospitals. Congregations, however, were disbanded. The houses of each congregation that were able to remain open, continued their life individually and independently from one another. At this point, one no longer speaks of the history of a congregation but rather a history of individual communities.

The houses of Saint-Omer distinguished themselves for their spirit of charity and selflessness during the terrible epidemics of 1636-1637. At the beginning of the French Revolution, 1789-1794, the hospitals of Saint-Omer had increased to three hospitals, and they joined together to form one House of Saint John in hopes of being better able to ride out the storm. But the Revolution made no exceptions and even the Sisters of Saint-Omer were evicted from the hospital. They were only able to return in 1813. At that time the civil administration of the hospitals and the absolute control which this civil administration exercised over the hospitals gravely interfered with the religious life of the sisters. "No novice could be admitted to make profession without the permission of the administrator." It seems that consent was given only if the administrator felt there was need for a new sister to serve in the hospital. "The sisters could be corrected and even dismissed from the convent by decisions of these laymen.... In most of these communities, the sisters did not have permission to pronounce the vow of poverty.... They retained their patrimony and the free disposition of their income and personal savings."[13]

In 1852 some of the convents which had survived (among them the unified convent of Saint-Omer) came together to form the new congregation of the "Franciscan Missionaries of Our Lady" with their mother house in Paris. Previously they had been called the "Franciscan Sisters of Calais." There were seven monasteries in this new congregation which represented "the remnants of the early Franciscan Tertiary congregations."

Before the French Revolution, there were seventy houses located in the north of France and in

---

[13]See Susan Moncla, *The Franciscan Missionaries of Our Lady*, in ANALECTA TOR, XIV (1981), p. 1066.

Flanders and the membership was around 12,000 sisters dedicated to the care of the sick, the wounded and those who were homeless. Therefore, they set themselves anew under the Rule of the Third Order of Saint Francis and chose to continue their service to the sick in hospitals and in private homes.[14]

So the most ancient congregation of Franciscan sisters for which we have certain documentation, survives even down to our own day under the name of the Franciscan Missionaries of Our Lady.

During the nineteenth century other convents of Grey Sisters, scattered here and there, but always in the same region, gave origin to new congregations of Franciscan Sisters with foundations and subdivisions. Each of these has been recorded in its own history.

---

[14]Mariano D'Alatri, *Francescane Missionarie di Nostra Signora,* in DIP, IV, col. 352. In 1974 the congregation comprised 110 houses with a membership of 1049 sisters. *Ibid.*

CHAPTER VI

THE CONGREGATION OF BLESSED ANGELINA OF MONTEGIOVE

The first congregation of the Franciscan sisters which received papal recognition in Italy was the Congregation of Blessed Angelina of Montegiove or of Marsciano. This recognition was received from Pope Martin V in the bull *Sacrae religionis* of August 19, 1428.

The beginning of this congregation is naturally associated with the noble standing of Angelina of Montegiove or Marsciano. A recent Congress of Franciscan Studies held at Foligno, September 22-34, 1983, brought great light on the origins and life of this congregation, even if it did not succeed in giving a final word about the dates that mark the various stages or phases of the life of its foundress. (The acts of this Congress were published by ANALECTA TOR.)[1]

1. Angelina of Montegiove

The biography of the well-known Foligno historian Ludovico Jacobilli, *La Beata Angelina*, has up to the present day been the "official text" for everyone who has been enlightened and inspired by Angelina or who has sought to establish a historical account of her life. This biography was published in Foligno in 1627.[2] Modern critics, who were at the Congress in 1983 noted above, have some reservations about this biography. They were especially concerned with the sources used by Jacobilli.

---

[1] R. Pazzelli - M. Sensi (editors), *La Beata Angelina da Montegiove e il movimento del Terz'ordine regolare francescano femminile*, Acts of the Congress of Franciscan Studies, Foligno, September 22-24, 1983. ANALECTA TOR, Roma, 1984. From now on cited as *La Beata Angelina*.

[2] L. Jacobili, *Vita della beata Angelina da Corbara, contessa di Civetella, institutrice delle monache claustrali del Terz'ordine di San Francesco e fondatrice in Foligno del monastero di Sant'Anna primo delli sedici che ella eresse in diverse province*. A. Alteri, Foligno, 1627.

Unfortunately, there was no official record of the process for Angelina's beatification. In the absence of any such documentation we must admit that the information we now have on hand is not complete enough to permit us to construct a biography that is certain in all its details.

Angelina was born at Montegiove, today a suburb of Montegabbione in the province of Terni in Umbria, about the year 1357. She was the daughter of Giacomo and Alessandra, of the family of Counts of Montegiove. The family was a branch of the Counts of Marsciano and for this reason Angelina is also known under the name of Angelina of Marsciano.[3]

We know very little about the youth of Angelina. It seems to be almost certain, from a constant tradition, that she was married to John *de Termis*, Count of Civitella. Today this place is in the province of Teramo in Abruzzo. Unfortunately, we have no documentary evidence for this event. Tradition affirms that Angelina soon after marriage became a widow and that they had no children. These were the years of battle, 1381-1385, between Charles III of Durazzo and Louis I of Angio for the control of the Kingdom of Naples.[4] We do not know on which side *de Termis* fought or whether or not he died from natural causes or in battle. Tradition says that

> Angelina then joined the penitential movement. She distributed her goods to the poor and gathered around herself a group of young women. Very soon suspicion fell upon her. She was accused of heresy by the Angevin King of a Naples, Ladislas, who wanted Angelina to be burned at the stake. The court of Naples beheld an outstanding miracle. Angelina was brought into the presence of the king and from the folds of her habit she brought forth burning coals. She was set free.[5]

---

[3]The paternal grandmother of Angelina was Fiandina della Corbara of the family of the Counts of Montemarte. She was the wife of Bindo, also called Binolo. For this reason Angelina is also called "della Corbara" by some of the earliest authors.

[4]Mariano D'Alatri, *Leggenda della beata Angelina da Montegiove, Genesis d'una biografia*, in *La Beata Angelina, op. cit.*, p. 42.

[5]Mariano D'Alatri, *op. cit.*, p. 42.

Angelina had to leave Civitella. This "could have been due to a good number of other reasons, the principal of which being that Angelina was a widow and could not inherit the title of countess."[6]

It was at this time that Angelina, according to tradition, left the kingdom of Naples "intending to go to Assisi to meditate and pray at the tomb of Saint Francis. According to Jacobilli, she began a solemn pilgrimage with her companions (*Vita,* p. 36) and reached Assisi on July 31, 1395." On August 2, while Angelina was making her visit to the Church of the Portiuncula, "she had her first inspiration to establish an authentic monastery for women Tertiaries professing the three vows of the Franciscan Rule."[7] She went to Foligno to present her plan to the bishop of that city. We know that at that time there were in Foligno five monasteries which observed the Rule of Nicholas IV.[8] Angelina chose the monastery of Saint Ann. "Jacobilli, in his *Vita della beata Angelina,* follows Wadding and places Angelina's arrival in Foligno in the year 1395 (p. 53). However, in *Additione e correctione alli 3 tome,* Jacobilli corrects himself: 'Blessed Angelina founded her congregation of Franciscan Tertiary Sisters of the Observance in Italy in the year 1385 in the monastery of Saint Ann of Foligno' (p. 498)."[9]

Original documents concerning this foundation have not come down to us. We know from other sources that "the Tertiary House of Saint Ann at Foligno was established *ex novo* by Brother Paoluccio Trinci before February 14, 1388."[10]

Among the faculties granted to Brother Paoluccio

---

[6]Mariano D'Alatri, *op. cit.,* p. 42.

[7]A. Alessandrini, *Angelina da Montegiove,* in *Dizionario biografico degli Italiani,* III, Roma, 1961, p. 208.

[8]Mario Sensi, *Il movimento francescano della Penitenza a Foligno,* in *Il movimento francescano della Penitenza nella società mediovale,* Roma, 1980, p. 404.

[9]Sensi, *Documenti per la beata Angelina, op. cit.,* p. 55, note 18. If we accept this date of Jacobilli, then we have to discard the "legend" of the trial in Naples and the Court of King Ladislas in 1384-1385. Ladislas was at that time still a child and did not come of age until 1399. See Sensi, *ibid.*

[10]Sensi, *Document per la beata Angelina, op. cit.,* p. 60. This "is deduced from the letter approving the work of Brother Paoluccio (a letter-dated in the year, 1399) sent by Brother Emilio Alferi da Asti, Minister General of the Minorites." *Ibid.*

was inserted authority to admit to the convent which he established "all those women he judged capable of persevering in the life in a praiseworthy manner and to admit them under the title of the Third Order until such time as the Holy See should decide otherwise." Pope Urban VI had approved the foundation in 1385.[11]

Angelina soon had to take over the direction of the monastery even if the date of this action is somewhat uncertain. Her task in providing direction is acknowledged in more than one document of the year 1400. From 1394 the monastery of Saint Ann was also called the monastery of the Countesses because it welcomed women from noble families. This might have been a monastery exclusively for the nobility in spite of the original words of the document of *authorization.*

Historical documentation soon shows that this monastery was associated with monasteries in Todi and Assisi. Pope Boniface IX recognized this monastery officially with the bull *Provenit ex vestrae devotionis* dated January 14, 1403. In this bull the pope "granted to Angelina, director, and her twenty-six 'poor nuns' of the House of Saint Ann in Foligno, the faculty of electing a confessor with full faculties to absolve them, at least at the hour of death (semel tantum in articulo mortis). It was the official recognition of the Tertiary House even though the policies of the Holy See concerning the cloister and the Rule of Nicholas IV remained."[12]

Some historians have thought that this official recognition of 1403 certainly was a strong invitation to other houses of Tertiaries or monasteries-in-formation that during this time began to multiply in central Italy. These monasteries began to form a federation first, then a union with the monastery of Saint Ann in Foligno in the strict sense of "congregation." Within a short period of time we have the union of six monasteries explicitly named in the bull of approval in 1428. These houses were San Giovanni in Todi, San Quirico in Assisi, Santa Margherita in Ascoli, Saint'Onofrio in Florence and Sant'Agnese in Viterbo.

---

[11]See Pierre Péano, *Le Religiose, op. cit.,* p. 23.

[12]Sensi, *Document per la beata Angelina, op. cit.,* p. 66.

The internal life of these quasi monasteries has not left us enough documentation that will allow us to reconstruct the broad outlines of that life. In the beginning it seems that Angelina was helped in the direction of the House of Saint Ann by Sister Cecca of Burgaro who was of the family of the Counts of Marsciano and Angelina's cousin. But all records concerning Cecca cease with the year 1406. We have nothing to tell us about the spiritual direction developed by the friars of Brother Paoluccio. Likewise no traces remain concerning Angelina's activity undertaken in behalf of the federation. Hagiographic tradition attributes to Angelina a great network of contacts and also twenty Tertiary houses personally founded by her.[13]

The road must have been fortunate and happy.

2. The bull *Sacrae religionis* (August 19, 1428)

Pope Martin V promulgated a most important document *Sacrae religionis* on August 19, 1428.[14] Even though some historians do not agree, we maintain this bull constitutes official recognition and even approval of the six confederated monasteries. When the last word on this document has been said, we believe that it will be correct to say of this document that it gave approval to Blessed Angelina's congregation.[15] In this document in fact the pope granted the convent of Saint Ann, and the six Tertiary houses (bizzocaggi) that had in the meantime formed the federation with it, the faculty of electing a minister (a ministra) in each house. The pope also granted the faculty of receiving the profession of novices. In effect, this was the legitimation of all that had already been accomplished in the Tertiary houses. Finally, the pope granted the federation the faculty to elect a minister general (a "ministra generale")

---

[13]*Ibid.*, p. 65.

[14]BF, VII, n. 1826., pp. 706-707.

[15]Sensi, who brought us so much knowledge about the events in the life of Blessed Angelina, considers the bull *Apostolicae Sedis* of May 2, 1440 as the solemn approval of the Tertiary congregation in Foligno and not the bull *Sacrae Religionis*. See *Documenta per la beata Angelina, op. cit.*, p. 74.

who had the right to conduct visitations, to correct the sisters, to remove unworthy local ministers from office. The minister general and the local ministers in their turn were subject to the visitation of the ministers and visitators of the Friars Minor. This document did not, however, define the exact limits of the jurisdictional and coercive authority the pope gave to the Friars Minor.[16]

By virtue of this document, a custom developed that for some years at least

> the ministers (le ministre) and the councilors (discrete) of each convent gathered together every three years in one of the monasteries to celebrate a Chapter. They elected the minister general (la ministra generale) who in the company of her most experienced sisters, made the periodic visitation of the various communities that she might have knowledge of the local situation, be able to maintain discipline, and be able to choose the local ministers. Angelina, as minister general, often travelled from one convent to another. However, her residence was the Convent of Saint Ann in Foligno.[17]

Unfortunately, soon afterwards, things were no longer peaceful. The same Pope Martin V in the same year 1428, December 9th, published *Licet inter coetera*. In this document the pope decreed that Tertiary men and women, those who were "regular" and those who were not, must be subject to the obedience of the superiors of the Friars Minor. This measure obviously brought the tendency toward complete autonomy and union to an abrupt halt. In that very period of history in Italy, not only in the female congregation of Blessed Angelina, but also in the male congregation of Lombardy of the Third Order Regular, the process of unification and complete self-government were well under way.

3. Evaluation of the importance of *Licet inter coetera* (December 9, 1428)

The text of the bull specifies the circumstances and

---

[16]Sensi, *Documenti*, *op. cit.*, p. 68.

[17]A. Alessandrini, *Angelina da Montegiove*, *loc. cit.*, p. 209.

reasons for the steps adopted. Thus, we know that the minister general of the Friars Minor, Father Anthony of Massa Marittima, had discussed with the pope the problem of some people, both clerics and seculars, both men and women, who were wearing a grey habit much like the habit of the Minors. The minister general said they were calling themselves Tertiaries of Saint Francis, that they professed the Third Rule. Some of them, either with authorization or on their own initiative, were living together in community, while others were leading a religious life according to their own whims without due reverence and obedience. The minister general concluded that such a state of affairs caused confusion in the Third Order and scandal to souls.

With the background of such reports, the pope took action to remove the habit of the minors from some would-be Tertiaries. To avoid further scandal, the pope entrusted Cardinal Giordano, Bishop of Albano, with the task of converting all the Tertiaries to obedience to the superiors of the First Order. The said superiors had authority to make official visitations, to reform, and if necessary, to impose suitable punishments on the Tertiaries.[18]

Some historians noted that the unpopular measures of *Licet inter coetera* were not taken by the pope because he had personal knowledge and conviction that the Third Order (at that point regular) needed correction. Instead they affirm, the pope acted unilaterally after the insistent requests of the minister general of the Minorites.[19]

The Friars Minor wanted to determine the application of the bull *Licet inter coetera*. They held a special General Chapter in Assisi in 1430, confirming the unity of direction for the female Franciscan movement in the famous Martinian Constitutions prepared at this Chapter. The pope seemed more than satisfied and a short while later sent the declaratory judgment *Pervigilis more* by which he "confirmed" the constitutions made by the Chapter. Among other things, the pope specified that the Poor Clare nuns "and all other monasteries or houses where the

---

[18]BF, VII, n. 1843, pp. 715-716.

[19]R. Pazzelli, *Il Terz'ordine regolare, op. cit.*, p. 115. The impartial De Gubernatis affirmed with prudent circumlocution, for example: "The letter of Martin V, sent only because of the requests of the Minister

common life was followed were strictly obliged to submit to the jurisdiction of the superiors of the Friars Minor or their delegates."[20]

What took place immediately at the Monastery of Saint Ann in Foligno gives a clear idea of the desires of the Tertiary Sisters of Blessed Angelina and the external circumstances which surrounded pontifical documents.

At the end of October, 1430, the new Minister General of the Friars Minor, Brother William of Casale, was in Umbria and specifically in Foligno to visit the houses of his order. "During his stay in Foligno," writes Sensi,

> Brother William of Casale, in all probability, met with Sister Angelina. Angelina, in accord with her office of minister general, offered her obedience in compliance with the norms of the Martinian Constitutions. However, the formal act of obedience was deferred until the third of November in the Church of Saint Francis in Foligno in the presence of Brother Glasso of Naples. Glasso had a few days before been elected Minister of the Province of Saint Francis and, hence, was the representative of Brother William of Casale. Sister Angelina promised for herself and for all the congregation which had elected her their head, obedience to the Minister General of the Friars Minor as established in the bull *Licet inter coetera* and confirmed by the decree *Pervigilis more*. Very soon it was clear to the majority of the sisters at Saint Ann's Monastery that the obedience offered by Sister Angelina in the name of and in behalf of the whole congregation would have the inevitable consequence of making cloistered nuns of the whole congregation. This is why, seven days later, all the Tertiary sisters gathered in Chapter at Saint Ann's. The chapter, at least for that day,

General (of the Minors) was revoked by the letter of Eugene IV." De Gubernatis, *Orbis seraphicus*, II, p. 890.

[20]"And all monastaries whatsoever, or places of regular life for women...all of their ministers, must submit to the jurisdiction and obedience (as) a most strict obligation." See the letter *Pervigilis more* in BF, VII, n. 1892, p. 737.

set aside the more than seventy year old Sister Angelina, and her place was taken by Sister Orsella Monaldi who was on record as *the most worthy minister general of the sisters of the monastery of the continents* [21] *of the Third Order of Saint Francis*. This Chapter named Brother Stephen of Giacomo from Como, a friar of the Third Order of Saint Francis, as their legal representative before the pope to defend the privileges and grants which the Tertiary Sisters of Foligno saw threatened by the Minister General of the Friars Minor. Therefore, the convocation was announced for a new Chapter to be held on the following November 22 by Sister Angelina of Giacomo of Montegiove, *most worthy minister general (ministra generale) of the monastery of Saint Ann*. This Chapter renounced the actions of Sister Angelina because they had not been done freely but under threat of excommunication when she offered obedience in the name of the whole congregation to the legal representative of Brother William of Casale, Minister General of the First and Second Order: "the above mentioned Lady Angelina asserts she made that promise for herself alone," therefore without the necessary authorization of her sisters. Such a promise actually was in conflict with the Rule they had professed: "se ab observantia et jugo earum regule et norme nullatenus velle recedere—no one wishes to withdraw herself from the observance and the obligation of their rules and norms." This formal protest which followed the appointment of a patron at the Roman Curia, resulted in the publication on November 15, 1431 of the bull *Ad apostolicae dignitatis apicem* and marked a victory for the Tertiary sisters of Saint Ann who from that moment on remained somewhat distant in their relations both with the Conventuals and the Observants. They chose as their visitators and

---

[21]"Continents" was another title used to indicate the brothers and sisters of penance during the first centuries of Franciscanism.

counselors the friars of the Third Order of Penance of Saint Francis.[22]

4. The appearance of the regular Tertiary friars

To explain the appearance of Brother Stephen of Como and the "Friars of the Third Order of Penance" in the life of the congregation of Blessed Angelina, we must remember that these were the years during which the activity of the regular Tertiaries of Italy "belonging to the Congregation of Lombardy," sought to obtain official recognition and unity of their members scattered all over Italy. These years increasingly saw the celebration of regional Chapters which had for their purpose the coordination of common resources in a single direction.[23]

The bull *Licet inter coetera* of Martin V also meant an abrupt halt, even a step backwards on the road to unity and autonomy for the regular Tertiaries. They sought to remedy the situation. The Sisters of Blessed Angelina immediately understood that if they wanted to defend their autonomy, which they believed they had a right to do because of the recognition given them by the Papal bull *Sacra religionis* received only four months earlier, they had to unite their forces with the regular Tertiaries. To do this they chose, "as their legal representative before the pope," Brother Stephen of Como. A short time later documents show Stephen as the Vicar of Brother Hubert of Mondavio, "Minister General of the Third Order of Penance."[24]

Their united efforts, it seems, must have been added to protests of various foreign congregations of brothers and sisters that already had received official recognition and presumed autonomy. Very soon their efforts were crowned with success. Of course, Martin V could not rescind the decisions taken during the brief time of life that still remained for him. But his successor Eugene IV, 1431-1447, immediately did so in the first months of his

---

[22]Sensi, *Documenti per la beata Angelina, op. cit.*, pp. 70-71. See the bull *Ad apostolicae dignitatis apicem*, in BF, n.s. I, n. 37, pp. 25-26.

[23]For the events leading to unification and centralization of the male Third Order Regular in Italy, see Pazzelli, *Il terz'ordine regolare, op. cit.*, pp. 416 and 419, note 40.

[24]See Sensi, *Il movimento francescano a Foligno*, in *op. cit.*, pp. 416-419.

pontificate with the bull *Ad apostolicae dignitatis*,
November 15, 1431.

5. The bull of Eugene IV *Ad apostolicae dignitatis* (November 15, 1431)

First of all, let us give a short summary.

> From the reports of trustworthy persons, we
> have learned that following the letter of Pope
> Martin V some measures were taken that have
> caused many arguments, scandals, and difficul-
> ties. Fearing that such a state of things would
> continue if due peace was not restored to the
> Brothers and Sisters of the Third Order, and in
> our desire to promote tranquility for all and
> especially for those who want to serve God in
> regular observance, we consider that it would
> not be fitting to lessen what has been wisely
> established after mature deliberation by
> Nicholas IV with regard to the direction of the
> Brothers of Penance. Therefore, desiring to pre-
> vent lamentable difficulties, We revoke by our
> apostolic authority and We rescind the decree of
> our predecessor Martin V. We annul all ordi-
> nances and statutes which were published fol-
> lowing that decree. We decree that the direction
> of the Tertiaries that was established by
> Nicholas IV be faithfully observed. We forbid
> anyone, especially the Friars Minor to harass the
> Brothers and Sisters of Penance in any way.[25]

This letter has been given the classification of "Ad
perpetuam rei memoriam," i.e. it is not addressed to a
particular individual person. Copies of the letter were sent
the same day to the Archbishop of Compostella, to the
Bishop of Perugia, and to the Archpriest of Saint Celsus
and Julien in Rome. It seems that these officials were
the executors of the letter and their addresses tell us
something about the regions in which the decrees of the

---

[25]BF, n.s. I, n. 37, pp. 25-26. By ordering the tertiaries "to observe
faithfully whatever has been established by Nicholas IV," it is clear that
the pope gave a restrictive interpretation to the dispositions of *Supra
Montem* concerning the direction of the tertiaries. Namely, he gave this
interpretation as "counsel" and not as a disposition of law.

pope had to be put into practice.

For some years things would go quite well for Blessed Angelina's congregation. Two more monasteries were united to the congregation between the time the bull of recognition was received and the death of Angelina. These were the monasteries of Saint Elizabeth in Aquila and Saint Anthony of Padua in Perugia.[26]

6. After the death of Blessed Angelina

The traditional date for Angelina's death is July 14, 1435. Even though some contemporary scholars hold contrary opinions,[27] existing documentation makes it clear that this date is the more probable one.

Unfortunately, Angelina's death occurred when the foundation of her organization had not become fully stabilized. It seems that the choosing of the regular Tertiary friars (as spiritual directors) was accepted without resentment, at least in the early years. In fact even the professions of the Sisters of Saint Ann's were no longer held in the Church of Saint Francis, the Church of the Minorites, but took place in the monastery chapel in the hands of the Tertiary Ministers. The body of the foundress, however, was buried in Saint Francis Church.

The following year, 1436, brought the joyful news that the pope had spoken officially and that the Church recognized the community life and the profession of vows by the Tertiary sisters as legitimate, despite whatever doubts there may have been before. The pope said that their way of life did not come under the prohibition of *Sancta romana* of Pope John XXII in 1317. Eugene IV made this declaration "vivae vocis oraculo"—orally, in the presence of the Friar Minor Giovanni da Capestrano, the future Saint John Capestrano, and Fra Onofrio (Hubert) di Antonio from Mondavio, Minister General of the Regular Tertiaries of Italy who had accompanied him at this meeting with the Holy Father.[28] The result of that pontifical audience was communicated by Capestrano that very day in a well known letter *Noveritis qualiter* addressed to all the

---

[26]See Sensi, *Il movimento francescano a Foligno, op. cit.*, p. 418.

[27]See Sensi, *Documenta per la beata Angelina, op. cit.*, p. 72, nota 65; *idem, il movimento francescano a Foligno, op. cit.*, p. 419.

[28]Until a few years ago it was said that the first minister general of the

communities of friars and sisters of the Third Order of Saint Francis already living the regular life.[29]

Just prior to these events, Eugene IV sent two bulls, both dated March 29, 1436, to the congregation of Blessed Angelina. The first document *Aeternae beatitudinis* had been requested some time before Angelina's death by Angelina and the other ministers (local superiors) from the seven monasteries at that time federated with Saint Ann's in Foligno. This bull confirmed those things done by the Bishop of Todi following the bull of Martin V, *Sacra religionis* of August 9, 1428. The second document, *Ad ea ex apostolicae sedis*, was addressed to the "beloved daughter, minister general "pro tempore existenti" of the federation or congregation of Blessed Angelina. It granted the faculty of designating a vicar general and a special vicar for each of the individual houses subject to her.[30] That the document lacked a name in the title of the bull is further indication of the death of Angelina. "Probably when the pope approved her request, the office of minister general was still vacant, since Angelina had died just a few months earlier."[31]

7. The bull *Apostolicae Sedis providentia* (May 2, 1440)

The congregation of Blessed Angelina, in this document, dated May 2, 1440, seems to have received its highest approval. We report Sensi's summary:

Regular Tertiaries in Italy was Brother Bartholomew *de Benamatis* of Perugia, elected in the first General Chapter held in 1448, probably at Montefalco consequent to the bull of unification and centralization of the order. *Pastoralis Officii* of Nicholas V, July 20, 1447, (See Pazzelli, *Il Terz'ordine regolare, op. cit.,* pp. 120-128.) The first study which produced documents attributing the qualification of "Minister General of the Third Order" to Brother Hubert (Onofrio) of Montavio in the year 1436 was the work of M. Sensi, *Il movimento francescano a Foligno, op. cit.,* pp. 416 and 419, note 40.

[29]For the circumstances surrounding the intervention by John Capestrano in behalf of the tertiaries living in community, see various studies of A. Matanic̓, *Il Defensorium Tertii ordinis beati Francisci di san Giovanni Capestrano,* in *Il movimento francescano della Penitenz a nella società medievale,* Roma, 1980, pp. 47-57; *San Giovanni da Capestrano e la vita communitaria del Penitenti francescani,* in *Prime manifestazioni, op. cit.,* pp. 81-90.

[30]See the digest of these two letters in Sensi, *Documenti per la beata Angelina, op. cit.,* p. 110, Appendice XIV, a, b.

[31]Sensi, *Documenti per la beata Angelina, op. cit.,* p. 110, b.

In the request sent to Eugene IV by Margaret, Minister of Saint Ann's in Foligno, Francesca of Saint Hubert's in Florence, Cecilia of Saint John's in Todi, Margaret of San Quirico in Assisi, and Clare of Saint Margaret's in Ascoli, the events that led to the forming of the institute of their young congregation are set forth. The petitioners were afraid of falling into the net which some zealous inquisitors, by virtue of the bull *Sancta romana* of 1317, could employ to entrap them. This document besides censuring the teachings of the Fraticelli, declared that the Rule of the Third Order did not allow for living in community, and this under pain of excommunication for doing so. The events leading to the forming of the congregation are then set forth: Pope Urban V orally, ("vivae vocis oraculo") authorized Sister Angelina of Foligno to establish a congregation of Tertiary Franciscan women. By virtue of this permission, Sister Angelina founded various monasteries. On the advice of some religious, Angelina turned to Pope Martin V "ut ipse concessionem huiusmodi erectionem ac omnia alia gesta et facta per dictam Angelinam...confirmare et approbare ac illa eis de novo concedere vellet—that the pope would himself confirm and approve the grant received and the establishment and all other acts and deeds of the above mentioned Angelina and that the pope would grant these things to her anew.

The pope entrusted the task of providing for the implementation of his decree to Bishop Anthony of Todi who was to provide for the canonical establishment in the very form those women had requested in their petition. The same sisters turned to Eugene IV again asking that he would confirm the letter of Martin V and the work of the Bishop of Todi. The positive response of the pope is contained in the two letters mentioned above, both dated from Florence on March 2, 1436. Now, however, the petitioners say, some jurists are saying that the pontifical letters as well as the work of the Bishop of Todi are null since they contradict the Constitution *Sancta romana.* This is the reason for the sisters' petition.

Pope Eugene IV, despite the above mentioned constitution, approves anew the congregation of the Sisters of Foligno and confirms its juridical structure (local minister and general minister, elected every three years). The pope then makes dispositions regarding the habit (a rough cord in place of the belt), the dispensation from the vow of poverty, the naming of confessors (secular or regular of any order). Finally the pope decrees that the minister general, when canonically elected, needs no further confirmation.[32]

This would seem to have been the last document, the harbinger of tranquility and assurance for some decades.

Instead when *Apostolicae Sedis providentia* reached Foligno, there were seeds of serious distress already afflicting the congregation. The trouble would be revealed in all its gravity within a short time. The very self-definitions in which the Sisters of Saint Ann had expressed their identity during these years, indicates an uncertainty about that identity. After all, it was not an easy thing for the sisters to describe their own identity because they set out along a road that had not been travelled by others in Italy. "In the monastery, it is affirmed that the *Rule of the Continents and the Observance of Saint Clare* was in force. The religious sisters called themselves the *Poor Women of the Observance of the Third Rule of Saint Francis,* and also of *the Rule of the Observance of Saint Francis.*"[33]

---

[32]Sensi, *Documenta per la beata Angelina, op. cit.,* pp. 110-111. See the bull in BF, n.s. I, n. 466, pp. 222-223. Sensi adds, among other things, these observations: "2. The Sisters of Foligno, while belonging to the great Franciscan family, enjoyed full autonomy. Amongst the tasks of the sister servant (or ministra) General: 'cum visitoris pro tempore existentis *concilio* loca huiusmodi reformare....' The minister general of the Friars Minor thus exercises his jurisdiction over the congregation through means of the visitators, whose field of action, does not go beyond giving counsel. 3. Because of papal privilege, the sisters of the congregation of Foligno may grant their confessors the faculty to dispense them from the vow of poverty: 'eidem confessori cum eisdem sororibus super quibuscumque votis – castitatis et religionis votis dumtaxat exceptis, dispensandi illaque in alia pietatis opera commutandi."

[33]Sensi, *Document per la beata Angelina, op. cit.,* p. 7. See appendix XI, d, e, h; XV, b, d, q on pp. 101-103, 114, 120.

The young congregation deeply felt the lack of a charismatic person who could take the place of Blessed Angelina. Still other difficulties presented themselves. First, there was the emergence of economic interests which ran contrary to the committed needs of a congregation. The monastery of Saint John in Todi was just such a case. In 1444 the sisters at Saint John's petitioned and obtained from the pope exemption from the jurisdiction of the minister general (*the ministra generale*).[34] It seems that the reasons that at one time gave a thrust towards federation, no longer existed. Now the preference was again for autonomy and independence.[35]

8. Events occurring in the male Third Order Regular

The Friars Minor, after being on the sidelines for some years, again returned and became involved with the affairs of the congregation of Blessed Angelina. The Friars Minor had observed the preference of Angelina's congregation for the regular Tertiaries who at that time were at the peak of their activity in seeking to effect unity and autonomy for themselves. Attempts of the regular Tertiaries of Italy for this unification ran into serious difficulties just two years after they had received the bull *Pastoralis officii* from Nicholas V on July 20, 1447. This document had established their unification and it ordered them to assemble in a General Chapter, to elect a general curia which would govern the institute in complete autonomy. It has now been confirmed in recent studies[36] that there was more

---

[34]Sensi, *Il movimento francescano, op. cit.*, p. 420.

[35]The reasons given to Pope Nicholas for the request was that he would free them "from the jurisdiction of the minister general (la ministra generale)" and allow them to govern themselves "through the local minister of this place" suggests that these sisters had not understood or accepted at that time, or a least, in that monastery, the vision and needs for life that ought to govern a true congregation. See the "digest" which Enrico Menestò made of the pertinent document. The Sisters of Todi requested exemption because "many scandals followed the visits of the minister general to Todi: The minister (ministra) general would apply to other places some of the bequests made to the above mentioned monastery and she had transferred some Sisters of the above mentioned monastery to other places." E. Menestò, *Le penitenti Lucreziei*, in *La beata Angelina da Montegiove, op. cit.*, p. 383, note 23.

[36]The merit here again goes to M. Sensi who treated this problem in *Dossier sul Clareni della Valle Spoletana*, in PICENUM SERAPHICUM, XI, 1974, pp. 315-404.

than a union of houses taking place. There was a confederation which involved in addition to the Tertiaries, strictly so called, the orthodox Clarians[37] of the Spoleto valley. One of the Clarians, Brother Bartholomew *de Benamatis* of Perugia, was elected the first minister general. The general curia elected with him had to follow his desire to prepare new Statutes which would regulate more uniformly the life of the old and new Tertiaries. These Statutes must have been judged by many Tertiaries as detrimental to the freedom of spirit and practice that had been seen in the order until that time. This would explain the fact that on August 5 of the following year, 1449, the General Curia met in Assisi and elected one of their General Counselors, Brother Andrew *Francheschini* of Milan, Procurator of the Causes of the Order, especially "contra rebelles et inoboedientes fratres Tertii ordinis et bullae apostolicae concessae dicto ordini per summum pontificem Nicholaum V—against the rebellious and disobedient friars of the Third Order who were against the apostolic bulls granted to the above mentioned order by Pope Nicholas V." The documentation of this election is preserved for us by Bordoni,[38] who lets us see what was taking place. "Whatever were the causes for dissension," writes Sensi, "and the reasons adopted by the factions, one fact is certain, contentions would prevail. Nicholas V, the same pope who had authorized and promoted centralization of the Italian Tertiaries, with the bull *Romanus Pontifex*, September 18, 1449, restored everything to the state that existed before 1447. Nicholas V annulled the bull *Pastoralis officii*. (We read in the papal document the words "we rescind, we revoke, we invalidate and annul.")[39]

After the study by Sensi, who affirmed that *Pastoralis Officii* had indeed united Tertiaries and orthodox Clarians, and that these Clarians were represented directly in the union by the minister general, and that they wanted to impose their interpretation of "Franciscan life" on all, we now agree with Sensi's interpretation of *Romanus Pontifex*,

---

[37]The Clarians (Clareni) were the heirs of the Spirituals, but orthodox as to their doctrine. They favored strict observance.

[38]See the document and circumstances in Pazzelli, *Il Terz'ordine regolare, op. cit.*, pp. 128-136.

[39]Sensi, *Dossier sui Clareni, op. cit.*, p. 336 (extract, p. 26).

abandoning our previously held position.[40] The pope dissolved that not entirely natural "union," and brought affairs back to a pre-1447 status. We likewise agree that the object of contention in the matter must have been the Clarians. Even though orthodox, they were heirs of the Spirituals. "After centralization," the pope affirms in his bull, "there were some friars who had undertaken the reformation of the Order of Penitents of Saint Francis, obliging the Tertiaries of both sexes to live a form of rigorous life neither foreseen by the Rule of Pope Nicholas IV, nor included in their profession. The pope clearly says to them (the Tertiaries):"[41] "If they desired to choose a stricter life, they have another order, also instituted by the Blessed Francis, the Order of Friars Minor, in which they can serve God under a stricter Rule."[42]

After the separation of the regular Tertiaries from the Clarians, the former no longer had much influence in Umbria. In 1451 the first General Chapter celebrated after the dissolution of the union, Father Francis Spineti from Genoa was elected minister general. The center of the male Third Order Regular had definitely shifted to the north of Italy, identifying itself anew with the *Congregation of Lombardy*, which had been very active in the years from 1430 to 1436. For the remainder of the fifteenth and sixteenth century, we speak only of this congregation in Italy.[43]

The congregation of Blessed Angelina thus was left without even the support of the male branch of the Third Order Regular.

---

[40]See Pazzelli, *Il Terz'ordine regolare, op. cit.,* pp. 133-134.

[41]Sensi, *Dossier sui Clareni, op. cit.,* p. 336 (extract, p. 26).

[42]"Si vitam strictiorem sibi eligere voluerint, alium habent et iam per ipsum b. Fanciscum institutum Ordinem, videlicet, Fratrum Minorum, in quo sub strictiori regula suum possunt Altissimo reddere famulatum." See the bull *Romanus Pontifex,* of 1449 in Pazzelli, *Il Terz'ordine regolare, op. cit.,* pp. 132-133, note 2.

[43]After Brother Bartholomew *de Benamatis* of Perugia, 1448-1451, there is only one Minister General during the fifteenth and sixteenth centuries who was not from the north of Italy. See Pazzelli, *Il Terz'ordine regolare, op. cit.,* Appendice, *I ministri (e vicari) generali dell'Ordine,* pp. 375-376.

CHAPTER VII

QUESTIONS ABOUT CLOISTER AND JURISDICTION

We have had the occasion before to note the problem presented by Church legislation on "the cloister." In the second half of the sixteenth century the cloister became a critical problem and remained so until after the Council of Trent, 1545-1563. Even before 1450 there were decrees which indirectly touched on this problem.

1. The bull *Ordinis tui* (February 5, 1447)

First we will consider the bull *Ordinis tui* of Pope Eugene IV, dated February 5, 1447.[1] Eugene IV sought to impose uniform direction for the vast female Franciscan movement. At this time an *uneasy peace*[2] had been arranged between the Conventuals and the Observants by having a general vicar from Cismontane[3] and another one from Transmontane for the Minors of the Observance under the authority of the one minister general. The bull reserved to the Cismontane Vicar General, Brother James Primadizzis, authority to visit all the "nuns and sisters whether of the First or Second or the Third Order or of any other Order of Saint Clare and of the Blessed Francis." Then coming down to particular directives, "it had been understood that Brother John of Capestrano singled out over 103 precepts in the Rule of Saint Clare whose transgression could be serious matter. The pope restricted such

---

[1]BF, n.s., n. 1045, pp. 524-526

[2]The expression of the bull is very meaningful: "post *concordiam* inter...fratres qui dicuntur conventuales et vos alios quibus de regulari observantia est apellatio...*semifactam.*" (A half peace.) "After the *peace* between the brothers who are called conventuals and you others who are named of the regular observance, has been half way accomplished."

[3]Cismontane, this side of the mountains, i.e., Umbria; Transmontane, the other side of the mountains, i.e., Lombardy.

transgression to those that pertained to the four vows of obedience, poverty, the cloister and chastity, and to the election and deposition of the abbess."[4]

Did Eugene IV, by the authority of this papal document, intend to impose the cloister on all Franciscan sisters?[5] We doubt that he intended this. The pope speaks clearly of "the first Rule of Saint Clare" and does not mention the Rule of Nicholas IV, the Rule the Sisters of Blessed Angelina certainly followed.[6]

The bull contained directives of a general character and the document was not provoked by the situation in Foligno. Nevertheless, the bull did directly touch the monastery at a delicate historical moment through which the monastery was passing. Spiritual direction of the Sisters of Blessed Angelina was very soon, in law and in fact, again in the hands of the Friars Minor. Thus began a long struggle between the sisters and the juridical inter- pretation of the Friars (Minor) on how the lifestyle of the sisters should be — with or without a cloister.[7] The Friars Minor wanted the monasteries of Blessed Angelina to observe the cloister just as any other monastery of Saint Clare would observe the cloister.

"So began a long painful journey for various houses," remarks Sensi, "a journey which would last until the Council of Trent when the cloister, one of the points of great friction between the Observants and the Tertiary sis- ters of Blessed Angelina's congregation, became obligatory for all sisters."[8]

[4]Sensi, *Documenti per la beata Angelina, op. cit.,* p. 113.

[5]Sensi affirms that "the end of the congregation was determined by the bull *Ordinis tui* of 1447. It was through this document that the congrega- tion of Blessed Angelina was subjected to the vicar general of the Observants and became a community of cloistered nuns." *op. cit.,* p. 75.

[6]In the notarized account of the Chapter of November 22, 1430, it was clearly stated that "in this monastery of Saint Anna, the Third Rule of the Continents of Blessed Francis is in force and is observed." See Sensi, *Il movimento francescano a Foligno, op. cit.,* p. 421, note 45.

[7]The phases of this struggle have recently been recalled by Anna Filannino in *Il monastero di Sant'Anna nell'età moderna e contemporanea,* in *La beata Angelina, op. cit.,* pp. 221-315. We must observe that with *Ordinis tui* only the "right of visitation" was reconfirmed for the Friars Minor. The bull did not say that the sisters had to follow the Rule of Saint Clare and therefore had to observe the cloister. The Minors did not see the possibility of a different direction of life for nuns and sisters.

[8]*Documenti per la beata Angelina, op. cit.,* p. 75.

From this time on until the Council of Trent, the history of Saint Anne's Monastery in Foligno is identified with the history of all the congregations of Franciscan sisters. It was the struggle of the congregations or "monasteries of Tertiary sisters who wanted to remain faithful to their original purpose and, therefore, did not want to accept being assimilated into the Second Franciscan Order."[9]

2. The bull of Pius II *"Ut tollatur discursus"* (December 3, 1461)

"The Fathers of the Province (of Saint Francis in Assisi-the Observants)," writes Augustino da Stroncone, "no longer wanted the excursions of the Mother General of the Tertiary sisters. They decided to abandon her. But since the Bishop of Corneto, Governor of Perugia, disagreed with this decision, they had recourse to the pope. Pius II, by the bull *Ut tollatur discursus,* addressed to the vicar general and to the provincials, abolished both the office and the title of minister general and the triennial Chapter."[10]

The bull *Ut tollatur discursus* was dated December 3, 1461, and the pope addressed it to the vicar general and to the vicars provincial of the Observants. It was the response of the pope to the lamentations of the superiors of the Seraphic Province. The pope abrogated the concessions of Martin V and Eugene IV in force of which "nine congregations"[11] had elected every three years a minister general who made canonical visitations with some companions. "It is dangerous," affirmed the bull, re-echoing the Constitution of Boniface VIII, "and not seemly for women, especially if they are young, to go on excursions to

---

[9]Filannino, *Il monastero d Sant'Anna, op. cit.,* p. 222.

[10]Agostino da Stroncone, *Umbria Serafica,* a. 1522, in MISCELLANEA FRANCESCANA, V (1890) p. 128; in Filannino, *op. cit.,* p. 223, nota 5. Also Monjaux clearly affirms that "it was consequent to the requests of Luigi da Vicenza, Vicar General of the Observants, that Pope Pius II in 1461 suppressed the office of mother general and commanded that in the future each monastery should elect a superior who would have in her monastery the same authority which the general had in the entire institute *quia periculosum et minus honestum est mulieribus praesertim juvenculis, per alienas discursare sedes,"* in *Les Religieuses franciscaines,* Paris, 1897, p. 18,

[11]The bull actually speaks of "congregations" and not of "houses" of the congregations of Sister Angelina, as if it considered it to be a "federation" rather than a union. The list of the houses follows: Sant'Anna of Foligno,

other houses ('per alienas discursare sedes')." The pope suppressed the office of minister general and granted the superiors of each single "congregation" the same privileges and authority over their own family which the sister minister general had enjoyed. All indults and permissions granted to the congregations of the Third Order were re-confirmed.[12]

That was the end of the congregation. The federation was dissolved and each house returned to a completely independent status.

"The Minors of the Observance," Filannino wrote,

> some time later threatened to break off their spiritual assistance to the monasteries which did not intend to accept the observance of the cloister...The Tertiary sisters refused to yield to commands or threats and sought to resolve the controversy by appealing to the protection they enjoyed with members of the Roman Curia and with civil authorities. From this situation there broke out in the Umbrian Province a conflict which the Vicar General of the Observants, Brother Peter of Naples, repeatedly referred to as a very severe war—gravissimum bellum.[13]

3. Questions concerning jurisdictions

Soon new questions concerning jurisdiction were added to the questions concerning cloister. We can start by saying that in the first half of the fifteenth century various male congregations of Regular Tertiaries were established in Europe, and that they all had received pontifical recognition and official documentation, i.e. papal bulls.[14] In Italy the Congregation of Lombardy had recovered its vitality after the pause of 1449, due to the unsuccessful

---

Sant'Onofrio of Florence, San Quirico of Assisi, Santa Margherita of Ascoli, Sant'Agnese of Viterbo, Sant'Antonio of Perugia, Sant'Elizabetta of Aquila, Santa Maria of Ancona and Santa Chiara of Rieti.

[12]See the bull in BF, n.s. II, n. 971, p. 506.

[13]Filannino, Il monastero di Sant'Anna, op. cit., p. 224.

[14]The Congregation of the Tertiaries of Holland in 1401, the Belgium Congregation in 1413, the Congregation of Cologne in 1427 and the Congregation of Spain in 1442.

attempt to fuse the Regular Tertiaries with the orthodox Clarians of Umbria. In 1467 this congregation asked the Holy See to be granted the rights and privileges given to the congregations of Regular Tertiaries in Belgium and Spain. Paul II granted this request in *Excitat arcanum* of May 26, 1468.[15] In addition, the pope granted the Congregation of Lombardy the faculty to affiliate with itself other communities of Tertiaries who would ask to join. And so "to the Friars of the First Order who were now divided into the Conventuals and the Friars of the Observance with different tendencies and ways of thinking, were added the ministers from the ranks of the many congregations of male Tertiaries."[16]

It was natural that some communities of the Franciscan sisters would desire to be united spiritually with the families of the Regular Tertiaries who followed the same Rule. However, such efforts were not always pleasing to the friars of the Observance. Here is where we find the so called conflicts concerning jurisdiction. To whom should the direction of the houses of Franciscan sisters be entrusted? Were these sisters obliged to remain associated with the Friars Minor, or were they free to choose visitators and confessors from another order?

"Only the popes," wrote Péano,

> would have been able to end this dispute. But it must be understood that the policy of the popes in this matter of jurisdiction revealed itself as inconsistent, if not self-contradictory. The popes who held office during this period of the fifteenth and sixteenth centuries and later, were influenced by the advocacy and pressures of religious and civil authorities. The popes took positions which differed from one region to another and in accord with the requests from interested parties. There was no lack of papal intervention in this matter. Toward the end of the fifteenth century, the problem became a burning issue as a result of the polemics that prevailed.[17]

---

[15]See this bull in Bordoni, *Archivium, op. cit.,* pp. 269-271.

[16]Péano, *Le religiose francescane, op. cit.,* p. 32.

[17]Péano, *op. cit.,* pp. 32-33.

4. The action of Sixtus IV (1471-1484)

In dealing with the problem of how to regularize relationships between the different Franciscan families and the problem over the cloister, there was much activity undertaken by Sixtus IV, ex-minister general of the Minors, who was pope from 1471 to 1484. But not all of it was consistent.

Sixtus had scarcely been elected to the papacy when he promulgated the bull *Romani pontificis*, December 15, 1471.[18] Here he again entrusted the direction of the secular Tertiary brothers and sisters to the Conventuals and to the Observants. Péano notes that "by virtue of his apostolic authority, Sixtus confirmed those previous pontifical letters which *attributed a certain (aliqua) supervision, pre-eminence and authority over the friars and sisters of the Third Order* to the minister general and the provincials of the First Order. The pope accorded the same privilege to the ministers of the Tertiaries."[19] Actually he does not speak of the Friars and Sisters of the Third Order, for so doing would indicate the Third Order Regular, but only of the Brothers and Sisters of the Third Order. What Sixtus does here is to recall to mind what Innocent IV in 1247 had ordained that the Friars Minor were to have care of the Penitents of Blessed Francis.[20] This enlightens us as to the true meaning of the papal document. It is very clear that the pope is speaking of the Third Order secular from the fact that "he granted the same privilege to the ministers of the Tertiaries."

"Sixtus IV confirmed these decisions in another letter of November 17, 1473, *Decet Apostolicam sedem*, giving in detail the duties of the ministers of the Third Order—to visit, to reform, to correct, to clothe with the habit, to admit to profession postulants and novices respectively, both men and women."[21]

There was still another question: Could the Regular Tertiaries, who numbered many priests among their members, be asked to function as visitators or confessors of

---

[18]See the bull in BF, n.s. III, n. 67, pp. 37-38.

[19]Péano, *op. cit.*, p. 33.

[20]See Pazzelli, *Saint Francis and the Third Order, op. cit.*, p. 263.

[21]Péano, *op. cit.*, p. 33.

the Secular Tertiaries as well as visitators and confessors of the houses of the Franciscan sisters?

A first reply was given to this question by the bull *Pridem per alia*, sent by Sixtus IV on April 21, 1476 to "the Friars of the Third Order of Saint Francis." The bull affirms that the pope, through another letter "ad perpetuam memoriam," had already granted to "the minister visitator and to the provincials of the Friars of the Third Order of Saint Francis who serve the Lord in the eremitical habit, the faculty to conduct canonical visitations, to reform and correct each and every friar of the same order as has been set forth in detail in the letter just mentioned." Having understood that some of these friars recently had refused this visitation and correction and had presumed to take on themselves the care of souls, even though they were sometimes unqualified to do so, and especially when they had not received permission to do so, the pope again exhorts each of the friars to show themselves reverent and obedient to the same minister visitator and the provincials.[22]

We note, that despite the affirmation found in the letter's *Incipit*, that a similar concession given previously by Sixtus IV cannot be demonstrated with documents. Until now in pontifical documents "a certain superiority, preeminence and authority over the friars and sisters of the Third Order" was attributed to the Friars Minor to whom belonged the right of making canonical visitation of the leaders and the members (in capite et in membris), the right of instructing, correcting and reforming.[23]

Only the bull *Pastoralis officii* of Nicholas V in 1447 had granted a similar authority to the major superiors of the Third Order Regular.[24] This bull had been revoked and the union of the Regular Tertiaries and the orthodox Clarians dissolved, despite the fact that we know, from within the Congregation of Lombardy of the Third Order Regular, the

[22]See the bull *Pridem per alias*, in BF, n.s. III, n. 867, p. 426.

[23]See similar terminology in the bull *Romani pontificis, loc. cit.*, note 17, p. 17.

[24]The bull in fact said: "To the visitators above mentioned and others... delegated by the visitators... we grant the faculty of visiting all kinds of places and persons, leaders and members, (in capite et in membris) reforming and if it is opportune, correcting and punishing." See in Pazzelli, *Il Terz'ordine regolare, op. cit.*, p. 123, note.

friars did continue to direct their regular life according to the prescriptions of that bull.

Within a short time "the Tertiary sisters," writes Péano,

> brought up questions in their own houses concerning spiritual government of the friars on whom they depended for spiritual assistance. Consequently, rights and privileges were questioned and some convents were torn with dissension. The Sisters of Brussels, Aalst (Limbourg) and other foundations in the dioceses of Cambrai, Therounne and Turnai experienced this kind of reaction. Some of these sisters asked the pope to intervene in the matter and settle the confusion. Some sisters at Brussels and Aalst claimed they lived outside the French Province since they lived near the city of Cologne. The pope then placed all these monasteries in Belgium under the care and direction of the Provincial of France with all the faculties necessary to settle the case by force of the bull *Ex apostolicae servitutis* of October 16, 1477.[25]

The bull *Apostolicae Servitutis*[26] actually decided that the Franciscan sisters of the Belgian houses which were under the jurisdiction of the ministers and visitators of the Friars Minor of the French Province, could remain under such jurisdiction even if, according to some, that territory had now become part of the Province of Cologne. The same bull directed the vicar of the French Province to continue to show care for these sisters and the bull expressly forbade the minister of the Third Order to involve himself in the affairs of these houses.

In the introduction to the bull the pope indicated that he himself — although he had said in the letter sent to the Minister General Zanetto da Udine and to all the ministers provincial of the Friars Minor that he had recognized and granted them a certain superiority, preeminence and authority over the Brothers and Sisters of the Third Order — in another letter had also extended the same authority to Ministers and Friars of the Third Order, even

---

[25]Péano, *op. cit.*, p. 34.

[26]BF, n.s. III, n. 1002, pp. 498-499.

outside Italy and the region of Sicily, that is to the whole world.[27]

5. Solemn vows and the cloister

Meanwhile Pope Sixtus IV declared (in the bull *Ad Christi Vicarii*, November 14, 1480 and classified in rank as "ad perpetuam memoriam") that the vows of obedience, poverty and perpetual chastity professed by the Friars and Sisters of the Third Order of Blessed Francis, living in community by permission of the same pope or of his predecessors, must be considered solemn in all effects and thus equal to those of any other order approved by the Apostolic See, when they are professed according to the law, that is after the year of novitiate and in the hands of the duly elected minister.[28]

Did solemn vows bring a *monastic formation* of the Franciscan sisters? That is, once their vows were declared to be solemn vows, did it follow as consequence that the cloister was obligatory for them? There were, and there are,[29] some authors who say yes, this is what happened. But in fact the bull says nothing about this matter. Still this must have been the position and reasoning of the Friars Minor, particularly the Friars of the Province of Umbria, concerning the houses of the ex-congregation of Blessed Angelina. From this moment on the Friars Minor gave preference to this interpretation. Still the sisters resisted. Then in the Provincial Chapter, probably held in the summer of 1482, the Friars Minor of the Province of Saint Francis (Umbria), seeing the uselessness of their efforts, decided that they would no longer offer their spiritual assistance (direction, confession, etc.) except to those communities which had accepted the cloister. The pope seemed to approve the matter. In fact, he sent the bull *Exponi nobis fecistis*, of September 24, 1482 to the Friars Minor. In this document the pope allowed the vicar provin-

---

[27]"Per alias nostras litteras...ad eosdem ministros generalem et provinciales Ordinis minorum de observantia...necnon ministro et fratres dicti Tertii ordinis, etiam extra Italiam regnum Siciliae huiusmodi per universum orbem, consistentes, eadem autoritate extendimus." *loc. cit.*, p. 498.

[28]See the bull *Ad Christi vicarii*, in BF, n.s. III, n. 1360, p. 681.

[29]On this point see how much Filannino has written, *op. cit.*, p. 224, note 6.

cial of the Friars Minor of the province to restrict their spiritual assistance to those sisters who had agreed to live "according to the established regulations and your decrees" ("iuxta regularia instituta et ordinationes vestras"), that is to those sisters who "according to your directives agreed to live the cloistered life in their houses" ("iuxta ordinationem vestram voluerint clausae in earum domibus vivere").[30]

Even after this it cannot be said that the sisters were defeated. Wadding writes:

> Regretting that they had either to be recluses in their convents or be deprived of the direction of the Friars Minor, they did everything possible to insure that neither the first nor the second possibility happened. They had recourse to many intercessors at the Holy See and obtained from the pope the letter *Quanto contentiones*, whose implimentation gave rise to many controversies.[31]

The sisters in their official request to the pope sought the abrogation of the decrees of *Exponi nobis fecistis*. The request was presented by the monastery of Saint Agnes and that of Saint Anthony of Padua in Perugia (monasteries of the ex-congregation of Blessed Angelina). The reply of the pope, the bull *Quanto contentiones* of December 16, 1482, was directed to the Archpriest and Prior of San Severo in Perugia and to the vicar general of the same diocese. The pope reviewed the preceding events and the reasons set forth by the sisters, especially the fact that the Rule of the Third Order did not oblige them to the cloister ("Regularia instituta Tertii Ordinis eas ad hoc non arctent") and that if they had wished to observe the cloister, there were other monasteries they could have entered. Moreover, if perchance they were constrained to observe the cloister, the majority of the sisters would return to their own homes ("quamplurimae ex eis...potius redirent ad paternas domos.") The pope asked those to whom the bull was addressed to persuade the vicar and the Friars Minor to abstain from such novelties as obliging the

---

[30]See the bull *Exponi nobis fecistis*, in BF, n.s. III, n. 1641, p. 834.

[31]Wadding, *Annales Minorum*, t. XIV, p. 385.

sisters to observe the cloister ("ut ab huiusmodi novitati-
bus prorsus abstineant...et ne eas ad clausuram inducere
tenent.") If the vicar and the friars refused to comply, the
executors of the bull had authority to provide for another
spiritual director who possessed the desired qualities of
age, integrity and holiness of life.[32]

"But the papal interventions," observes Péano,

> did not calm agitated spirits. The Friars of the
> Observance remained firmly attached to their
> position, especially the Vicar Provincial Battista
> of Montefalcone, who had applied to the letter
> the decision of the Chapter by withdrawing all
> spiritual help from the sisters. In still another
> letter *Intelleximus quod longo iam tempore*[33] and
> dated September 15 of the following year, Sixtus
> IV asked the Vicar General of the Cismontane
> family, Brother Peter of Naples, to restore har-
> mony between the two parties. The pope wrote:
> "We have considered that the observance of the
> cloister, although it guarantees a more perfect
> reputation of a good moral life, and is a compo-
> nent (as a work of 'supererogation') of a more
> strict observance, a life of stricter observance
> cannot be forced upon a person unwilling to
> embrace it. Moreover, we consider that excessive
> distraction of women is highly dangerous and
> not at all suitable for religious life. As is just and
> proper, we wish to put an end to this dispute."
> The pope then authorized the vicar general to
> undertake the task of executing this decree.
> History shows us that from that date (September
> 1483) the Reformed Friars Minor of Blessed
> Amedeus da Silva assumed the spiritual direc-
> tion of the Tertiary sisters of the Province of
> Umbria.[34]

The "Amadean Friars" (for thus were called the followers of

---

[32]See the bull *Quanto contentiones*, in BF, n.s. III, n. 1677, pp. 848-850.

[33]See BF, n.s. III, n. 1778, pp. 893-894.

[34]Péano, *Le Suore Francescane, op. cit.*, p. 26. The details of this dispute between the Sisters of Saint Ann's Monastery in Foligno and the
Minors of the Observance have been recorded by Anna Filannio, *op. cit.*,
pp. 225-228.

the Portuguese reformer, the Conventual Franciscan, Amedeo of Silva, +1482[35]), had the care of the spiritual direction of the Sisters of Saint Ann for about forty years. After that the monastery again received spiritual assistance from the Friars Minor of the Observance.

The question of the cloister and the interpretation of various pontifical ordinances regarding the Franciscan sisters, remained troubled water for the whole first half of the sixteenth century until the Council of Trent, as we shall be able to consider in the following chapter.

---

[35]Pope Sixtus IV was the protector of Blessed Amedeus. In fact, the pope "granted Amadeo full control of his own houses; appointed him his own personal confessor, and gave him the Roman convent of Saint Peter in Montorio." See Lazzaro Iriate, *History of the Franciscan Order*, Franciscan Herald Press, Chicago, 1982, pp. 68-69.

CHAPTER VIII

FRANCISCAN SISTERS IN THE SIXTEENTH CENTURY

The events and questions which closely touched the general history of the Franciscan sisters during the sixteenth century are chiefly three: the new Rule of Leo X (1521), the definitive prescriptions of the Council of Trent regarding the cloister, and the ongoing development of questions concerning jurisdiction. This century is one of the more complex and momentous centuries in the history of the Church.

1. The Rule of Leo X (1521)

The Rule of Leo X was promulgated by the bull *Inter coetera nostri regiminis* and dated January 20, 1521.

The birth of this Rule must be seen in the context of the reform that was already present in the Church at the beginning of the century and in the decision of the Roman Curia to bring about a certain uniformity in the various movements of the Third Order Regular, male and female.

Spiritual conditions in the Church were not the best. The spirit of humanism which for more than a century had dominated in Italy and Europe, had caused a certain secularization in ecclesiastical circles and was not entirely absent from religious orders. The simple, living faith fed by the desire of Heaven which had characterized the Middle Ages had by this time been substituted for by a more precise perception of earthly values. First among these human values was a sense of self-sufficiency with regard to religion itself.

The movement which had begun at the end of the fourteenth century was affirmed and grew very rapidly in the following century.

Philosophy was separated from theology and

became the science of man and nature. It was a new way of conceiving life that developed both spontaneously and through the influence of ancient Greek and Roman thought. It acknowledged man as having his autonomy; it made the earth his kingdom.... The knowledge of ancient thought was also an encouragement to speculate without the limits placed by medieval transcendency.[1]

All this did not have a very beneficial influence on the various aspects of Christian and Church life which were, so to speak, reclothed with a certain worldly style.

The Church soon began to react. It did this especially, and clearly, at the Fifth Lateran Council held during the years 1512-1517. This Council called for a reform of Christian society in its structure and in its members, including the Franciscan world of the Third Order.

The congregations of Franciscan friars and sisters which arose during the fifteenth century and were neither followers of the first Rule of the Friars Minor, nor of the Rule of Saint Clare, followed the Rule of Nicholas IV, the Rule of 1289. But now it was evident to all that this Rule had a predominantly lay character. There was no mention in this Rule of community life, not to mention religious vows.

The pressing situation was that many congregations of Friars and Sisters of the Third Order Regular of Saint Francis needed a suitable Rule. There was need also for a greater uniformity among the congregations. The regular congregations of friars and sisters which arose in the most varied of circumstances showed a remarkable diversity even in external aspects, in the style of life, in the government of the communities, in regulations, etc. Thus it was necessary to give all these communities a correct Rule for religious life which would also be capable of bringing about a greater uniformity.

These must have been the goals of Pope Leo X who asked for the preparation and the publication of the new Rule which bears his name. This rule was addressed to

---

[1] A. Momigliano, *Storia della letteratura italiana*, Principato, Messina, 1938, pp. 107-108.

"The Brothers and Sisters of the Third Order of Blessed Francis, living in congregations under the three essential vows."[2]

In the brief presentation of the Rule, (which forms the *beginning* of the bull), the pope recalls the evolution which took place in the Third Order of Saint Francis from the time of Nicholas IV onwards:

> under the inspiration of the Holy Spirit, not only married persons entered into this order, but also virgins and continent persons who have built the monasteries in which they live under the three essential vows, some even observing the cloister. Because in the "third Rule" approved by Nicholas IV there are regulations (precepts) which are suitable for married people, but not for virgins and celibates, a fact that many times keeps these persons from entering this order,

the pope eliminated from the Rule of Nicholas IV whatever was not suitable to the new state. He confirmed and approved what was precious in it and presented it to the brothers and sisters so that they would observe that Rule.

This Rule is divided into ten simple and organic chapters. What had been contained in the previous Rule is conserved here with only an adaptation for religious men and women. Here one is explicitly reminded that "the friars and sisters of this fraternity are said to be *of penance* (Chapter VI) and here the fundamental characteristic, which had by then become traditional, is repeated: the *religious man* must exhort them and instruct them and lead them to "penitence-metanoia and to the exercise of virtue" (Chapter IV). With regard to the question of the cloister, this Rule "established that cloister would be obligatory wherever it had already been vowed."[3]

Reading the text critically we must really agree that the bull prescribed cloister for those monasteries or congregations whose Statutes intended to have it ("Tenentur etiam ad clausuram servandum illae, quae ipsam expresse

---

[2]"Dilectis filiis Fratribus et Sororibus Tertii ordinis beati Francisci sub tribus votis essentialibus in Congregationibus viventibus." See Bordoni, *Archivium, op. cit.*, p. 380.

[3]See Frascadore, *Francescane Suore, op. cit.*, p. 212.

servare voluerint") and whose sisters had thus explicitly promised to observe the cloister. The Rule grants the cloister, as if it were some kind of grace or favor, to any monastery which wanted it, provided that the cloister would not interfere with any of the activities of hospitality and care that had usually been extended to the sick.[4]

And so it would be false, if not dishonest, to affirm that the Church had established "univocally" (even before the Council of Trent) that solemn vows automatically implied obligation to observe the cloister. Pope Sixtus IV with the bull *Ad Christi Vicarii* of 1480[5] had declared the vows of the Friars and Sisters of the Third Order were to be considered *solemn.* But the Rule of Leo X affirms (and this was in 1521) that the cloister was obligatory only for those congregations or houses which "explicitly wanted the cloister."

The weak point of this Rule, a weakness that does not make the entire Rule feeble, was the lack of clarity in determining "for whom" this Rule was intended, that is, who should be obliged to accept and follow this Rule.

When the Rule speaks of government or jurisdiction (Chapter V, Concerning Prelates and Officials) the Rule prescribed that every superior of the local community of Friars and Sisters of the Third Order had to be obedient in everything that pertains to the observance of the Rule, to the ministers provincial of the Friars Minor and to the visitators delegated by him. For everything else, they had to observe their own Statutes. Thus the Rule granted direct "visitation" once a year, as specified, to the Friar Minor minister provincial in whose territory the Tertiary community was located. This right of visitation implied, according to the custom, the right of correction of faults observed and even the right of dismissal of incorrigible subjects.

The Rule of Leo X did not seem to take into account that very important reality so clearly evident throughout the fifteenth century, the reality of the several congregations of the Friars and Sisters of the Third Order which

---

[4]"Quod omnibus et singulis Conventibus concedimus, dummodo hospitalitas et caritas quam exercere solent apud infirmos, nullum cum honestate patiatur detrimentum": Bordoni, *Archivium, op. cit.,* p. 384.

[5]See above, p. 89.

had received pontifical recognition. This recognition generally implied the authority to elect a minister or visitator general who had been exclusively granted the right of canonically visiting the friars and sisters of that particular congregation. The Rule of Leo X did not speak at all of this visitator general just as it did not speak of the ministers provincial of those autonomous congregations.

Did Pope Leo X really intend to revoke all previously given privileges with the promulgation of the new Rule? The bull of promulgation of the Rule does not say so, nor does it hint at it. Rights of such primary importance had been granted by means of official seals affixed to those documents.[6] It was necessary that those grants be explicitly revoked by name, had such been the pope's intention.

The consequence of all this ambiguity was that the congregations of friars and sisters who had their own visitator or minister general thought that the new Rule did not apply to them. It was clearly directed, they thought, to those autonomous houses of Friars and Sisters of the Third Order, or even to those federations of houses, improperly so called congregations, which had always in fact been subject to the direction and the right of visitation by the Minorite authorities. "This Rule," writes Frascadore, "was not accepted by all the congregations of Regular Tertiaries. It raised enormous conflicts and polemics especially in nordic countries."[7] The Regular Tertiary friars and sisters, who had received above mentioned pontifical recognition, sought to keep the Rule of Nicholas IV as their own, integrating their own Statutes with the Rule. Their own Statutes often had the aspect of a new Rule, so complete were they and so adapted to the religious life.[8]

---

[6]For the Third Order Regular in Italy Pope Julius II had just a short time earlier in 1508 explicitly decreed (the bull *Romani Pontificis providentia*) that the Minorites must not enter into the houses nor the affairs of the Third Order Regular and that they were to abandon completely the right of making a visitation by their visitator general. See more on this point, p. 104.

[7]Frascadore, *op. cit.*, p. 212.

[8]The male Third Order Regular in Italy would have these Statutes approved "with apostolic authority" by the Cardinal Protector, Rodolfo Pio of Caprion April 28, 1549. These Statutes remained in force as the official Rule of the Order until 1927, that is, until the Rule of Pius XI.

None of the congregations which actually refused to follow the Rule of Leo X was ever reproved for this refusal and no congregation was asked by individual request to accept this Rule.[9]

2. The Council of Trent and the cloister

The second important event which gave a new face and a new direction to the congregations of Franciscan sisters was the Council of Trent (1545-1563). We know that there was no aspect of Christian life which was not stirred to new life by the influence of this ecumenical council. It is good to remember here that the primary purpose of the Council was twofold: "1) to fight against the errors of Luther and the other Protestant reformers by identifying Catholic doctrine in these controversial themes; 2) to promote Catholic reform for so long a time seen as necessary and urgently called for by all those who had become aware of the serious state of catholicism."[10]

If the Council of Trent produced a more systematic formulation of the truths of faith on the doctrinal side, on the practical side of life, that is in the area of reform, the Council imposed a "most strict order" on all aspects of Christian life.

In addition the decisions which were taken, in the Council and immediately after it, concerning the Franciscan friars and sisters were many in number and differed from order to order. The prescription which dealt more directly with the life of the Sisters of the Third Order was concerned with the cloister."[11] In the 25th Session of

---

[9]Pope Saint Pius V, when he wished to reform the male Third Order Regular in Italy on the observance of the Rule, explicitly prescribed the continuation of its own Rule, that is, those Statutes approved by the Cardinal Protector, and Pius V did not allude to the Rule of Leo X. See Pazzelli, *Il Terz'ordine regolare, op. cit.*, p. 165, note 2.

[10]*Dizionario dei Concili*, edited by Pietro Palazzini, Rome, 1966. Vol. V, p. 383.

[11]"New prescriptions for the cloister had been decreed by the Friars Minor for all nuns and sisters who depended on them for spiritual assistance. In the General Chapter of Salamanca in 1553 it was decreed that the "nuns and sisters of the Third Order who lived in community and depended on the Friars Minor (tibi creditarum) in order to aviod scandals and the 'admiratio' of the faithful, all religious women must be cloistered in perpetuity according to the custom of the nuns of the Second Order,

the Council, by this time very near its conclusion, the Council published the constitution *De regularibus et monialibus* on December 3, 1563. In Chapter V of this document, the Council explicitly referred to the Constitution *Periculoso* of Boniface VIII in 1298, and ordered all bishops to restore with all diligence the cloister in the monasteries subject to them. The constitution sought the compliance of the disobedient by prescribing ecclesiastical penalties and other punishments, not excluding, if it should be necessary, recourse to the secular arm.

> It is not licit for any nun to go out of the monastery after profession even for a brief period of time, under any pretext whatsoever, if this exit had not been approved by the bishop. It is likewise unlawful for anyone of whatever age or sex to cross the threshold of the monastery without the permission given in writing by the bishop or the superior under the penalty of excommunication to be incurred *ipso facto*.

The Council also determined that "because monasteries of nuns outside the cities are exposed to dangers of wicked people, bishops and other superiors shall take care, wherever it seems useful, to transfer the nuns to monasteries, old or new, within the city walls."[12]

3. Particular prescriptions of Pius V concerning the cloister

About three years after the conclusion of the Council of Trent, Pope Pius V sought to specify in detail how the laws dealing with the cloister established by the Constitution *De regularibus et monialibus* and promulgated by the Council, should in practice be observed. The pope issued a new Constitution *Circa pastoralis officii* on May 29, 1566. In this Constitution the pope decreed:

> 1) All nuns, at the present time and in the future, in any order whatsoever, even if they are

---

the Order of Saint Clare, and that men would not be admitted into their cloister for any reason without the permission of the Apostolic See." See Wadding, *Annales*, t. XVII, p. 297.

[12]See *Conciliorum Oecumenicorum Decreta*, Herder, 1962, pp. 753-754.

called "lay" nuns (conversae) must remain in their monasteries under perpetual cloister once they have made their profession, even if they were not bound to observe the cloister by the prescriptions of their own Rule, or even if in their own monasteries from time immemorial they had never observed the law of cloister. This was to be in conformity with the constitution *Periculoso* of Boniface VIII and the decrees of the Council of Trent.

2) In case there should be some nuns who resist or would be in disagreement with the above suggestions, their ordinaries and major superiors shall compel them as rebels and disobedient persons that this cloister be observed in perpetuo.

3) Even the women who are called Tertiary sisters or Penitents, of every order, who live in a congregation (in common life), if the solemn vow of cloister forms part of their profession, they are obliged to observe the law of cloister in its entirety. If this solemn vow has not been made, their ordinaries shall exhort and persuade them to profess the vow and submit to the cloister. If the sisters refuse, and if they are found to be leading a life that gives scandal, they must be punished most severely.

4) Those who insist in living without making profession of the vows and without cloister are forbidden to admit any candidate to their order or congregation in the future. If any such candidates were received or admitted contrary to this decree, we declare such receptions or professions null and void.

5) So that the above mentioned nuns or Tertiary sisters would not be lacking the necessities of life because of the cloister, we establish and command their ordinaries to designate pious lay sisters who are not professed to the task of collecting alms. If these women are professed, they must be at least forty years old and be lodged in premises adjoining the convent. They may not enter the cloister except for special cases set

forth in the Constitutions and likewise they may not go out of their houses to gather the above mentioned alms if they do not have the permission of the ordinary or their superiors.

6) If this system should not be sufficient for their maintenance, the ordinaries are to provide for the collection of alms by other pious persons. And because the cloister may not be violated by reason of an excessive number of nuns, we decree that the nuns and their superiors shall not admit into a monastery a number of persons greater than that which can be maintained with their own efforts combined with the ordinary reception of alms.[13]

These dispositions had to be published in every monastery. And if, in this matter, there had been disobedient sisters, they were to be punished by calling on the "secular arm," if necessary. Every disposition or privilege previously granted which is contrary to what has been here determined must be considered abrogated and annulled.

The dispositions of the Council of Trent and those which followed[14] de facto had the result of causing Franciscan sisters to pass from the status of being Franciscan sisters to the status of being cloistered nuns.

This transition was not immediate everywhere. For many monasteries decades had to pass before the law of the cloister was applied in all its rigor. It is true that "the interventions of the Observants on behalf of the nuns of monasteries which depended on them, from that time on relied on Pontifical documents. The Observants intended to be and were the executors of these documents."[15] But the local situation was such that it would have been

---

[13]See *Bullarum, Diplomatum et Privilegiorum Sanctorum Romanorum Pontificium Tauriensis editio*, 1862, t. VII, pp. 447-452.

[14]Besides *Circa pastoralis officii*, Saint Pius V published in 1568 the apostolic constitution *Lubricum vitae genus* which confirmed 'even more drastically' the prescriptions of *Circa pastoralis officii*. In practice, affirms Frascadore, "the pope suppressed communities with simple vows and forbade the erection of such communities in the future." *Op. cit.*, p. 212.

[15]Filannino, *Il monastero di Sant'Anna, op. cit.*, p. 229.

impossible to enclose all the sisters of a city in their monasteries all at the same time. At Foligno, for example, "in the first half of the sixteenth century more than five hundred nuns, that is ten percent of the urban population, lived in eleven monasteries and the income was absolutely insufficient."[16] The constitution *Circa pastoralis officii* prescribed that a number of nuns "greater than that which could be sustained with their own income and ordinary alms" should not be admitted into the monastery. But to carry out of the plan called for years during which the increase of the number of deaths would progressively reduce the number of nuns. For these and other reasons, the cloister in the monastery of Saint Anna was fully imposed only in the year 1615.[17]

4. The question concerning jurisdiction

The question over jurisdiction continued to be debated and continued to hurt relationships between the Observants and the Third Order until the drastic provisions undertaken by Pius V in the years 1566-1568. In practice the question touched the Third Order Secular and the male Third Order Regular. In those nations where the Third Order Regular had received pontifical recognition of a kind, there was immediately a theoretical and practical question: Are the members of the Third Order Regular with their own visitator general and ministers provincial subject to the right of the visitation by the Friars Minor? Must the members of the fraternities of the Secular Franciscan Order who started under the direction of priests of the Third Order Regular also be "visitated" by the Observants? To these questions the responses were in the affirmative for the Minors, and, of course, in negative for the Tertiaries. From this difference of opinion came disagreements and conflicts. The Franciscan sisters had earlier received a definitive response (the bull *Ordinis tui* of Eugene IV, 1447) in which the right of visitation by the

---

[16]*Ibid.*, p. 230.

[17]From the study by Filannino we know that in 1573 the monastery of Saint Anna had forty-two nuns. In 1630 there were thirty nuns "while the monastery had admitted only eleven, which hindered the observance of laws regarding the cloister." The number at a much later date stabilized at about twenty. See *op. cit.*, p. 242.

Friars Minor was reaffirmed for all nuns and sisters of Franciscan inspiration.[18] The nuns and sisters thus were for the most part passive spectators, remaining partial towards one side or the other of the disputed question, depending on their community and religious formation.

Concerning the two questions mentioned above, there was a succession of several pontifical documents which did not always make a precise distinction between the Third Order Secular and the Third Order Regular. And thus these documents were interpreted in different ways by the interested parties. As a matter of fact down to the present day inexact interpretations have been given regarding the controversy.

These could be corrected by a more careful examination of the sources. We suggest the following clarifications:

a) The popes, even in the sixteenth century, repeatedly reaffirmed that the right of visitation and correction of Secular Tertiaries was reserved to the Friars Minor. The outstanding documents in this matter are *Exponi nobis fecistis* of Pope Julius II, October 15, 1507 and *Exponi nobis fecistis* of the same Pope Julius on January 7, 1509.[19] These two bulls were exclusively concerned with the Secular Franciscan Order. In the first document (dated 1507) everything that was clearly established in the previous decrees of Sixtus IV is repeated, that is, all the "ministers, brothers and sisters" of the Third Franciscan Order remain under the "correction, the supervision and obedience of the Friars Minor."

The evolution of a part of the Third Order towards the regular state was not mentioned at all in this bull. Neither such evolution nor the common life are mentioned. So this aspect clearly did not form part of the pontifical instruction because it did not belong to the purpose of the document. The pope's intervention had been caused by the conduct of some "Ministers, Brothers and Sisters of the Third Order" of the province of Saint James in Spain.[20]

---

[18]See above chapter VII, p. 81.

[19]See the two bulls in Dominicus de Gubernatis a Sospitello, *Orbis Seraphicis, Historia de tribus Ordinibus a Seraphico Patriarcha Santo Francisco institutis,* t. II, Lugduni, 1685, respectively pp. 898-900 and 901-903.

[20]See De Gubernatis, *op. cit.,* II, p. 899.

The pope repeats the same matters in the second document *Exponi nobis fecistis* of 1509. This letter, too, was occasioned by further resistance on the part of the same Spanish Secular Tertiaries to be subject to the Minor's right to "visit, reform and correct." Moreover, since the bull was addressed not only to the Observants but also to the Conventuals, the pope decreed that "those who had at one time made the choice of your obedience are to remain in it without change (in perpetuo). Those who have abandoned the obedience they once made to one of you"[21] are to return to that obedience within the period of ten days after the promulgation of this letter. Those "Brothers and Sisters" who till now have not chosen obedience to either of you, as was established previously by Sixtus IV and by Us, "are held to choose obedience to one of you within the space of ten days and to remain in that obedience without further change (in perpetuo)." This document speaks only of the "Brothers and Sisters of the Third Order" without any qualification of meaning. Therefore these are the Brothers and Sisters of the Franciscan Secular Third Order.

b) Concerning the congregations of the Third Order Regular which had already received pontifical recognition in the preceding century, there are two important bulls which witness to their exemption from the right of visitation by the Friars Minor.

1) The bull *Romani pontificis* of Pope Julius II, February 8, 1508 was concerned with the male Third Order Regular in Italy. It was published in between the two *Exponi nobis fecistis* documents of 1507 and 1509, as we have already mentioned, and thus acquires a particular importance. "We have ascertained," says the pope,

> that some *curators* would defend the rights of the Friars Minor, compelling certain ones to obey the Minors when they are unwilling to do so. (There the pope alludes to the Secular Tertiaries mentioned in *Exponi nobis fecistis* of 1507.) But it was never our intention that

---

[21]"Illi vero, qui obedientiam alterius vestram semel electam dimiserunt, ad eamdem intra spatium decem dierum a die institutionis praesentium revertantur." De Gubernatis, *op. cit.*, p. 903.

Exponi nobis should be understood to include the houses of our beloved sons of the Third Order of the regular observance who are called of Penance of the Congregation of Lombardy, which cannot be "visitated" by anyone except the visitator general of their own congregation.[22] We command the above mentioned *curators* and judges appointed by the Friars Minor or by the Apostolic See—under penalty of excommunication to be incurred *ipso facto*—not to interfere in any way with the houses and affairs of the Third Order and that they are to leave the right of visitation to the above mentioned visitator general.

In this bull the pope appoints as executors of the document the Archbishops of Florence and Cremona and the Bishop of Imola.

2) The bull *Ad uberes fructus* of Pope Clement VII, March 10, 1527 concerning the Franciscan Third Order in Spain was published

following on the request of Antonio di Tablada, who was presented as the visitator general and principal master of all the Tertiaries of both sexes, secular and regular in Castile, Leon, Galicia and Andalusia. Having reviewed the principal points of the Rule of the Order of Penance, the pope granted to the Minister Antonio all the rights and privileges that the Mendicant Orders in general enjoyed. Furthermore, the pope affirmed that "the Tertiaries of Compostella never had been subject to the obedience of the Friars Minor" but had always lived under obedience to their own prelates, the visitators. The pope then confirmed the right to celebrate a general chapter every three years, with the nomination of a council of definitors, who would be for

---

[22]"Cum autem nunquam fuerit, nec sit nostrae intentionis quod dicti Conservatores de domibus...Fratres Tertii Ordinis eiusdem S. Francisci de Poenitentia nuncupati regulari observantiae sub habitu eremitico Congregationis Lombardiae degentium...se intromitterent...quae ab aliis, quam a Visitatore Generali dictae Congregationis visitari non possint." De Gubernatis, *op. cit.*, pp. 900-901.

"the nuns, the hermits and married people who lived in the world." Clement granted even wider authority to the superior general, including power to transfer friars and sisters from one house to another in case of necessity, to establish and change Statutes lawfully and freely (licite e libere), to dispense even from the vow of poverty, declaring that the friars and sisters and the hermit nuns of the Order of Penance should be considered as true religious living in community, and that it was forbidden to call them by names which showed lack of respect for them. No one, not even the Minors and high Church dignitaries had the right, for any reason whatsoever, to involve themselves in the government of *this congregation of the Order of Penance*.[23]

c) The Friars Minor, however, did not yield to such decisions. They continued to block the independence of Tertiary congregations until the two bulls of suppression were promulgated by Pius V: the *Superioribus mensibus* of April 16, 1567 which decreed the suppression of the Regular Tertiaries in Spain, transforming them into Friars Minor[24] and the bull *Ea est officii nostri ratio* of July 3, 1568 which suppressed the office of visitator general and subjected "all the friars and sisters, the professed, the lay-brothers, the houses, monasteries and religious houses of men and women, the commissaries and provinces established in any part of the world ("per universum orbem"), the entire flock of the Third Order Regular of both sexes, to the minister general and to the provincials of the Order of Friars Minor called of the Observance."[25]

Of all the congregations of the male Third Order Regular, the only one to regain full autonomy and independence was the Italian congregation which, after an interval of eighteen years,[26] would again have its minister general by force of the decree of the papal bull *Romani*

---

[23]Péano, *op. cit.*, p. 36. Also see Pazzelli, *Il Terz'ordine regolare, op. cit.*, pp. 309-312.

[24]For details of this event see Pazzelli, *op. cit.*, pp. 313-318.

[25]*Ibid.*, pp. 173-180.

[26]See *ibid.*, pp. 180-183.

pontificis providentia of Sixtus V, dated March 29, 1586. From that time on until our own time, the Third Order Regular has remained autonomous.

The other congregations all remained dependent on the Friars Minor until the time of their disappearance, occurring at different times and for different reasons for each congregation.[27]

d) A different aspect of jurisdiction more directly interested the Franciscan sisters in the sixteenth century. They were not so much interested in questions concerning on whom they had to depend, but whether or not they had the right to be considered true religious. For centuries the continuous insistence of ecclesiastical authority on the necessity of the cloister, even before the Council of Trent, as already seen, had created such a mentality in the Church that many bishops, including high Church dignitaries, believed that these "pious women" who did in fact live in community with religious vows but who refused to accept the cloister, did not merit the designation of being true religious women. They were considered lay persons, and therefore had to submit to the laws for the laity.

Early in the century the intervention of Pope Leo X was necessary to bring peace to souls. In the bull *Ea quae per sedem apostolicam* of August 31, 1517,[28] the pope

> indicated first of all that Sixtus IV had already established that "the Sisters of the Third Order of Saint Francis pronouncing the three essential vows and living in common were true religious...that their vows made in the hands of their superiors had the force and validity of solemn vows and produced the same effects...as vows in religious orders approved by the Holy See." As a consequence of this, the sisters enjoyed all the privileges of the Friars Minor, as had been acknowledged by the Fifth Lateran Council.

In spite of all these efforts, this same pope declared,

---

[27]See causes and circumstances in Pazzelli, *op. cit.*, pp. 219-221, 315-318, and 367-369.

[28]See the bull in Bordoni, Archivium, pp. 370-372.

many prelates and pastors of parishes, especially in France and Germany, said that "these
sisters are not true religious" and therefore are
not entitled to the privileges of religious, such as
the right of having their own oratories and cemeteries, the right of having the Blessed Sacrament
in their Chapel, of having the Holy Oils, or
singing of Masses. But as true *laywomen* they
are obliged to assist at Mass and receive the
Sacraments of the Church in parish churches.

This attitude and way of doing things has
been the source of difficulties for the sisters and
the cause of great scandal for the Christian
world.[29]

The pope concluded: "We approve the declarations of our
predecessor (Sixtus IV) and we forbid all prelates under
penalty of excommunication, to interfere with these sisters
in the exercise of their rights for we also 'declare them to
be true religious.'" It would seem clear that such intervention would have removed all doubt and discussion about
the matter and put an end to the dispute. History says
this did not happen. The aversion to the idea of religious
life for women who did not accept the cloister remained
deeply rooted in the mentality of ecclesiastics—and indeed
not only of ecclesiastics but of the sixteenth century itself.
The aversion continued to be experienced. "The social-
political-religious climate of the time," Péano adds, "did
not in any way favor the existence of convents of sisters
who were confused with the beguines (sometimes for ulte-
rior motives). This did occasionally happen, especially in
certain regions of the Upper Rhine Valley."[30]

All these considerations formed the dominant element
in the process that formed the provisions of the Council
of Trent and the decrees which came after the Council
concerning the matter of the cloister.

---

[29]Péano, *op. cit.*, pp. 38-39.
[30]*Ibid.*, p. 38.

CHAPTER IX

FRANCISCAN SISTERS IN THE SEVENTEENTH AND EIGHTEENTH CENTURIES

1. Events following the Council of Trent

The decrees of the Council of Trent concerning religious women and especially the decrees of the constitution *Circa pastoralis* of Saint Pius V were meant to have as a natural consequence the passage from the status of being "sisters" to the status of being cloistered nuns.

In order to understand the radical change which the decrees mentioned above really brought into the lives of religious women, we briefly recall the state of affairs at the time of the Council of Trent.

"From the time of the publication of the constitution *Periculoso* of Boniface VIII in 1298 and continuing after that," writes Creytens, "solemn profession unfailingly implied the observance of the strict cloister and an absolute prohibition of going out of the monastery except in some cases of emergency...'Religious woman' properly so called, solemn profession and the cloister were terms that indicated (their) condition of life."[1]

To avoid equivocation we must add that "religious women properly so called" were considered to be only those who were solemnly professed and who followed one of the four traditional Rules: Saint Basil, Saint Augustine, Saint Benedict, and Saint Francis (that is, the Rule of Saint Clare for the Poor Clares).

The Rule of the Franciscan or Dominican Third Order was not considered to be a Rule that obliged observance of the cloister.

---

[1] R. Creytens, *La riforma dei monasteri femminili dopo i decreti tridentini*, in *Il Concilio di Trento e la riforma tridentina*, Atti del Convengo Storico Internationale (Trento 2-6 settembre, 1963) Roma, 1965. p. 46.

Consequently at the time of the Council of Trent there existed the so-called "closed monasteries" and the "open monasteries" corresponding to the actual situation in which the cloister was or was not observed. Besides those monasteries in which the law of the cloister was in force, other monasteries were considered "closed"

> where the sisters had embraced the cloister even if they were not held to this by their Rule or their profession.... The inhabitants of these monasteries were Tertiary sisters. Thus they were not nuns in the strictest sense of the word because their Rule was not strictly speaking a Rule, but a way of life (a modus vivendi) approved by the Church and so did not imply obligation of the cloister.[2]

On the other hand, open monasteries were those in which the cloister was *de facto* not observed, either by law or by dispensation or by custom. The constitution *Circa pastoralis* decreed the cloister for all these monasteries even those of the Tertiary sisters. Their vows, even though declared solemn by Sixtus IV in 1480, as mentioned above,[3] did not oblige the sisters to observe the cloister because they did not follow any of the four traditional Rules, but the Rule of the Third Order.

Saint Pius V wanted to eliminate this exception, and he did so with point three of the above mentioned constitution *Circa pastoralis.*[4]

"But not all Tertiary sisters living in community, belonged to this category. Many Tertiary sisters had not wanted solemn vows and were living in community with only simple vows." The pope also considered their case (number four of the constitution) and

> left them freedom to choose one of these two options: either make their solemn profession or

---

[2]Creytens, *op. cit.*, p. 47.

[3]See above, p. 123.

[4]See above, p. 125-126. Here is the Latin text: "Mulieres quoque, quae Tertiariae seu de Poenitentia dicuntur, cuiuscumque fuerint Ordinis, in congregatione viventes, si et ipsae professae fuerint, ita ut solemne votum emiserint, ad clausuram praecise, ut praemittitur, et ipsae teneantur." See Creytens, *op. cit.*, pp. 63-64.

retain their present status. In the second case, however, they must bear in mind that they were no longer able to receive novices and, should anyone make profession in their community, the professions were to be null and void. The pope, as we have seen, did not suppress communities of Tertiary sisters with simple vows, but he condemned them by force of his constitution to a slow but certain death.[5]

The application of the constitution *Circa pastoralis* provoked "pandemonium among the nuns of the open monasteries. The first monasteries to experience the painful effects of *Circa pastoralis* were the monasteries located in Rome where the pope's decrees were carried out immediately with firmness and severity." By the tenth of August of that same year of 1566, this notation was given: "they are making the visitation of all the monasteries of women, and monasteries of all sorts of Tertiary sisters and beguines are being closed."[6]

The manner of carrying out the decree must have seemed, at times, excessively severe even to the civil authority as we see in the address of Tiepolo to the Senate of Venice:

It seems great severity has been employed by him (the pope) towards some religious...such as the friars and nuns, obliging them against their will to regulate their lives more strictly than the way in which the same friars and nuns had chosen to bind themselves. Hence not only lamentations and tears have followed upon this action but also desperation and flight.... The *Avisatore* of Rome mentions explicitly that some Tertiary nuns, hearing that Monsignor Carniglia (one of those entrusted with the task of the reform) intended to reform them, wanted to poison themselves.[7]

In spite of everything, the reform continued in Rome and was extended to other dioceses of Italy.

---

[5]Creytens, *op. cit.*, p. 64.

[6]*Ibid.*, pp. 66-67.

[7]*Ibid.*, p. 67.

There were nevertheless some bishops who were strongly opposed to such hasty destruction of the open monasteries in their dioceses.... Moreover, the Council of Trent, had conferred on the bishops the faculty of dispensing from the cloister "ex aliqua legitima causa—approved by the bishop." Thus no one was able to blame the bishops for violating the Tridentine decrees, because it was the bishops' task to judge the legitimacy of the reasons for going outside the cloister.[8]

But Pius V, when it was noticed that the bishops frequently used their power to grant permission to leave the cloister, intervened again with a new document, the bull *Decori et honestati*, dated January 24, 1570. The pope taught that "from now on, nuns were permitted to leave the cloister only for three reasons: a great fire, an epidemic of sickness and leprosy; in accord with this norm the bishop and the superior of nuns were to decide whether one of the reasons obtained."[9]

Based on many different motives, much opposition continued. A good number of Tertiary sisters were well disposed and would willingly have embraced the cloister "if there had not been the insurmountable obstacle of the extreme poverty of their monastery.... Thus many refused to make their solemn profession and returned to the world."[10]

There were also social and moral reasons due to the customs of the time. There were regions in which many of the nuns had been forced to enter religious life by relatives who were seeking a way "to avoid diminishment of family resources." Generally, these people chose "open monasteries." "None of these women thought, when they became

---

[8]*Ibid.*, p. 69. "The forbearance of the bishops–Hermans wrote–permitted the continued existence of many convents of penitents or tertiaries. Under the very eye of the pope, the Oblates of Saint Frances of Rome continued their peaceful life of contemplation and charity." Istituti di *voti semplici*, in DIP, V, col. 1562. "The constitution *(Circa pastoralis)*–adds Gambari–did not even hinder the rise, with the approval of the bishops, of new women's communities without solemn vows." *Congregazione religiosa*, in DIP, II, col. 1562.

[9]Creytens, *op. cit.*, p. 70.

[10]*Ibid.*, p. 76.

nuns...that they would one day be enclosed in a monastery of strict enclosure by reason of their religious profession."[11]

Let us not omit some considerations of a political nature: these customs of society were defended by authorities of the states and the republics. Thus the Senate of Venice sent a formal note of protest to the Holy See. The Holy See had "no intention to disturb good relations which it had with certain civil governments simply over the question of the cloister of some monasteries.... Thus, in a letter of December 31, 1580 the Holy See made it known that it did not want to force the nuns to greater restrictions than those to which they were accustomed."[12]

Confronted by similar pressures, especially in Italy, the Holy See gradually

> became less severe in applying the law.... The Holy See understood that, to be accomplished with ease, change in the institutions of monasteries of women required a transformation of the structure of society and of civil institutions and customs, changes which could not be effected in a few years' time. Therefore it had decided, where necessary, to adapt itself to the circumstances and to be content with a less rigid cloister than that which had been called for by the bull *Decori e honestati* of Pius V.[13]

So "quite a few monasteries in Italy and elsewhere remained as they were before 'open monasteries.' Here and there some monasteries were successful, thanks to the protection of powerful civil leaders.... Others remained open because they did not find the necessary means for their support."[14]

Particular events concerning the monastery of Saint Ann in Foligno, have already been mentioned. Such events can be considered typical, for they were repeated in dozens of sisters' monasteries, at least in Italy. Several decades would have to pass before one could say that the

---

[11] *Ibid.*, p. 72.

[12] *Ibid.*, p. 73.

[13] *Ibid.*, p. 73.

[14] *Ibid.*, pp. 77-78.

laws concerning the cloister were being everywhere observed.

Outside Italy, especially in the nations or regions where the Protestant reformation was on the ascendancy, the question was entirely different: preoccupation centered on the survival of "religious life and not on having a cloister." Thus little importance was given to the decrees of *Circa pastoralis* even by the bishops themselves. In the Low Countries the instructions of *Circa pastoralis* were not accepted. "So in 1607, thirty-five years after the publication of the bull of Gregory XIII, it was said at the Provincial Council of Malines that closing of the "open monasteries" had so far been impossible because of the meagerness of the funds intended for the poor...."[15]

If, however, we take an overall view of the situation we must agree that "the majority of the open monasteries accepted the cloister." In the first decades of the seventeenth century for the most part the transformation had taken place. There no longer were Franciscan *sisters* dedicated to great external charitable activity but only Franciscan nuns dedicated to prayer and to the internal activities of their monasteries. Thus there disappeared "an ancient institution which the Church had officially recognized from the time of Sixtus IV until Pius V,"[16] or rather from the time of Martin V in 1428. "The transformation of the status of the Tertiary sisters to the status of being nuns of the cloister," Frascadore has written (and we fully support his position), "certainly was in opposition to the original charism of the Order of Penance of Saint Francis which had been preserved for about four hundred years in a great number of communities."[17] "It will be a long time," concludes Creytens,

> before the Church will again recognize "open monasteries" among the female religious institutions of consecrated life. This time will come

---

[15] The reference here is to the bull of Gregory XIII, *De sacris virginibus* of December 30, 1572. In this document precise instructions are given for providing for the support of the tertiary "nuns" so that the decrees of the Council of Trent and Pius V concerning the cloister could be carried out in practice. See Creytens, *op. cit.*, p. 78.

[16]*Ibid.*

[17]Frascadore, *Francescane, Suore,* in DIP, IV, col. 212.

when, because of the great changes in social and religious life in the seventeenth and eighteenth centuries, the Church will be obliged to appeal to "religious women" to dedicate themselves to public teaching and to the works of charity.[18]

2. Franciscan sisters in the cloister

We must not think that the substantial change in female religious life, i.e. the universal application of the law of cloister, caused a major crisis of the kind which today we would describe as a vocational crisis. This change was not a sudden change, as we have seen. It was accomplished during the lapse of more than one generation, and thus allowed for the gradual formation in Christian people of a new idea of what the Franciscan sister now was, i.e., a nun.

Feminine vocations to the Franciscan religious life were plentiful. In large part this was due to the climate of a more intense and more deeply felt religious spirit, one of the more readily discernible results of the *Catholic reform*. This term *Catholic reform* is understood as including all that intense theological and practical activity which the Catholic Church put forth in order to contrast with, and if possible, to frustrate the effects of the Lutheran Reform. This reform, begun in 1517, had during the years 1530-1560 gradually widened its sphere of influence in a large part of Europe. The Council of Trent had been summoned to take appropriate steps to offset the spread of Lutheranism. Its decrees touched on every area of life and had in fact caused and promoted this new climate of counter-reform. "The desire for reform," writes Péano,

> the desire for a return to the Franciscan ideals manifested itself everywhere but especially in the First Order which saw the establishment of the Reformed Friars Minor in Italy, the institution of the Discalced Friars in Spain, the Recollect Friars in France, Germany and England. Nor should we forget the foundation of the Capuchin Friars who became an autonomous group in the family of Saint Francis. This new situation was

---

[18]Creytens, *La riforma dei monasteri, op. cit.*, p. 78.

beneficial to the Franciscan Sisters of the Third Order. And even though their cloister life was accentuated, this fact seems in no way to have hindered their growth and expansion.[19]

a) *The "Reform of Limbourg" (Holland)*
Perhaps the most significant example of this new reality was the rise and development of the desire for cloistered life where external conditions did not oblige it, that is in the Low Countries. This movement crystallized in the famous *Reform of Limbourg*, a reform of the Penitent Recollectines.

The beginning of this reform was due to Jeanne Neerinck who was born in Gand, Belgium in 1576. She died in Limbourg in 1648. Jeanne was unable to fulfill her desire for the religious life until she was twenty-eight years old in 1604. She was accepted into the convent of the Grey Sisters in her city. This was one of the many convents of the Grey Sisters which still existed in the Low Countries. These sisters followed the Rule of the Third Order Regular of Saint Francis given by Leo X in 1521 and for the most part they dedicated themselves to the care of the sick.

Jeanne wanted to introduce among her sisters a more contemplative life of prayer and penance with a strict cloister, following the example of the Friars Minor Recollect.[20] With some of her sisters from Gand, Jeanne founded in 1623 a new monastery in the city of Limbourg (hence the name of the reform). This was a strictly cloistered life, with the members divided into choir sisters and lay sisters. They continued to follow the Rule of the Third Order Regular and they observed the constitutions, called Apostolic Constitutions, which were prepared by the Belgian Recollect Father Pierre Marchant (1585-1661) who had been of great assistance to the foundress. Jeanne

---

[19]Péano, *Le Religiose Francescane, op. cit.*, pp. 47-48.

[20]This reform of the Recollects is the reform of the Friars Minor which came from Spain and would flourish in France, Flanders and Germany, especially after the first part of the seventeenth century. "The Recollects won very great prestige with all social classes. They wore their own habit, which had a pyramidal hood and in their way of life they were similar to other reformed families.... In the eighteenth century the number of Recollect provinces rose to twenty-five with 11,000 members." Iriate, *History of the Franciscan Order, op. cit.*, pp. 181-182.

adopted the name "Jeanne of Jesus." Their constitutions were approved by Urban VIII in 1634.

This reform was very successful and it spread quickly to various monasteries.

> External activity was severely excluded. However, the convents were able to have a small convent school with some ten to twelve students whose life was regulated by suitable norms. The students could leave the convent only when they finally went back to their families again on completion of their studies. All the convents were autonomous and juridically they depended on the Recollect Friars Minor. While Jeanne Neerinck was still living, the convents of the Reform numbered sixteen, and just before the beginning of the French Revolution there were more than forty convents spread throughout Flanders, Belgium, France and Germany.[21]

b) *The Franciscan Sisters of the Sorrowful Mother (Mexico)*

Another typical example to be remembered "in this context of fervor and renewal" is the foundation of a convent of Franciscan sisters with papal cloister, but who were not Poor Clares. They were founded by a missionary of the Observance, Father Antonio Margil of Jesus in the territory of the missions. He founded this institute in 1683 at San Juan del Rio in the province of Queretaro in Mexico with the collaboration of Beatrice Flores (1665-1745) "for the purpose of offering to souls who so desired the opportunity to live the cloistered life."[22] They were called—and are still called today—the Franciscan Sisters of the Sorrowful Mother. They are perhaps the oldest convent of nuns of the Third Order who from the beginning have observed the papal cloister. During their history "the community on four occasions had to suffer being excluded from their monastery, in 1863, 1867, 1914, and 1926. These religious women always succeeded in returning to the convent of their origins."[23]

---

[21]Van Hulst, *Penitenti recollettine, di Limburgo*, in DIP, VI, col. 1371-1372.

[22]G. Rocca, *Francescane dell'Addolorata*, in DIP, IV, col. 254.

[23]*Ibid.*

3. The spread of charitable communities in the seventeenth century

Along with these typical examples of cloistered monasteries, which remain somewhat isolated examples, there continued to flourish in the female religious world the desire for an active life of charity with a strong disinterest in the cloister.

During the seventeenth century there arose some extraordinary apostolic figures who gave validity and vitality to new forms of the works of charity. Even if they did not realize it, they gave birth to many new institutes. We recall some of them here.

Saint Vincent de Paul gave shining witness to the ideal of brotherly love with the founding of the Daughters of Charity. These sisters had their beginning in Paris through the work of Saint Vincent de Paul and Saint Louise de Marillac in 1633. She gathered in her home a "community of young women from the countryside who had come to the capital city with the desire to serve the destitute." In 1642 some of these women began to pronounce a private vow. Thus was created "an intermediate type of consecrated life between the lay and canonical religious life of the seventeenth century."[24]

John Baptist de la Salle excelled in the field of education for the common people. In 1682 he founded the Brothers of Christian Schools. During this same period (besides the Ursulines who had been founded in 1535 by Saint Angela Merici) the Visitation sisters were established in 1610 for the education of young women by Saint Frances Frémiot de Chantal (+1641) who worked with the encouragement and under the direction of Saint Francis de Sales.

Drawing upon the example of these most interesting beginnings, there followed various new foundations.[25]

As a cause of this phenomenon, one must also remember that the evolution of society during the Renaissance

[24]G. Rocca, *Figlie della carità*, in DIP, III, col. 1540. First approved by the Archbishop of Paris in 1646 as a "confraternity and then by Cardinal De Retz in 1655 who then placed the confraternity in perpetuo under the direction of the superior general of the Congregation of the Missions, the association acieved its definitive character with the approval of Cardinal Vendome, Legate *a latere* of Pope Clement IX in 1688." *Ibid.*

[25]In Italy there were twenty-two new foundations and in France about

had greatly increased the role of women in the religious state. Indeed, even before this time, beginning with the appearance of the Grey Sisters and their employment as nurses which they exercised primarily in their hospitals, religious women—Franciscan and non-Franciscan—had begun a life of seeking spiritual perfection by placing themselves at the service of their most needy brothers and sisters.

To understand the spirit which animated the innovators of these new forms of religious life for women, we must especially note that the efforts to form the new communities which began in the 1600's were not made in a spirit of opposition to the cloister stemming from a love of greater freedom. Rather these women sought a greater availability for the exercise of the works of charity, many of which were incompatible with the observance of a cloister. Their position with respect to the legislation or canonical thinking of the Church was not born out of prejudice.

The founders and foundresses of the seventeenth and eighteenth centuries were not preoccupied with quibbles of the canonical order. "Living the Gospel," writes Hermans, "they felt impelled to give answer to this or that need of the people of their time, abandoned children, the sick in need of assistance, young people or adults separated from the faith community, entire populations deprived of the proclamation of the Gospel, clerics needing formation or spiritual assistance."[26] It is a fact that the new initiatives collided with the restrictive decrees of *Circa pastoralis*. They were in fact different from the traditional female monasteries of the Poor Clares, the Benedictines or the Augustinians because the new religious women did not profess solemn vows and were not obliged to the cloister. They constituted a new reality in comparison with the religious life as decreed by the Council and the constitution which came after it. Boaga reminds us:

---

forty. Among the institutes for women the following may be mentioned: the Sisters of Borromeo of Nancy (1652), the Daughters of the Blessed Virgin Mary (1610), the Daughters of the Presentation (1627), the Daughters of the Cross (1625), the Magdalenes (1618) and many others. See E. Boaga, Aspetti e problemi degli ordini e congregazione religiose nei secoli XVII e XVIII, in Problemi di storia della chiesa nei secoli XVI-VIII, Dehoniane, Napoli, 1982, p. 118.

[26]A.M. Hermans, *Istituti di voti semplici*, in DIP, V, col. 123.

In that decree the pope imposed the strict cloister perpetually for all the professed women of any institution, even in those cases in which their own statutes did not impose the cloister, or where such a cloister had never been observed. Religious life, according to this pontifical document, was conceivable only in orders with solemn vows and also for women observing the strict cloister. As a consequence, sisters belonging to groups or societies of Tertiaries, if they professed solemn vows, had to be placed under the laws of papal cloister as nuns. If they professed simple vows, however, granted that according to the jurists of that time these simple vows had no juridical force, these women had to be persuaded to make their solemn profession and to accept the cloister. All other groups of women who persisted in living the common life without solemn vows and without cloister, were prohibited from receiving new members and in practice were condemned to extinction.[27]

To understand such great severity at the distance of four hundred years, we must keep in mind the purpose of the legislation, which was to establish absolute stability in religious or consecrated life. Solemn profession was then irrevocable. A nun could return to the lay state or be reduced to the lay state, only by a declaration of the nullity of her religious profession.[28]

4. The very first of the "new congregations"

From the beginning of the seventeenth century, due to the pressure of the new factors mentioned above, there were attempts to establish institutes of sisters who should dedicate themselves to the active life and should place themselves at the service of their neighbors either in the field of education or some other form of assistance. It is not that these people wanted to go against what the Church had established concerning the cloister. They simply wanted to come to the assistance of those who were in

---

[27]E. Boaga, *Aspetti e problemi, op. cit.*, p. 120.

[28]See A.M. Hermans, *Istituti di voti semplici*, in DIP, V, col. 122.

need because of life's circumstances. We mention only the most significant of these efforts.

a) *The English Dames of Mary Ward (1609-1610)*

This institution was not Franciscan, but we feel, nevertheless, it should be of interest to us because it was the first to open a new way which would then be followed by a great number of other attempts by new congregations both Franciscan and non-Franciscan in the following two centuries. "The evolution of events of this institute," as Gambari has noted, "had great influence on the history and development of the female congregations of simple vows."[29]

It is also interesting to note right away that this congregation arose in the very land and almost at the same time in which flourished the Recollectine Penitents of Limbourg, a strictly cloistered institute.[30] This fact cautions us not to be excessively rigid in determining the characteristics of a historical period, even in Church affairs. We are aware that examples of religious life which are exactly opposed to each other can flourish in the same period.

The English Dames started through the work of Mary Ward, an English noblewoman living in the city of Saint-Omer (then in Flanders and today in France in the diocese of Arras) during the years 1609-1610.

In the English community of Catholics, transplanted to Belgium because of the Anglican persecutions, there had been for some decades an impulse towards female religious life with the establishment of several convents. Mary Ward, a member of this Catholic community, was certainly not lacking in virtue, talent, or initiative. She desired to enable women to carry on an active apostolate under "unique and vigorous guidance."[31] Mary Ward thus established an association of religious women who took care of schools and boarding houses for English nobility along with a school for the young girls of the neighborhood. The foundress envisioned different categories or grades of

---

[29]E. Gambari, *Congregatione religiosa*, in DIP, II, col. 1563.

[30]See above, pp. 154-155.

[31]Léopold Willaert, *La restaurazione cattolica dopo il concilio di Trento*, in Flesch-Martin, *Storia della chiesa*, vol. XVIII, 2a ed. italiana, AAIE, Torino, 1976, p. 198.

those belonging to the institute: novices, scholastics with simple perpetual vows, coadjutors with simple perpetual vows and professed sisters with solemn vows. Mary omitted, of course, the obligation of observing the law of cloister and choir. The new institute followed the constitutions of the Society of Jesus and for this reason the sisters were also called the "Jesuitesses." The plan was put into practice in different houses, first in the Low Countries beginning at Saint-Omer and then elsewhere. Very soon the work was extended to Germany, Italy, Austria and Hungary. The innovations in their religious life that brought "first and foremost freedom from the cloister, stirred up very strong opposition in the Roman Curia."[32] "Mary accepted misunderstanding to such an extent that, suspected by the Inquisition, she was imprisoned and her institute suppressed."[33] This suppression was decreed after twenty years of fruitful activity with the publication of the bull of Urban VIII *Pastoralis romani pontificis*, January 13, 1631.

The companions of Mary Ward continued to live together privately with her. After the death of the foundress, they continued to dedicate themselves to the education of young women under the name of the "Institute of the Blessed Virgin Mary." Soon the congregation was able to spread again to different countries with the approval of the bishops or at least their toleration.

Much later in 1877 this Institute was approved by the Church. In 1908 Pius X recognized Mary Ward as the foundress of their institute. Today "the plant that is the institute of Mary Ward extends its three branches to every continent," (*Institutum Beatae Mariae Virginis—IBVM, the Institute of the Blessed Virgin Mary of the Sisters of Loreto in Ireland and the Institute of the Blessed Virgin Mary of the*

---

[32]The restrictions, to which the foundress was subjected, have left a sinister memory in the constitution of Pope Benedict XV *Quamvis justo* of 1749. These restrictions detailed the activities of the congregations under the supervision of the bishops in the dioceses in which her schools and the boarding schools were located. See the bull *Quamvis justo* in *Benedicti Papae XIV Bullarium*, tom. III, Romae, Congreg. de Propaganda Fide, 1753, pp. 54-68.

[33]Maria Forno, *Ward, Maria*, in *Bibliotheca Sanctorum*, Prima Appendice, Roma, 1987, c. 1456. Also see E.M.I. Whetter, *Istituto della Beata Vergine Maria "Dame Inglesi,"* in DIP, V, col. 130.

Sisters of Loreto in Toronto, Canada) and today has about five thousand members.[34] The process for the canonization of Mary Ward, begun decades ago, is very well advanced and has reached the *positio* phase of its development.

b) *The Daughters of Saint Francis of Assisi (Pisa, Italy, 1611)*

On the Franciscan side of things we note as the first institute the Daughters of Saint Francis of Assisi of Pisa. Two Franciscan Tertiary sisters began to live in community in 1611 under the direction of the Reformed Friars Minor in Borgo a Mozzano in the neighborhood of Lucca. For some time the community was made up of just four sisters who dedicated themselves to the education of young girls. The congregation which still exists with the same name has always remained modest in numbers. However it is significant because of its historic origins at the beginning of the 1600's.

c) *The Elizabethans of Aachen, Germany, (1623)*

A short time later in 1623 the Elizabethans of Aachen arose in Germany. They give us a fuller and more fortunate example of the same development in religious life: works of charity, absence of cloister. Its beginnings were due to Apollonia Radermecher (1571-1626). From the year 1611 Apollonia had dedicated herself to the care of the sick and assistance to the poor in several hospices. In 1622 the authorities of Aachen entrusted to her the direction of the local hospital. Since she was unable to guarantee the presence of sisters for the service of the hospital, Appollonia was advised to give life to a new religious community. This was done with the help of the Observant Friars Minor of Cologne.

> In 1626 Apollonia Radermecher together with two companions took the habit of the Franciscan Tertiary sisters. The new community and the hospital were placed under the patronage of Saint Elizabeth and because of this the religious were called the Hospital Sisters of Saint Elizabeth or the Elizabethans of Aachen....The young community recruited its members from families of high social standing. Soon it was

---

[34]See M. Forno, *loc. cit.*, col. 1456-1457.

possible to send sisters to Duren (1650) for the service of the local hospital and then to Luxembourg (1671) and Graz (1690). From Duren a community was founded in Julich (1687) and another in Graz (1698). From the latter departed religious who gave origin to still more autonomous communities, some of which later became mother-houses of congregations.[35]

d) *Franciscans of the Immaculate Conception of Sebenik (1673)*

One of the few examples of congregations that arose near the end of the seventeenth century was the congregation of the Franciscan Sisters of the Immaculate Conception of Sebenik. This congregation started in lowly circumstances because of local needs and it exists as such even today.

> It drew its inspiration and beginning from the Penitent Franciscan Tertiary Sisters who had even from the fourteenth century lived in Sebenik and other regions of Croatia where the Franciscan friars were missionaries. It began as a religious community of common life in Sebenik in 1673. The sisters dedicated themselves to the assistance of the sick and the poor and they helped the clergy in the churches. They made their living from their work and from receiving alms. They professed the Rule of the Third Order Regular of Leo X, translated into Croatian and preserved in an ancient manuscript.... Because of their generosity and humility they were be called the *Minjurice*, that is "the little sisters."[36]

Until 1922 the apostolate of these sisters was restricted to the city of Sebenik. Today the institute is present in France, Austria and Germany as well as in various dioceses in Croatia and Dalmatia where it had its beginnings.

The few examples which we have selected are the classic examples of how the communities of "evangelical life-style" began to appear in the seventeenth century in Italy

---

[35]G. Rocca, *Elisabettine di Aquisgrana*, in DIP, III, col. 1115-1116.

[36]G. Rocca, *Francescane dell'Immacolata di Sebenico*, in DIP, IV, col. 293-294.

and elsewhere. From a community that in the beginning was involved with a quasi-community task, the members gradually assumed a form of life that involved promises and even the emission of one or more simple vows. The one requisite for the founders or foundresses was that their institute should not be constrained to observe the cloister. They sought and in fact obtained permission to remain societies of common life and institutes of simple vows; equally distant, it might be said, between religious orders and secular associations.[37]

In practice this is how the rise of communities—and later on—the congregations of sisters arose.

The religious congregation of sisters as we know it today, writes Gambari,

> is the result of a long and complex historical-juridical process inserted into a phenomenon of still greater dimensions, namely the movement inspired by the Holy Spirit, which brings persons attracted by the gospel to follow the virgin, poor, obedient Christ in forms of life different from those which the Church had accepted and organized. At a given moment the Church herself welcomes this new form of common life as the state of the profession of the evangelical counsels.[38]

5. The conservatory and the houses of charity

One of the characteristic structures which the new communities of Franciscan and non-Franciscan sisters adopted was that of the conservatory. The official acceptance and, let us say, the history of this term was that of a "convent of women without cloister and without vows, maintained by alms and also with the assistance of public funds, open to receive poor girls without a dowry." The term in the seventeenth century was not new. Towards the end of the middle ages this name was given to an asylum

---

[37]Hermans, *op. cit.*, p. 124.

[38]Gambari, *op. cit.*, p. 1560. Today after the promulgation of the Code of Canon Law (January 25, 1983) we no longer speak of Orders, nor of religious Congregations, but only of "Religious Institutes" which canon 607.2 defines as "a society whose members profess public perpetual vows

for children and adolescents in any kind of need whatsoever. The inmates of the institution were "conserved" or protected from danger. An education was given to the young and also a trade was taught. In some conservatories a careful instruction in music was given to the children who had the gift for it.[39]

The word "conservatory" would have a long life with the meaning of the term somewhat different according to the times. "In the nineteenth century the term frequently included both convents connected with a boarding school or a primary school as well as other charitable institutions in order to distinguish them from the monasteries of contemplative nuns."[40]

Ecclesiastical authority was not able to offer opposition: the conservatory was in practice, a house of devout women who were doing good works.

Another term or institution was that of the "house of charity" or the name of a saint followed by the expression "of charity," e.g. Saint Clare of Charity. This meant that the institution welcomed young girls for the purpose of educating them.

6. The eighteenth century. Characteristics of the new institutes

In the eighteenth century one sees a continual decrease in the number of nuns or women religious "properly so called," those of the traditional orders with solemn vows and living in cloistered monasteries[41] but not a decline of female vocations to the consecrated life. Among the various causes of this phenomenon, religious and social, "the

---

according to their own proper law or else temporary vows renewed when they expire and live fraternal life as community."

[39]This type of conservatory would be successful and gave uniqueness to some of the others. At Naples during the sixteenth century four conservatories of this kind were established. They had their eminent teachers such as Allesandro Scarlatti, Durante, Pergolesi, and Vinci. The same situation obtained in other cities which gave the term "conservatory" the meaning of "a professional school of music," a meaning that the word still keeps in Italian. See T. Ledòchowska, *Conservatorio*, in DIP, II, col. 1628.

[40]T. Ledòchowska, *Conservatorio*, in DIP, II, col. 1627.

[41]One can mention here "the drop in the number of nuns recorded in Tuscany: in 1550 there were 4403, declining in 1738 to 2201 and in 1806 to 1769." See E. Boaga, *Aspetti e problemi, op. cit.,* p. 105.

change in the condition of women in the Church, with the coming of the new congregations of women involved in apostolates outside the cloister and in the midst of the people must be considered one of the most important."[42]

"It is important for us to consider," adds Boaga,

> in these new male and female congregations, the variety of the typical orientation of life in comparison with previously experienced forms of religious life. In the new forms we note a larger field of activity for religious life with strong involvement of religious in apostolic activity and with a special attention to local needs. The new congregations of men and women earned a reputation for their lives of prayer and austerity as well as for their apostolic tasks. These new congregations sought to involve themselves in the practical work of the religious formation and instruction of the people, the education and instruction of young people, the care of the sick and other works of charity, and pastoral ministry in urban centers and rural areas. This meant that religious men and women were authentic forces for good in the apostolate of the time.[43]

Officially these new forms of religious life continued to find a lack of warm welcome, if not clear cut opposition, in their relationships with the Roman Curia. The more frequent attitude which they encountered was that of tolerance. In various ecclesiastical documents which pertained to the affairs of the new congregations and which at times even included documentation of "approval," these new organizations were designated confusedly with varied terminology, such as "confraternity," "sodality," "society," "congregation," "pious union" and "association." The meaning was not precise, but very broad. This varied terminology "did not imply any official change of attitude by the Holy See. The style of life of these new entities could not be approved positively and officially because

---

[42]E. Boaga, *Aspetti et problemi, op. cit.*, p. 105.

[43]*Ibid.*, pp. 118-119.

it contrasted with current legislation. Therefore it was tolerated."

However, the severity of *Circa pastoralis* did not de facto hinder the more or less spontaneous phenomenon of the multiplication of female communities which were foreign to the outline of the constitution. This was, at least in part, due to the attitude of bishops who did not hesitate to test the usefulness of these communities in the pastoral ministry.

"The bishops," writes Gambari,

> were firmly convinced that they were authorized to establish congregations of simple vows in their dioceses. The Holy See implicitly admitted the legitimacy of these foundations, but refused to admit that they could be considered "religious communities and their members could be considered as true religious." For this reason the Holy See, although it sometimes did approve rules and statutes, nevertheless never wanted to approve the institute or the congregation as such. On the contrary, the above mentioned acts...explicitly excluded the confirmation of the institute which was thus simply "tolerated."[44]

The famous constitution *Quamvis justo* published by Benedict XIV on April 30, 1749 concerning the institute of the "English Dames" founded by Mary Ward, repeated this same position. While recognizing the office of the superior general, it openly said that the approval of the constitutions did not imply the approval of the corresponding congregation. "It was at that time," notes Torres, "that with the approval of the constitutions of a female religious congregation, the Holy See started to add the clause 'absque approbatione instituti—without the approval of the institute.'"[45] Only towards the end of the eighteenth century did

---

[44]E. Gambari, *Congregazione religiosa*, in DIP, II, col. 1563.

[45]J. Torres, *Approvazione delle religioni*, in DIP, I, col. 769. "Until the end of the eighteenth century," affirms Gambari, "the "Apostolic See, when even if at times it confirmed rules and statutes with its approbation, never intended to approve the institute or congregation itself. So in any act relating to this society, the Apostolic See explicitly excluded approbation of the institute with the insertion of a so-called safety clause by which the female religious congregations were only tolerated:"

this clause first begin to be omitted in documentation. The first explicit approval of a female congregation occurred in 1777 and was granted in favor of the Oblates of the Immaculate Conception of Ascoli.[46]

7. The new congregations

We have already observed that the constant characteristic of the majority of the new institutes or congregations which arose in the eighteenth century was their offering of self to the service of the Church with various apostolic and charitable activities.

If there is a common element running through the institutes or congregations of Franciscan sisters which in a certain way qualifies and distinguishes them, this could be the special attention given to the care of the sick in hospitals, in rest homes, in homes for the elderly, in charitable activity among the very poor, sheltering homes for the orphans and educational programs for children and youth, particularly for young girls. The Franciscan congregations which arose in the eighteenth century and which continue in our own day are many. Among them we mention the following:

a) *The Franciscan Missionaries of Assisi (formerly called "del Giglio," 1702)*

This institute began in Assisi in 1702 through the efforts of Father Giuseppe Antonio Marcheselli of the Friars Minor Conventual and Angela Maria del Giglio, a Franciscan Tertiary. The purpose of the community was "to serve in the work of education, specializing in the area of education for little children and orphans, of caring for the poor, assisting in parish ministry, caring for the sick and missionary activity."[47] This community began as a "Conservatory" which, in addition to the sisters, welcomed "young girls as aspirants." This modest beginning grew

---

Institutorum secularium et Congregationum religiosarum evolutio comparata, in "Commentarium pro Religiosis," 29 (1950), p. 230. The additional clause reads thus: "Through these present letters we do not intend among other things to approve in any way the Conservatory itself"—from the Constitution *Quamvis justo*. See above p. 122, note 32 (pp. 58-59 of the *Bullarium* there indicated).

[46]E. Gambari, *Institutorium saecularium, op. cit.*, p. 231.

[47]G. Odoardi, *Francescane Missionarie del Giglio*, in DIP, IV, col. 342-343.

and became an academy, a boarding school for students, as was recorded in the documentation of 1730. This educational institute had the protection of the Bishop of Assisi and of the ministers general of the Friars Minor Conventual to whom the institute has always remained affiliated. Pius VII in 1822 gave the Conservatory the title of "Monastery of Giglio." In the nineteenth century the institute suffered from suppression twice as did many or almost all others; the Napoleonic suppression in 1810 and the Italian suppression of 1860. Losses in both cases were made up for by new educational and charitable enterprises which today include "day care centers for children, elementary and catechetical schools, after school and boarding schools, schools for dressmaking, sewing and embroidery, orphanages, homes for runaway children, clinics, out-patient clinics, hospitals and dispensaries."[48] At the beginning of this century, missionary activity was added and later became important enough for the institute to adopt the title "The Franciscan Missionaries of Giglio of Assisi."

b) *The Franciscan Tertiary Sisters of Bressanone (1700)*

By way of introduction, let us say, first of all, that the city and territory of Bressanone were under the control of the Austro-Hungarian Empire until the treaty of Saint Germain in 1919. The history of the Franciscan Sisters of Bressanone developed in a very large part under the influence and actions which the Austro-Hungarian civil authorities exercised over religious corporations.

The date of birth of this congregation is considered to be the year 1700. It had its beginning through the efforts of Maria Hueber (1653-1705) who lost her father at a very young age. She was raised, educated and instructed by her devout mother who was a dressmaker by trade. Because of poor health and filial devotion to her mother, Maria was unable to fulfill her desire of consecrating herself entirely to the Lord. However very soon she became a member of the Third Order of Saint Francis.

> Upon the death of her mother in 1696, the doors of the convent still remained closed to her, this time because of her age. At that time Father

---

[48]*Ibid.*, p. 344.

Isidore Kirnigl, a Friar Minor, who was her confessor and spiritual director, encouraged her to take an interest in poor young girls of the city by giving them instructions in reading, writing, religion, and sewing. At the same time Father Kirnigl placed at her side her first spiritual daughter, the young dressmaker Regina Pfurner. In spite of difficulties of every kind this activity continued even after the death of Maria Hueber.[49]

The development of the institute was extremely limited at first because a quota was imposed by the civil government on members of the institute and remained in force for 150 years after the foundation. Only slowly did the civil authority grant an increase in the number of members of each convent from six to twenty.[50]

There could now develop an outstanding organization for the instruction and education of young girls. For a long time the schools opened by the institute were the only ones in the centers of the Dolomites. In due time the sisters obtained regular diplomas and were asked to train other teachers. In the meantime the sisters professed the Rule of Leo X of 1521 which was integrated with constitutions approved by the Provincial Chapter of the Reformed Friars Minor (1724) and by the Bishop of Bressanone. The sisters made their profession of simple perpetual vows "with episcopal cloister as was suitable to their scholastic apostolate."

Father Capistrano Soyer (+1865) who was their counselor and director for half of the nineteenth century, "developed the foundation with the establishment of daughter houses which remained autonomous. A motherhouse of religious congregations was formed. Thus in the last century there were established four independent religious congregations, the Franciscan Sisters of Bressanone, of Bolzano-Bozen, of Caldaro-Kaltern and of Rio Pusteria-Muhlbach,"[51] all dedicated to the apostolate of

[49]*Suore Terziarie Francescane in Bressanone, in Annuario Cattolico d'Italia* 1984-85, *Editoriale Italiana*, Rome, 1984, p. 844.

[50]See M. Vettori, *Francescane de Bressanone* (Bolzano), in DIP, IV, col. 225.

[51]*Ibid.*

the education of young girls. But in this century, under the direction of Bishop Adriano Egger, episcopal commissary, the three houses were united with Bressanone (1928) where the Mother General resides. "The congregation embraced the Rule of the Third Order Regular given by Pius XI in 1927, and in 1929 new constitutions approved by the ordinaries of Bressanone, Trent and Innsbruck were added." In the period between the two World Wars other fields of activity were undertaken: household administration in retirement homes and in colleges directed by religious men, the work of nursing and health care assistance in hospitals, clinics, rest homes and missionary activity in Bolivia (1928) and Cameroon (1935). In 1974 the congregation had 74 houses with 614 professed members.

CHAPTER X

THE END OF THE EIGHTEENTH CENTURY, THE ERA OF NAPOLEON AND THE "RESTORATION"

1. The Enlightenment

The well-known position of Church authority concerning new congregations of sisters who wanted to live religious life in "open monasteries" without the cloister is already sufficient to explain why there were not a great number of new institutes of this kind in the seventeenth and eighteenth centuries.

In the second half of the eighteenth century, as a joint primary cause of this dearth of new religious communities of women must be noted and emphasized the growing hostility towards religious orders as an integral part of the policies of civil authority in many European countries. This was one of the more visible effects of that complex philosophical and social movement which today we know as the "enlightenment." This current of thought was founded on the affirmation of the absolute self-sufficiency of human reason against every form of transcendentalism. This "enlightenment" not only exalted "thought, reflection and reason," and hence man, as was done during the Renaissance period. It also claimed the sovereignty of man, carrying the theory to excesses never before known, even to the extent of including contempt and the denial of values—such as religion—which at one time had exercised great influence on the vast majority of people or had been held in highest esteem by them. Affirms Lortz: "It is the birth of autonomous civilization, independent of the Church."[1]

---

[1] J. Lortz, *Storia della Chiesa*, II, Paoline, 1973, p. 17. Bianca Magnino outlines the "enlightenment": "Reason inspires moral 'intuition,' and it is reason that guides man along the way to the good. Not only does reason

In the fields of politics and government, the "enlightened" monarch himself alone could make decisions for the "welfare" of his people without any need to consult his advisors or parliament. In the area of religion the enlightened monarch equally believed he could make all arrangements without consulting traditional spiritual authority, that is, the Church. Hence, "enlightenment" in the area of religion, produced Josephinism or jurisdictionalism,[2] while in social matters enlightenment was the ideological presupposition which contributed to the French Revolution.

It is extremely difficult if not impossible today to estimate how many monasteries were closed, or how many congregations were suppressed in their very beginnings, the sisters sent home to their own families, generally with a small annuity or pension, in different countries where this political-religious tendency sooner or later would gain the upper hand. It became a characteristic of the great family of the Bourbons who ruled from the thrones of Austria, Spain, France, Naples and Sicily, as well as in the

show the stages of the way but it almost constrains one to follow it through to the identification of virtue in physical well-being, morality in pleasure and progress in the joy of living.... Away with asceticism which seeks to smother life and render people incapable of happiness. If an individual has fallen into that trap, the enlightened state must liberate him. How? By forcibly closing convents, monasteries. This will be the policy of the enlightenment and in fact later on the French Revolution." *Alle origini della Crisi Contemporanea, Illuminismo e Rivoluzione, Raggio,* Roma, 1946, pp. 266-267.

[2]The name "Josephinism" comes from Joseph II of Hapsburg-Lorain (1741-1790) Emperor of Austria from 1765. He is the incarnation of the ideal *enlightened* absolute monarch and asserted the right of his jurisdiction in relations between the state and Church. This implied distinct tasks in the two spheres of action, but with interference and control by the state in those matters that concerned ecclesiastical temporalities. And not in these matters only: the Emperor intended his jurisdiction to cover ecclesiastical areas such as teaching, theology, the universities, on whether or not religious orders and congregations would survive, depending more or less on their usefulness to civil society. The judgement on this matter was naturally reserved to the state. For this purpose a mixed commission of laity and ecclesiastics was established (whose members were dutifully obedient to imperial authority and were above the authority of the Church). They were called the Commission of Regulars. This Commission adopted measures in accord with the pleasure of the Emperor. In 1781 this Commission suppressed "the male and female institutes which did not dedicate themselves to teaching or some health-care activity." So "many hundreds of monasteries were suppressed without hesitation because they would not have been useful to civil society." Lortz, *op. cit.,* p. 348.

duchies of Parma, Lucca and other smaller places (that is over the greater part of Europe) in the second half of the eighteenth century.

2. A typical example: The Franciscan Teaching Sisters of Hallein (1723).

We find in the case of the Congregation of the Franciscan Teaching Sisters of Hallein a typical example of what the new female congregations would have to suffer from the policy of the "jurisdictionalist" regimes (even if their activity was external and of the kind that rendered assistance and education to the people).

This institute had its beginnings with the work of Maria Therese Zechner, a Franciscan Tertiary. In 1723 Maria Therese began to welcome little children into her home to give them the first "elementary instructions on devotion and employment." Very soon other young girls came to associate themselves with Maria Therese and began to live together. Well organized, they developed rapidly, and although they were still living in the spirit of the Rule of the Secular Franciscan Order, they suffered the first suppression in 1750. In 1758 the Prince-Bishop of Salzburg allowed the small community to regroup itself, but only for a short time. The new Prince-Bishop, Girolamo Colloredo, "wanted to prohibit not only the Third Orders but everything that proximately or remotely was connected with convent life. The sisters were forced to wear civilian clothing."[3] The bishop forbade them even to follow the Franciscan Rule. To renew their simple vows the sisters used the subterfuge of going to a convent of the Franciscan Friars outside the diocese of Salzburg. The people, for their part, appreciated the educational work of the sisters, and so the association was able to grow. In the following century, taking advantage of the fact that the government was then favoring schools, the congregation was able to undergo expansion. In 1819 the Rule of Leo X for the Third Order Regular was officially adopted. In 1822 a decree of the Consistory recognized the institute but

---

[3]Pierre Péano, *Francescane insegnanti di Hallein (Austria)*, in DIP, IV, col. 314. These decisions clearly indicate that "in the higher clergy and prince-bishops the customs and culture matching the French Enlightenment took root in a particular way": Lortz, *op. cit.*, p. 350.

only "as a simple temporary religious union."

The sisters meanwhile widened their field of action and established a day care center and a house for training young girls for domestic work. "In 1842 the Empress Carolyn Augusta called some of the sisters to establish a house of formation in Vienna,"[4] and in this way permitted the opening of other daughter houses. "Hallein was the cradle for two other congregations which circumstances caused to be autonomous: the Sisters of Vienna" who were called the Scholastic Franciscans of Vienna or the Franciscan Teaching Sisters of Vienna, and the Franciscan Teaching Sisters of Amstetten. In 1902 the Bishop of Salzburg finally granted canonical establishment as an institute of simple perpetual vows. The activity of the congregation today includes "elementary and high schools, centers of professional formation, kindergarten schools, orphanages and hospices for the sick and the elderly...." The three congregations, besides being in Austria, are working in Argentina and Brazil.

3. The French Revolution

The French Revolution, in the order of time, came after Josephinism and completed what remained to be done concerning religious orders and congregations. The French Revolution should have achieved the destruction of medieval institutions. Most important of these institutions was the Church. Actually, the French Revolution marked the end of past development and laid the foundations for new beginnings. And so one can say it was a mixture of catastrophe and positive opportunity. "The conflict between the French Revolution and the Church," writes Lortz,

> was not only the consequence of a social movement struggling against the feudal system; instead political-social and frequently anti-clerical religious tendencies flowed together here.... The French Revolution was the logical result of ideas of the enlightenment such as those developed in France beginning in 1750 with Voltaire, Diderot, and Rousseau. These ideas, founded on

---

[4]Péano, *Francescane insegnanti, op. cit.,* col. 315.

natural law, tended towards equality for all but also cherished a declared hatred against all revealed religions and every hierarchical church.[5]

As a natural consequence of this approach, persecution against the Church was an important component of the Revolution itself. In practice this persecution furiously attacked the nerve-center of the Church symbolized by the clergy and religious orders. The new National Assembly on February 13, 1790, decreed "the abolition of all monasteries belonging to contemplative orders."[6] Theoretically those religious who gave themselves to the care of the sick and to education were spared. But these religious also passed under the direct control of the State even in those matters which pertained to the internal life of the community such as admission of new candidates and religious professions. On April 14, 1790 the National Assembly "declared as an article of the Constitution that the law no longer recognized monastic vows. Orders and regular congregations in which such vows were made, were suppressed and remained suppressed in France; they were not able to establish similar organizations again. All individuals of both sexes presently living in cloisters would be able to leave the cloister."[7]

The Franciscan sisters (and not only these sisters) had to leave their monasteries, be separated, find refuge with relatives, or live clandestinely for many years. The Penitent Recollectines of the Reform of Limbourg, for example, who were, as we have mentioned, nuns of the Third Order with strict cloister saw more than half of their more than forty convents suppressed.

A little later, on July 12, 1790, the "Civil Constitution of the Clergy" was proclaimed. Within a short period of time (by November 27 of that same year) the clergy were

---

[5]J. Lortz, *op. cit.*, p. 362.

[6]*Ibid.*, p. 357. On the French Revolution and the Church see the following works: Charles Ledre, *L'Eglise de France sous la revolution*, Paris, 1949; Edmund Pressense, *L'Eglise et La Revolution francaise*, Paris, 1864; Bernard Plougeron, *Les Reguliers de Paris devant le serment constitutionel: Une Option, 1789-1801*, Paris, 1964; Lazzaro Papi, *Commentari della Rivoluzione francese*, Milano, 1840.

[7]Barruel, *Storia del clero in tempo della Rivoluzione francese*, translated into Italian by Giulio Alvisini, Roma, 1794, Vol. I, pp. 38-39.

required by law to take an oath to uphold "complete detachment from the Papacy and adherence to the service of the enlightened State."[8] The priests who refused to take the oath lost all civil rights. Later in September of 1792 there was a further angry reaction against those priests who had refused to take this oath. (These priests were by far the majority.) More than three hundred priests and three bishops were massacred in the notorious "September Slaughter."[9] But in doing so, the Revolution went too far, exceeding all limits. There was a reaction. "The courage to profess the faith and the blood of martyrs once again mysteriously became the seeds of a new Christianity."[10]

The French Revolution came to a close officially with the violent death (on July 27, 1794) of Maximillian Robespierre, the cruel dictator of the "revolution of the proletariate." When the royalists wanted to rekindle the revolution in October of 1795, they found opposing them in the streets the cannons of a young General Napoleon Bonaparte who had received the task of defending the new parliament called the Convention. This was positively the end of the Revolution. Even if "hatred towards religion and priests had become a dominant feeling, and still lasted" for some time, of the Revolution there would remain the one thing that was positive. The principle of equality for all persons, even if put into practice laboriously and with different degrees of intensity in various countries, would become the foundation of the modern world.

4. Napoleon Bonaparte

Bonaparte, whose period of glory (1796-1815) is wedged in between the modern and contemporary age, was a son of the French Revolution. In part he symbolized a going-beyond that revolution: "As an 'enlightened' man, Bonaparte was absolutely relativistic in religious questions

---

[8]J. Lortz, *op. cit.*, p. 363.

[9]Among these martyrs was the priest of the Third Order Regular of France, Father Severinus Girault, "First victim of the Massacre of the Carmelites." Pope Pius XI on October 1, 1926, recognized one hundred and ninety-one martyrs from the French Revolution with the title of blessed.

[10]Lortz, *op. cit.*, p. 363.

and in questions of Church politics he was Gallican"[11] and a promoter of the all powerful state. He was also a realist in political matters. Convinced that ecclesiastical order and religious devotion in France were necessary for the good of the state, Bonaparte supported and promoted both of these realities.[12] In 1801 by means of the Concordat with the Holy See (on July 16) and the free return of priests to their parishes, "the laborious work of pastoral reconstruction had its beginning." Napoleon, who personally did not want to have anything to do with religious orders, in a certain way favored the teaching sisters when dealing with the matter of the congregations of sisters. He "had even conceived the project of a single teaching congregation which would reunite all French sisters under a single Rule which, according to him, ought to be that of the Ursulines because in the eighteenth century almost all the schools for women (in France) were in their hands."[13]

All this took place, as it were, in the first act. But when Pope Pius VII (1800-1823) began to stand up to his arrogance, not recognizing, for example, his divorce of Josephine Beauharnais, Napoleon resorted to a decisively anti-clerical policy. In vain he sought to bend the pope to his absolutism. He put the pope in prison on July 5, 1809 and subjected him to harassment and outrage. He also laid the blame on religious orders, suppressing those which, outside France, had been able to save themselves from the persecution of the Bourbons.

5. The Restoration

The Church was only able to begin its reorganization after the downfall of Napoleon, at the time of the "Restoration" decreed by the Congress of Vienna, September 1814 to June 1815.

With the fall of Napoleon, Pius VII, in the eyes of the world, became "the heroic martyr and the moral victor."[14]

---

[11]Upholder of that teaching which in France affirmed a strict union of the Church with the State (a national Church) and challenges the absolute authority of the pope.

[12]Lortz, *op. cit.*, II, p. 399.

[13]Robert Lemoine, *Le droit des religieux, du Concile de Trent aux Instituts séculiers*, Bruges, 1956, p. 345.

[14]See Lortz, *op. cit.*, II, p. 401.

This brought prestige to the Church which was treated with respect at the Congress of Vienna. This Congress of the "Restoration" decided to return to the *status quo antea*, that is, to the political boundaries which nations had prior to the onslaught of the Napoleonic fury and all that went with it. So concerning Pius VII, the diplomats at Vienna were in substantial agreement to recognize the territories which had for centuries constituted the Papal States. This agreement was also due to the ability of the Papal Secretary of State, Cardinal Ercole Consalvi who was the shining light of the Papal States, especially during his second mandate from 1814 to 1823,[15] because of his moderate policies which were received with general approval. It is true that the Congress of Vienna did not seek anything more than a political restoration. Thus it did not give directives for internal policies of the countries, but de facto it helped to create that climate of renewal of which we are going to speak, a climate which also favored the creation of a great number of congregations of sisters in the active life.[16]

Among the results stemming from the decisions of the Congress of Vienna the following are to be noted:

a) the Church in various countries was free again to take up its institutional life;

b) the Papacy was recognized as a sovereign power, even though this sovereignty was predominantly in the realm of the spiritual order. Because of this recognition a large number of juridical treaties called "concordats" were signed to regularize relations between the state and the Church in each country for the rest of the nineteenth century. In these concordats the free exercise of religion was always affirmed, a positive factor for the birth of congregations of sisters since this meant freedom from possible interference and restrictions by the state.

On the other hand, the illuminist ideas of the previous

---

[15]Cardinal Conslavi had been Secretary of State from 1800 to 1806 and had concluded the Concordat with Napoleon in 1801. When results contrary to those hoped for took place, Conslavi left office and was practically exiled. He was entrusted again with the Secretariat of State in 1814.

[16]See Ilario Rinieri, *Il Congresso di Vienna el la Santa Sede (1813-1815)*, Roma, 1904, pp. 420-428.

century, reached a critical point in the years from 1815 to 1830 and the weakness of these ideas became clear. "The advantages of the new situation now became apparent, that is, the possibility in the new climate for taking up again the work of Catholic reconstruction.... It was the beginning of a new era...more profound in a religious and pastoral sense."[17]

The enlightenment and the French Revolution had been a violent smothering of the basic need for religion and tradition. With its bloody passing, it was inevitable that there would be a nostalgic return to religion and tradition. This return was held back in the beginning by the shining star of Napoleon. But after him the return was able to spread freely. We are not speaking of a violent reaction. It was more a subtle change of feeling, a change of interior attitudes: this nostalgia for religion and for the Church, humiliated by the enlightenment, by the French Revolution and Napoleon, was transformed "into a prevailing urgency of public life."[18]

Even external social conditions seemed to contribute to the fostering of this atmosphere. An obvious poverty reigned everywhere following the disasters brought on by the Napoleonic wars. Religion had for a long time been known as a refuge for the poor. On top of all this add "a series of outstanding men capable of translating religion into their written works, a series of writers whose temperament seemed suited to the needs of the times" and who exercised "a strong influence on individual persons and on particular groups and who became the center of movements of wide proportions."[19]

A new climate was created, extremely well adapted for the growth of the congregations of sisters. Never before had there been such a succession of births of new institutes year after year. "From the tables recorded in the

---

[17]See Lortz, *op. cit.*, II, p. 371.

[18]*Ibid.*, p. 406. In the field of philosophy and literature, this attitude would be called "Romanticism" which can be defined as "a movement of eager search or an unsatisfied nostalgia for an ideal."

[19]Lortz, *op. cit.*, II, p. 408. Among these note G. Michelle Salier (+1832), Joseph de Maistre (+1831), Hugh Lamennais (+1854) and somewhat later Henri Lacordaire (+1961), Charles Montalembert (+1870). In Italy especially we remember Allessandro Mazoni (+1873).

Collectanea of Bizzari[20] it is noted that from 1816 to 1822 there were as many as 124 institutes which received some kind of approbation of their status."[21]

6. Franciscan sisters congregations

Notable among these institutes were Franciscan congregations, the only ones in which we are interested at present. First of all, the

> early communities of sisters scattered during the times of crisis, now re-established themselves in France, Germany, Belgium, Italy and other places. Such communities included the Elizabethans, the Grey Sisters and the Recollectines who gathered their members together and founded new houses, dividing and subdividing themselves into autonomous and independent congregations according to the circumstances of persons and places....

"After the French Revolution," notes van Hulst,

> it was not possible to return to the cloister even though some convents desired to do so. Religious women were engaged in an important apostolic activity, teaching and caring for the sick. Despite all their good will, it was impossible to continue to observe a Rule drawn up for the nuns of the cloister with Divine Office during the night hours, austere corporal penances, lengthy fasting and abstinence, etc. Thus it was that, with the encouragement of the local bishops, the Penitent Recollectines up-dated their constitutions and slowly their convents became transformed into centralized religious congregations.[22]

---

[20]Bizzari, A., *Collectanea in usum Secretariae Sacrae Congregationis Episcoporum et Regularium*, Romae, 1863.

[21]See R. Lemoine, *Le droit des religieux, op. cit.*, p. 279.

[22]C. van Hulst, *Penitenti recollectine di Limburgo*, in DIP, VI, col. 1372. The author gives names and data for twelve centralized congregations of religious sisters who constitute the Recollect Penitents of our time: *ibid.*, col. 1372-1381.

"The education of boys and girls," observes Péano,

> was about to become the field of the apostolate
> for many institutions. The middle of the nine-
> teenth century saw the horizons of the aposto-
> late broaden to include a missionary dimension
> following many appeals from remote foreign
> lands for "laborers for the harvest." In the course
> of time and with the increase of local vocations,
> many indigenous independent congregations
> were established.
>
> The new foundations had small beginnings
> and had to pass through many difficulties, not
> to speak of outright persecutions and misunder-
> standings. The majority of them began with a
> few members of a Secular Franciscan fraternity
> who came together to live the common religious
> life with the Rule of Nicholas IV. This they did to
> promote their spiritual life and to consecrate
> themselves fully according to the charism of the
> founder or foundress. Gradually these religious
> women accepted the "form of life" of Leo X with
> the approval of the diocesan bishops. They made
> their simple profession of the three vows of reli-
> gion. There was hardly any more discussion
> about a question of cloister. In this context, each
> Institute had its own special history, including
> the trials attendant to its foundation and the
> internal and external events that it faced in the
> course of time. Each institute followed its own
> line of development in living the experience of
> the regular life and the demands of the apostolic
> activity chosen by the founders. But although
> the forms of apostolic activity differed according
> to needs, the spiritual vision of the Poverello
> remained unchanged and gave unity to all these
> generous efforts of the one ideal.[23]

Among the new congregations of Franciscan sisters
which arose during this period the following deserves
particular mention.

---

[23]Péano, *Le Religiose Francescane, op. cit.*, pp. 52-53.

7. The Franciscan Elizabethans of Padua, 1828

These sisters are an example of the originality and the special character surrounding the origins of some congregations of Franciscan sisters in the first half of the nineteenth century. The Elizabethans began in Padua in 1828 when the Secular Franciscan Elizabeth Vendramini began to live a life in common with other Tertiaries having as their purpose their dedication to the total education of poor and abandoned young girls. However, the members of the community remained Secular Franciscans who followed the Rule of Nicholas IV (1289). Their institute was neither a convent nor a conservatory. There the young girls spent the day in school, in study or in other activities, returning to their families (when these existed or were able to support their children) for supper and for the night. Otherwise, the "sisters" shared with the children whatever they had, including lodging. This form of life, which provided solutions for many local problems, also pleased the civil and Church authorities; it provided professional teachers who continued to live in community. The nascent institute was more than ever a great asset to the city of Padua, when, in 1836 the "Asiatic flu" ravaged the city. The "sisters" suddenly found themselves without students because they obeyed the health decrees to close all places of public association in order to avoid the spread of the epidemic. The "sisters" therefore, used their house as a refuge for those who were ill because of the epidemic. This was a circumstance which later on broadened the activity of these Tertiaries of the common life, and let us say, widened their scope. In 1838 the Rest Home "Beata Angelina" in Padua was entrusted to the Tertiary sisters. This home was established for the education of abandoned children gathered there; it also took care of sick and elderly women as part of the same hospice. In 1845 infant homes were opened in Padua and were also entrusted to the care of these "sisters." Thus a few years later they were asked to take care of the institute for the blind, the civil hospital in Padua and the Hospice of Venice. For many years civil and ecclesiastical authorities would have liked a more juridical form to this "special institution but Vendramini affirmed that her own institute was already approved by the Holy See simply because it was made up of Tertiaries to whom Pope Nicholas IV had given the Rule in 1289, and she had never thought of the creation of economic funding."[24] Only in 1910 did the institute receive the Pontifical Decree of Praise and in 1913 the first approval of its Constitutions. Among the superiors general who have succeeded to the guidance of the congregation must be remembered Mother Agnes Noro. During her twenty-one years as general, 1923-1944, "she succeeded in opening sixty houses, in obtaining final approval of their Constitutions and the beginning of the process for the beatification of the foundress at Padua, 1938."[25] During this period also the first foreign missions were undertaken. Today the institute, besides being in the country of its origin with concentration in the region of the Veneto, has spread to Switzerland, Argentina, Egypt, Kenya and numbers more than 1,600 professed religious.

---

[24]G. Rocca, *Francescane elisabettine, di Padova*, in DIP, IV, col. 285.
[25]*Ibid.*

CHAPTER XI

PRINCIPAL EVENTS OF THE NINETEENTH CENTURY

1. The evolution of juridical status

The special character of the new institutes and their strange relationship with Church authority invites us to set forth briefly the evolution of the Church's legislation dealing with religious congregations of women living the active life and not observing the cloister. Earlier we caught a glimpse of this problem. We now need to have some knowledge of the juridical status in which every new congregation found itself and some understanding of why particular difficulties were experienced in so many ways by every new congregation of sisters.

Summarizing the situation from the sixteenth century to the end of the nineteenth century, Lemoine says that after a period of "simple tolerance" which prevailed in the seventeenth and eighteenth centuries, the new-born congregations began "to receive the praise and approval of *episcopal* ecclesiastical authority" without this way of approval being interpreted as an abandonment of the traditional concept of the "religious life." The vows of these Congregations were not in fact recognized as public vows. The congregations themselves were not thought of as "religious," properly so called. Only at the end of the nineteenth century were "simple vows admitted as sufficient to constitute the religious state."

This very long and slow road to growth was inaugurated forcibly, as it were, by the French Revolution. Before the Revolution, communities or congregations not having a cloister used to meet innumerable difficulties when they sought to obtain some kind of official recognition. With the evolution of civil society that followed from and as a result of the French Revolution, there also corresponded an evolution of religious legislation. Particularly we must remember that for a large part of Europe directly or indirectly (by force of Napoleon's victories) there existed the effects of French law. "The position of religious, in the full meaning and civil law understanding of the word, was changed in an essential way. Not only did religious not enjoy any recognition or legal protection, but a cruel persecution struck them and proscribed them indifferently."[1] Giulio Alvisini, translated and published in Italy the work of Barruel, *History of the Clergy at the time of the French Revolution*, in the year 1794 when the Revolution was still raging. Alvisini noted in his introduction: "The Church saw her religious women forced to flee from their institutes, to seek sustenance among a thousand dangers in the world."[2]

In such circumstances the Holy See was forced "to grant certain nuns the privilege of professing only simple vows."[3] The Church was unable to impose the cloister on congregations which arose at that time. Civil legislation which did not recognize vows and no longer protected those who made them, constituted a serious obstacle to the profession of solemn vows. In the meantime, congregations which from the beginning were local in character arose in France. They began during the Revolution to make up for the lack of the proscribed and exiled clergy. These sisters and their Statutes received approval of diocesan bishops who certainly did not intend to circumvent the decrees of Saint Pius V, but simply sought a remedy for existing needs. "Encouraged later on by the number of vocations and requests from different dioceses, these congregations desired to broaden their apostolate and asked for the support or approval of the Holy See."[4]

[1]See R. Lemoine, *Le droit des religieux, op. cit.,* pp. 283-300.

[2]Barruel, *Storia del clero della Rivoluzione francese,* translated into Italian by Giulio Alvisini, Roma, 1794, t.I, p. xxiv. Concerning Barruel, Alvisini wrote: "He himself (a French Jesuit, editor of a daily paper) was in Paris an eye witness and participant...he was able more than any other to enrich the literary public with a most authentic history of the frenzy of his country against the Catholic Church, of the persecutions, massacres and exile of the French clergy. This history which he published last year (1793), has just appeared in England in a London edition in three parts." *Ibid.,* p. xxxi.

[3]Lemoine, *Le droit des religieux, op. cit.,* p. 275.

[4]*Ibid.,* p. 274.

After the French Revolution, civil society had needs that had not existed in preceding centuries such as a generalized desire on the part of the people for education and the need of health care for the sick. Frequently the State did not know how to satisfy these needs. The great number of newly formed congregations actually prospered because they dedicated themselves with great enthusiasm to works of mercy and to teaching. Delighted because of this wonderful fruitfulness in the Church, the popes favorably welcomed these congregations in consideration of the services rendered. "But the Roman Curia did not abandon its usual prudence and for a long time continued to refuse, as it did in the eighteenth century, to give the name 'religious' to members of 'congregations of simple vows' lawfully founded by bishops in their respective dioceses."[5]

From 1816 to 1822, as we have reported, there were 124 new institutes which received definitive approval of the bishops. But from 1816 to 1850 (the time which includes the above mentioned institutes) "only seven institutes (two of which were male congregations) with their Constitutions were fully approved by the Holy See. Thus little by little the distinction was introduced between institutes of Pontifical right and institutes of Diocesan right."[6]

At any rate, with the passing of years, the "severity of language" used by the Church maintained the outward form only for appearances. The Church still refused to call "religious" those sisters from congregations of simple vows. Lemoine observes "congregations, especially those of women, enjoy a period of expansion at this time that is without precedent. It seems that the Church sees in them a new form of religious life better adapted to new times."[7]

Little by little things returned to normalcy. The most remarkable decree in this respect was perhaps *Ecclesia Catholica* of 1889. This document helped congregations of simple vows to obtain, however indirectly, the desired title of "religious" women. The above mentioned decree stated that it was not possible to recognize as "religious" those associations or societies "without common life and without

---

[5]*Ibid.*

[6]*Ibid.*, p. 279.

[7]*Ibid.*, p. 281.

religious habit." Thus the document implicitly affirmed the religious character of congregations with simple vows, "with common life, and religious habit." Their vows would be recognized as "public vows." These vows, remaining simple vows, would be accepted as sufficient to constitute the religious state.[8]

All these understandings were sanctioned by the Constitution *Conditae a Christo*, published by Pope Leo XIII on December 8, 1900. As we shall see, this constitution was the foundation of modern legislation in the Church concerning congregations of sisters of active life.

2. Some congregations founded in the middle of the nineteenth century

Among the congregations of Franciscan sisters which began about the middle of the century, we note the following:

a) *The Franciscan Sisters of Oldenburg, Indiana (1851)*

Fr. Francis Rudolf, an American missionary who came from Strasburg, Alsace in 1842 to work in the diocese of Vincennes, Indiana, saw a great and pressing need. The children of that region were without instruction in the Catholic faith.[9] Through the help of a friend who was visiting in Europe, Fr. Rudolf asked for help from the sisters of a Franciscan Convent in Vienna. After some delay one sister arrived at Oldenburg on January 6, 1851, Sister Teresa Hackelmeier. Three young women from the area joined her in the founding of a new Franciscan congregation. A short time later a postulant, Teresa Dreer, was received into the community from Rorscach, Switzerland and received the name Sister Antonia at her investiture. Sister Antonia was a gifted and well-educated person. The responsibility of training the sisters as teachers was entrusted to her by the foundress. As the community grew, the congregation increased its commitment to education and other apostolates.

After the death of Mother Teresa Hackelmeier on September 27, 1860, the community chose Sister Antonia Dreer to take up the leadership of the young congregation.

---

[8] *Ibid.*, pp. 282, 283.

[9] See Sr. Laverne Frietsch, O.S.F., *Sisters of Saint Francis, Oldenburg, Indiana*, in ANALECTA TOR, XIX, no. 141, (1986), pp. 189-212.

Sister Antonia exerted a strong and lasting influence on the educational apostolate during her twelve year administration. The congregation was blessed in choosing a series of able leaders who gave strong affirmation and direction to the expansion of the congregation. These leaders were assisted by some strong helping factors that fostered the growth of the congregation and its apostolic activity.

The first of these factors is seen in the constitutions, adopted in the early years of the congregation which received final approbation from the Holy See in 1899. These early Constitutions were deeply imbued with Scripture and Francis' vision of Gospel-living, unusual in their completeness and their practical wisdom.

A second factor is seen in the initial, cohesive, national character of the early community. Because of their Austrian foundress, many vocations were received from German families living in the Mid-West and encouraged in the many German parishes in which the sisters conducted their educational apostolate. This made an easy transition for the new postulants as many used the German language equally as well as the English.

A final reason for the great progress and rapid growth of the congregation can be seen in the strong emphasis on the educational apostolate. This work of the community received great emphasis in the United States with special attention being given to the growing need of secondary education in the twentieth century. Today the work has widened to include a diversity of ministries throughout the country.

In recent years the Franciscan Sisters of Oldenburg have undertaken a mission outside the United States in Papua, New Guinea. There, sixteen sisters work in the apostolate of education and pastoral ministries on the diocesan and local levels. They are also assisting in the establishment of a native community of sisters.

b) *The Poor Daughters of the Holy Stigmata of Saint Francis (The Franciscan Stigmatines, 1855)*

The beginnings of this congregation go back to 1846 when Secular Tertiary Anna Maria Fiorelli Lapini, having become a widow, decided "to become mother for many poor and defenseless children and young people." Right away, Anna Maria had some companions with whom she began to live a common life in a house called "la Fantina" near Florence, Italy. These women dedicated themselves to providing free education for poor and abandoned children. The newly begun institute, at once, had the applause and help of religious and civil authorities with the result that in a short time it received the Decree of Praise on July 23, 1855. These sisters called themselves the Daughters of the Holy Stigmata. As the foundress desired, the institute was aggregated as the Third Order to the Friars Minor in 1856. By papal decree the minister general of the Friars Minor became protector and counselor of the Office of Superior General of the Stigmatine Sisters, having authority to nominate a commissioner for the direction of the institute. This authority lasted until 1950 when the Congregation for Religious abolished a similar commissary's office. The institute had a rapid expansion for at the death of the foundress in 1860 it numbered thirty-seven houses spread throughout central and southern Italy. The institute received final approval in 1888. Its growth continued in a steady manner. During the nineteenth century the only activity outside Italy was in Albania where a flourishing mission was established from 1879 to 1944. In the present century the Stigmatine sisters have enlarged their sphere of activity to include Brazil, Spain and Ecuador. "The institute reached its highest development about 1970 when it numbered more than 1250 members."[10] In 1986 the institute counted 950 professed sisters. The activity of the Congregation is today described as involving "community building and evangelization of the working people, educational activities through schools, catechetics, hospices for the young and for workers."[11]

c) *The Sisters of Saint Francis of Philadelphia (1855)*

The Sisters of St. Francis of Philadelphia consider St. John Neumann, C.SS.R., fourth Bishop of Philadelphia, and Mother Mary Francis Bachmann as their co-founders.[12] Bishop Neumann, in Rome for his *ad limina* visit, sought

---

[10]G. Rocca, *Povere figlie delle suore stimmate di san Francisco*, in DIP, VII, col. 208.

[11]*Francescani in Italia, Annuario, op. cit.*, p. 327.

[12]See Sister M. Adele Francis Gorman, O.S.F., ANALECTA TOR, vol. XVI, n. 136, (1983), pp. 147-170. Translator's note: I am most grateful to Sister M. Adele Francis Gorman, O.S.F., Congregation Historian, and

the permission of Pope Pius IX to bring a European community of sisters to America. The pope thought it wiser that Bishop Neumann establish a new foundation in America. A Franciscan Tertiary himself, the pope believed the Franciscan spirit could best adapt itself to the needs of the country.

While he was still in Rome, Bishop Neumann received a letter from one of his priests concerning a request of three young women who were asking the bishop's approval to form a community of Franciscan sisters. It was clear to the bishop that the foundation of the community he sought was this Franciscan community.

Upon Bishop Neumann's return to America in March of that year of 1855, he met with the three aspirants: Anna Maria Bachmann, who had come from Bavaria in the 1840's and who was a recently widowed mother of four, her sister, Barbara Boll, and Anna Dorn, a Tertiary of St. Francis of Assisi. The Bishop was highly pleased with the interview. On Easter Monday of 1855, April 9th, these women received the habit of the new congregation from the hands of the bishop together with new names: Sister Mary Francis Bachmann, Sister Mary Margaret Boll, and Sister Mary Bernadine Dorn.

Centering the sisters in a life of union with God through prayer and penance, Bishop Neumann directed them to the service of the needy. Within a very short time this small community was called to serve the needs of people far beyond Philadelphia in Syracuse. Sister Mary Bernadine Dorn became the leader of the group of sisters taken by Mother Francis to Syracuse. After the death of Bishop Neumann in 1860, his successor separated the New York sisters, forming a first daughter congregation among whose outstanding apostolates was work among the lepers of Molokai.[13]

Responding to the request for sisters in Buffalo, Mother Francis took three sisters and her daughter Johanna, who was a postulant, to Buffalo for the new mission. After the death of Mother Francis, Bishop John Timon of Buffalo

---

Sister Andrew Persing, O.S.F., Archivist, for supplying material used here concerning the Sisters of St. Francis of Philadelphia.

[13]Mother Marianne Cope, leader of these missionaries, is being proposed for canonization.

separated the sisters from Philadelphia; Mother Francis' blood sister, Mary Margaret Boll, became the first provincial minister of the Buffalo congregation. Consequently, within eight years, the three founding sisters had each become the general of a religious institute.[14]

In the course of time, three more branches were formed from the vine, offshoots of the Buffalo community. In 1865 sisters were sent to Pittsburgh, who later became the Franciscan Sisters of Millvale. In 1882 sisters were sent from Buffalo to the metropolitan area of New York. From the sisters working in the New York area another new congregation was formed. On July 16, 1893 they became known as the Sisters of St. Francis of the Mission of the Immaculate Virgin. Finally, in 1922 the Sisters of Saint Francis of Providence were founded with the assistance of the Franciscan Sisters of Millvale, and thus became the sixth congregation of the "Neumann Heritage Family."

In accord with the practice common in the nineteenth century, all these foundations became independent communities under the direction of the local bishop.[15] When the Franciscan Sisters of Philadelphia celebrated the fiftieth anniversary of their founding, the number of sisters had grown from nine in 1863 to 790. "At the peak of the collective membership, the Sisters of St. Francis who trace their origin to Saint John Neumann and Mother Mary Francis Bachmann numbered over four thousand."[16]

A review of the apostolic service of the Sisters of St. Francis of Philadelphia exemplifies the service of the Church to the needy. Under the leadership of Mother Mary Francis the sisters staffed the first school, in St. Alphonsus parish, in 1858 and opened the second Catholic Hospital (St. Mary's) in Philadelphia in 1860. Like most United States congregations, this community has expanded its ministries from the original education and health care commitments to include a wide variety of service in pastoral,

---

[14]See Sister M. Adele Francis Gorman, O.S.F., *Franciscan Tertiary Congregations: The Sisters of St. Francis of Philadelphia*, ANALECTA TOR, vol. XVI, n. 136, (1983), p. 152.

[15]See our fuller treatment of this practice in this chapter, p. 160.

[16]See Sister M. Adele Francis Gorman, O.S.F., *Franciscan Tertiary Congregations: The Sisters of St. Francis of Philadelphia*, ANALECTA TOR, vol. XVI, n. 136, (1983), p. 153.

health, social and educational endeavors, including missionary activity outside the United States.

d) *The Franciscan Sisters of Allegany, New York (1859)*

The Franciscan Sisters of Allegany, New York, trace their beginnings to April 25, 1859, when, in the chapel of St. Bonaventure College and Seminary, Father Pamfilo da Magliano, O.S.F., gave the habit of the Third Order of Saint Francis and the name, Sister Mary Joseph, to Mary Jane Todd. Father Pamfilo, the Custos-Provincial of the Friars Minor of the Immaculate Conception Custody, had come with three other friars to western New York in 1855 at the invitation of Bishop John Timon, C.M., of the Diocese of Buffalo and Nicholas Devereux, a Catholic layman and landowner. The friars had come to educate young men at St. Bonaventure College and to carry on pastoral work in the area. Bishop Timon had also asked Father Pamfilo to "seek for sisters of the Third Order" to provide education for the young women of the area, and his search led him to form a new congregation, the Franciscan Sisters of Allegany.[17]

After the reception of Sister Mary Joseph, Ellen Fallon was received on June 24, 1859, and took the name, Sister Mary Bridget. Several months later, these two sisters were joined by Mary Anne O'Neil, a fifteen-year old girl from New Jersey who had been exhorted by Father Pamfilo to be generous with the Lord despite her young years. Mary Anne was received on December 8, 1859, and took the name, Sister Mary Teresa.

These three women formed the nucleus of the new community which soon began to attract other young women from the surrounding areas. From the beginning of the Congregation, the sisters were under the jurisdiction of Father Pamfilo. He appointed the officers of the new community until 1865, when he presented the sisters with their first statutes which had been adapted from those of the Franciscan sisters in Glasgow, Scotland. That same year the sisters held their first Chapter and elected Sister

---

[17]From information supplied by Sister Ann Kelly, O.S.F., Archivist, presently in manuscript form, *A Heritage, History of the Franciscan Sisters of Allegany, New York*, by Sr. Veronica Inez Rodrigues, O.S.F. See also Sr. Veronica Inez Rodrigues, *The Franciscan Sisters of Allegany, New York*, in ANALECTA TOR, XIV, n. 134, (1981), pp. 1035-1053.

Mary Teresa O'Neil as their general superior. She was to serve in this capacity for fifty-five years (two by appointment, fifty-three by election). It was Mary Teresa O'Neil who was to give the leadership and formative vision to the new community, and whose spirit and influence were to continue to the present time. The new community grew and the sisters sought to serve the needs of the Church in a variety of ministries. In 1860, St. Elizabeth Academy was opened in Allegany for the education of young women. It grew rapidly and from this beginning the sisters branched out to open schools in Connecticut, New York, and other states along the eastern coast of the United States.

In 1879, three sisters were sent to Jamaica, British West Indies, and the Franciscan Sisters of Allegany became the first American-founded congregation of religious women to send sisters to the foreign missions. Missions were opened in Brazil in 1946 and in Bolivia in 1965. Sisters also went to serve the poor in the southern United States.

The year 1883 marked the beginning of involvement with apostolates other than schools. The original purpose of teaching children expanded to include hospital administration and health care, homes for the young and the elderly, pastoral and social work, and many more ministries, which continue to this day although some are in different forms.

The Franciscan Sisters of Allegany in 1959, responding to the needs of the Church by love and full joy in Christ's gospel sought to promote a deeper life of prayer by establishing a cloister. Eight years later the Council approved the substitution of the Ritiro concept. The Ritiro would allow professed members for a period of time to join the permanent nucleus of sisters in giving expression to the contemplative aspect of the Franciscan charism.

e) *The Franciscan Missionaries of the Immaculate Heart of Mary (called "of Egypt," 1868)*

This community represents another typical example of how a Franciscan congregation was able to begin with a particular goal which was the unique or chief reason for its beginning. Afterwards, the institute, responding to the necessities of place, widened its activities to embrace many tasks, but always within that common characteristic: "works of active charity exercised in the spirit of Saint Francis."

The institute had its beginning in Cairo, Egypt, the work of Maria Caterina Troiani. In 1865 the cloistered monastery of Saint Clare of Charity in Ferentino (Frosinone) decided to suspend missionary activity which they had begun in Egypt in 1859. The sisters who had labored in the mission remained there in Egypt. Three years later the Sacred Congregation of the Propagation of the Faith established them, by a decree on November 10, 1868, as an autonomous institute called "the Franciscan Missionaries of Egypt." Their name was changed to the present name in 1950. Their Rule was the Rule of Pope Leo X for the Third Order Regular. The central house of the Institute remained at Cairo until 1907 when it was transferred to Rome. The organization of the congregation has remained centralized even to the present time in the sense that the ministers provincial are named by the central government, and the ministers depend on that central government.

The apostolate of the institute has progressively been broadened in scope. Missionary activity, education of youth, and care of the sick were their early apostolates. To these have been added parochial and pastoral activities. The area of assistance to the sick has been broadened to include health care assistance of all kinds, especially in the areas of the missions, care of lepers and children of lepers, care of the abandoned elderly and the alienated. "Like Francis, itinerant and penitent in whatever place indicated by obedience, we seek to be the bearers of peace and joyous witness of the Lord Jesus 'to the nations' and also to countries of Christian tradition."[18] Emphasized are some noteworthy services or "charitable activities": "in Brazil, young widows with their children find a room with the sisters to take care of their children while they work during the day, and a small room to stay with their offspring during the night." In China, after the Red victory in 1949, "the Chinese Sisters of the Institute continued their

---

[18]*Francescani in Italia*, Annuario, coordinatore padre Umberto G. Sciamé, Movimento francescano, 1986, p. 271.

activity in secret and in disguise."[19] Today the institute is found on four continents: Europe, Africa, Asia, America and numbers about 1200 professed sisters. The foundress, Maria Caterina Troiani, was declared Blessed by the Church on April 14, 1985.

f) *The Franciscan Teaching Sisters of Christ the King (1869)*

The congregation traces its remote origins to the Teaching Sisters of Graz in Austria who were established in 1843. In 1864 four sisters of that congregation established themselves at Maribor in Yugoslavia for the purpose of "the Christian education of young women." In 1869 the local bishop made the foundation independent and named one of the sisters, Margaret Pucher, as superior general. The young congregation continued to follow the Statutes of the Teaching Sisters of Graz and the Third Order Regular Rule of Leo X. The congregation quickly grew due especially to the "Franciscan spirit of service in the apostolate with the young and especially in activities on behalf of the poor and children." The sisters were able to spread beyond their country beginning first in Egypt and then in the United States. With the promulgation of the Code of Canon Law in 1917, the superior general at that time, M. Lidvina Purgaj, decided the time was right for the congregation to have its own Constitutions approved by the Holy See and thus the institute became a congregation of Pontifical Right. In spite of the initial opposition of the Bishop of Maribor, the congregation received the Decree of Praise in 1922, and the Constitutions were finally approved in 1931. The congregation had already been divided into four Provinces: two in Yugoslavia, and one each in Italy and the United States. In the period between the two World Wars there had been an enormous expansion of the congregation geographically speaking and also in areas of the apostolate. Beginning with teaching and educational programs, the sisters added such activities as care for the sick and domestic assistance in Church institutions. During World War II the motherhouse was transferred to Rome. Following the directives of Vatican Council

[19]E. Frascadore, *Francescane missionarie del Cuore immacolato di Maria, dette d'Egitto*, in DIP, IV, col. 338.

II, the Constitutions were revised in accord with new demands of the times. These revised Constitutions were approved on May 28, 1984. The charism of the congregation has been thus described: "To live the gospel in religious community for the love of God and in the Franciscan spirit of penance, joy and simplicity, to educate the youth, to fulfill other apostolic activities in the service of the Church" (Art. 2). To the Provinces already mentioned, soon were added five others: two in Yugoslavia, and one in Argentina, Austria and Paraguay. The congregation in 1987 numbered 1510 sisters.[20]

3. The Storm in the Middle of the Century

It is necessary to keep in mind the ideological and political developments which took place during the mid-nineteenth century if we wish to understand the various events to which the sisters of active life were subjected, events which affected their foundation and growth. Every congregation had to experience these effects though the manner differed from one institute to another.

We have noted that with the "Restoration" there was a return to the political geography of the European states to what it had been before the French Revolution. But the ideals of liberty born of the French Revolution very quickly spread everywhere. In Italy in the area of politics, these ideals merged with the movement toward national unity. The accomplishment of this unity would mean the uniting of kingdoms and duchies, and the extinction of some individual independent states. Among these latter would be the Papal States. "Now," as Lortz correctly observes,

> the process of national unification of the Italian peninsula tragically found itself in direct opposition to the temporal sovereignty of the pope and, unfortunately, to the teachings of the Church. Too few were the spirits endowed with such inner openness that they would know how to reconcile these two things: ardent love for the

---

[20]From the information furnished by the Generalate. See their latest publications: M. Similjana Kodric - B. Natalia Palac, *Suore Scolastiche francescane di Cristo Re, Storia - Missione - Vita*, Roma, 1988, and K. Celina Saric, *Suore Scolastiche francescane di Cristo Re nella regione di Roma*, Roma, 1989.

unity of the fatherland and ardent love for the Church.... Anti-religious and anti-clerical liberalism profited from the situation.... Opposition and even hostility against the papacy as such grew from this consideration[21]

with the consequence that the greater part of the Restoration Movement, *il Risorgimento*, had an anti-religious and anti-clerical spirit. All this became clearly visible following the proclamation of the Kingdom of Italy, March 17, 1861, and through various laws which in practice closed or suppressed religious houses and institutes.

A short time before, in 1855, in the Kingdom of Piedmont, a law of May 29 decreed: "Those moral entities recognized by civil law which are not engaged in preaching, education or assistance to the sick shall cease to exist."[22] A decree, also dated May 29, specified the orders and religious communities whose houses were affected by that law. For the Franciscans, besides the Poor Clares and the Capuchin Sisters, the decree explicitly named "Tertiary Franciscan Sisters" (N. 11) and "Franciscan women," (N. 12) without any further clarification.[23]

Such laws were extended to all the various regions of Italy, section by section as these regions were annexed to Piedmont. The particular difference was that the exception inserted in the original laws of Piedmont, that is, that the suppression would not touch those moral entities "engaged in preaching, education or assistance to the sick," was left out or forgotten. Thus in Umbria, the first region after Sicily annexed to the new Kingdom of Italy, the Commissioner Gioacchino Pepoli, referring to the laws of 1855, applied them in the following way:

> We consider that (the suppression) was and is greatly justified in as much as the religious corporations do not fulfill the purpose for which they, for the most part, were so richly endowed. As they do not cooperate with the progress of

---

[21]Lortz, *op. cit.*, pp. 413, 420.

[22]See in Italo Mario Laracca, *Il patrimonio degli ordini religiosi in Italia, Soppressione e incameramento dei loro beni (1848-1873)*, Roma, 1936, p. 89.

[23]*Ibid.*, p. 95.

> public education and bring relief to indigent
> peoples...it is decreed: All the corporations and
> establishments of whatever kind of monas-
> tic orders and regular or secular corporations
> existing in the Provinces are suppressed.

Particular religious houses were excluded, but not an order or congregation in itself, as in the laws of 1855.[24]

In 1866 a new "comprehensive recapitulation law" was promulgated to give uniformity to the already decreed suppressions. In practice this law suppressed houses and institutes which had been able to evade the decrees of 1861. From a "list of houses of religious suppressed in 1866," it is evident that the Franciscan sisters (not Poor Clares) had twenty-one houses suppressed with 501 sisters dispersed; "Franciscan Sisters of the Observance" (not better identified) had eight houses suppressed with 183 sisters dispersed. In this list there were other groups such as the "Stigmatines," "Sisters of Saint Ann," "Sisters of St. Joseph," etc. some of whom were probably Franciscan sisters.[25]

On September 20, 1870, Rome and its Province became part of the Kingdom of Italy. The government soon sought to extend to Rome also the laws by which the Kingdom was able to suppress religious congregations and other ecclesiastical entities in other regions.[26] This was accomplished by the law 1402 of June 19, 1873.[27]

4. New Congregations by subdivision

Here we must note a phenomenon verified remarkably often, especially in the nineteenth century: the rise of new congregations of Franciscan sisters through subdivision from the mother community. Just as in horticulture, many kinds of flowers and ornamental plants are multiplied chiefly by planting a slip or cutting from the parent stock, so many religious congregations recognize their own

---

[24]See *ibid.*, p. 101.

[25]See Laracca, *op. cit.*, Appendice IV, pp. 195-196.

[26]See *ibid.*, p. 139.

[27]By force of this law ninety-three houses of men with 1819 religious and forty-one convents of women with 1069 Sisters were closed in Rome. See Laracca, *op. cit.*, p. 154.

beginnings in this kind of procedure. The phenomenon is especially verified when the original congregation establishes new branches or daughter-houses in a different country or in a different diocese. When relations between the country where the community was founded, and the country which is the site of the new community have become difficult for the most varied of reasons the problem may find its solution through subdivision, that is the granting of autonomy to the daughter community. Again when relations between the congregation of origin and the new off-shoots encounter substantial difficulties also for a variety of reasons differently considered by both sides, the separation of the two entities takes place and there is the establishment of a new independent entity. More often still does this happen when houses of a congregation of Diocesan Right are established in a diocese different from the place of origin. The bishop of the diocese with the daughter houses does not care to have religious sisters who work in his diocese dependent on "outside" authority who can move them or change them from house to house. To insure that in his own diocese there will be a well-planned apostolate and that he will be able to count on stabilized components, the same bishop will promote or benevolently consider the aspirations towards independence of daughter houses existing in his diocese. He will proceed thus to the establishment of a new congregation. Sometimes for the sake of distinguishing the two entities, the bishop changed the name and sometimes also the habit. In the United States there are a noticeable number of congregations of Franciscan sisters who have had their origins in this way.

5. Some more important congregations of the second half of the nineteenth century

In this period of time some of the largest and most important congregations of Franciscan sisters had their beginnings. Among them are recorded the following: We will speak of them in chronological order.

a) *The Franciscan Alcantarines (1869)*

Because of the circumstances of its beginning, as well as its scope or purpose, this institute can be considered as an example of the congregations of Franciscan sisters originating in southern Italy in the second half of the nineteenth century.

With the end of Bourbon absolutism that had done very little for the betterment of the social classes, the new political forces "immature and badly organized, were unable to resolve the problems which had been left unresolved."[28] On the contrary, more problems arose; the introduction of liberal systems by the Piedmontese, and the demolishing of customs barriers did not bring positive results for an economy almost exclusively agricultural and incapable of competing with the economy of the north. In the hands of the great non-caring landowners, the monopoly of the land was another negative factor. The masses grew frightfully poor. Illiteracy and the phenomenon of lawlessness were wide-spread. To this situation must be added the difficult problem of the discord between the Church and the State, and the suppression of thousands of religious entities which were the principal points of religious reference for the poor.

In the Church documents of this era, one can notice preoccupation over the spread of religious indifference and the presence of a troubled atmosphere poisoned by masonic liberalism, an atmosphere saturated with hate towards the Church and its institutions. It was then from the deep Christian spirit rooted in the people that there sprang up examples of victorious reaction to evil. Among these examples, the new congregations of sisters hold a preeminent place. In various places institutes with quite visible qualities of charity arose coming to assist the spiritual and material needs of under-privileged classes, to care for the education of semi-abandoned boys and girls, and the training of young people, especially women, for gainful and honest work.

Among such institutes, the Alcantarine Franciscan Sisters are chosen as typical. This institute began at Castellammare di Stabia in the Province of Naples in 1869 through the efforts of a diocesan priest Vincenzo Gargiulo and a Franciscan Tertiary, Maria Luigia Russo.

The institute was founded for the purpose of the

---

[28]A.Scirocco, *Governo e Paese nel Mezzogiorno nella crisi dell' Unificazione*, Milano, 1963, p. 3.

instruction and education of girls, especially orphans, to assist boys and young men within the ages established by the ordinary of the place, and to protect from vice the young girls who were likely to fall, and those already having addictions. With the passage of time, these first goals were widened to include the care of the sick in hospitals and in the home, and assistance to the poor.[29]

The need for such activities was great indeed. For this reason the congregation was quickly successful. Given the fundamentally religious climate of the people of the place, vocations were abundant. Since the co-founder, Maria Luigia Russo, was enrolled in the Franciscan Third Order, it was decided from the beginning to aggregate the foundation "to the Franciscan Order with the Alcantarine reform" and to call it "the Poor Daughters of Saint Peter of Alcantara." The Bishop of Castellammare di Stabia, Bishop Francesco Saverio Petagna on October 17, 1874 "declared the nascent institution canonically erected...and approved its form of life and its educational and charitable purposes."[30]

In 1890, there were ten houses located in Campania, Lazio, Abruzzi, Basilicata, and Puglie with one hundred twenty religious not counting novices and candidates. In 1894, Pope Leo XIII examining the Constitutions and letters of commendation sent by the ordinaries who hosted the Alcantarine Sisters in their dioceses, granted the Decree of Praise, "reserving the granting of final approval of both the institute and its Statutes to a more suitable time."[31] The final approval of the pope was received on January 14, 1903.

> The Congregation had a rapid development. In 1919 it numbered thirty-three houses, all in Italy, with 225 religious. The apostolate abroad began in 1932 with the opening of a mission in Brazil where today there are fifteen houses with

---

[29]G. Rocca, *Francescane Alcantarine*, in DIP, IV, col. 259.

[30]E. Marchitelli, *Le Suore alcantarine ieri e oggi*, Marietti, Torino, 1981, p. 41.

[31]See *ibid.*, p. 116.

101 religious. In 1962 a house was opened in Spain at Arenas, in the province of Avila, the land which preserves the remains of the patron Saint of the Congregation, Peter of Alcantara. In 1963 the Franciscan Alcantarine Sisters were established in Canada.[32]

"On July 31, 1976 the institute numbered ninety-two fraternities with 708 professed sisters with perpetual vows."[33]

(b) *The Franciscan Sisters of Mary (FSM, 1872)*

The Sisters of Saint Mary were founded on November 16, 1872 in Saint Louis, Missouri. Mother Mary Odilia Berger, foundress of the Sisters of Saint Mary of the Third Order of Saint Francis, had been a member of the Poor Franciscans of the Holy Family in Pirmasens, Germany. While visiting Paris, Mother Odilia was appalled by the exploitation of German working girls there and heard a call from the Lord to serve these women. This meant requesting a dispensation from vows as a Poor Franciscan to be a member and superior of the Sister Servants of the Sacred Heart of Jesus in Paris. She and five companions later emigrated to the United States in November, 1872.

When she and her companions arrived in St. Louis, they were assisted in establishing their foundation by the Vicar General for German Catholics, Monsignor Henry Muehlsiepen. The sisters' ministry was in the home care of victims of small pox and others who were ill. It was this compassionate care for the sick and living in faith that proved to be an attraction to other women who became members of the community. They had temporary housing before occupying their own convent adjacent to St. Mary of Victories Church. The name "Sisters of St. Mary" was given them by the people of St. Louis who observed them going in and out of their convent through the doors of the church. Mother Odilia wrote a Constitution for the Sisters of St. Mary from her copy of the Rule of the Poor Franciscans in Pirmasens, and a partial draft from the rule of the Sister Servants of the Sacred Heart of Jesus. Approval was received from the Church authorities in St.

---

[32]G. Rocca, *Francescane alcantarine*, in DIP, IV, col. 259-260.

[33]E. Marchitelli, *op. cit.*, p. 229.

Louis. On October 4, 1880 Mother Odilia and sixteen of the first sisters made perpetual vows.

Mother Odilia became ill days later and died on October 17, 1880 at the age of fifty-seven. Before she died she requested that Sister Mary Seraphia Schlochtermeyer be her successor. It would have been difficult for anyone to follow Mother Odilia at this time and Mother Seraphia was, apparently, rather severe and strict in discipline. Unrest and growing doubt and unhappiness emerged among some of the sisters. Two of the sisters spent three months studying the novitiate program of the Sisters of the Poor of St. Francis in Hartwell, Ohio. Filled with fervor and a renewed appreciation of the Franciscan spirit they returned to share that spirit with their companions. The actual facts surrounding the separation and the appearance of two communities are not detailed in the chronicles of either the Sisters of St. Mary or the new community of the Sisters of St. Francis. But on January 17, 1894 Sister Augustine Giesen, who had been novice mistress, together with four other sisters set out for Kansas City to form a new congregation under the title of "Sisters of the Immaculate Conception," which was changed a year later to "the Sisters of St. Francis."

The Sisters of St. Mary worked mainly in city apostolates, gaining recognition in the areas of health care, nursing, medicine and hospital administration. They also entered the field of foreign mission work in Bolivia, Peru, and Brazil. The Sisters of Saint Francis worked mostly in rural areas and one large city with apostolates in health care services and education. Both congregations became pontifical institutes.

In 1979, the Sisters of St. Francis initiated a discernment process in search of a Franciscan community open to unification and whose scope and spirit were similar.

The Sisters of St. Mary were also involved in a study of their own charism and were working to present the request for the approval of their Constitutions. In 1968, at the beginning of a special chapter, a possible reunion of the congregations was considered. In 1972, on the occasion of the centenary celebration of the founding, the Sisters of St. Francis were invited to join in the celebration. In 1981 the Sisters of St. Francis made a decision in their chapter to study reunification with the Sisters of St. Mary. The charism of both congregations surfaced many values held in common and the minor importance of superficial differences. Both congregations adopted resolutions requesting permission for reunion and the Sisters of St. Francis decided unanimously to adopt the constitutions of the Sisters of St. Mary on the receipt of the decree of ratification. On January 20, 1986 the Congregation of Religious and Secular Institutes decreed that the Sisters of St. Francis might once again be united with the Sisters of St. Mary. The public proclamation of the reunification was celebrated on August 2, 1986. On November 1, 1987 the name "Franciscan Sisters of Mary" was formally chosen and a new leadership team elected by the combined membership assumed office.[34] Until recently members of the reunified congregation serve in various healing ministries in the United States and in two foreign countries.[35] In 1992, the only foreign mission is in Brazil. (The one in Africa was discontinued.)

c. *The Franciscan Missionaries of Mary (1877)*

The Congregation of the Franciscan Missionaries of Mary is remembered especially as an example of the marvelous development that many new congregations had immediately after their founding. With its 9,181 members, present in 1984 in 73 countries and five continents, the institute is today the largest among the congregations of Franciscan sisters. In its high ideal, expressed in its dedication to universal mission, its members must be ready to be sent into any country where there is need for evangelization.[36]

---

[34]From information furnished in this short history of the Franciscan Sisters of St. Mary, we are most grateful to Sister Marylu Stueber, F.S.M., Congregational Archivist. Also see *Priceless Heritage*, Franciscan Sisters of Mary, 1987; Mary Ellen Lewis, "Reunification of Two Congregations As Culture Change," *Review for Religious*, January-February, 1990, pp. 65-73; Mary Teresa Noth, "An experience of Reunion: One Divided—Becomes One," *Review for Religious*, May-June, 1987, pp. 383-406.

[35]See *Congregational Identification Statement*, Franciscan Sisters of Mary, 1100 Bellevue Avenue, St. Louis, Missouri: "...members of the reunified congregation serve in...Missouri, Oklahoma, Wisconsin, Illinois, South Carolina, Texas, Florida, Virginia, Minnesota, Brazil and Africa."

[36]Article 43 of their Constitutions states: Every Sister is "sent" on mission and is just as ready to leave her own country as to remain there

The congregation was started in India in 1877 by Mother Mary of the Passion (Hélène de Chappotin) who was born at Nantes in 1839. In 1876, following internal crisis in the missions of Madurai where the Congregation of Mary Reparatrix had worked from 1860, twenty religious separated from the community. Among them was Mother Mary of the Passion. With three companions she went to Rome where on January 6, 1877, she obtained from Pope Pius IX permission to found a new congregation of the Missionaries of Mary with the declared purpose of universal mission. This congregation was to be established at Ootacamund in the Vicariate Apostolic of Coimbatore under the authority of Bishop Joseph Bardou, M.E.P.

The adjective "Franciscan" was added to the title of the institute when it entered the great family of the Third Order Regular in 1885 and accepted its Rule. The institute received the Papal Decree of Praise in 1885, final approval in 1890, and the approval of the Constitutions in 1896. Beginning in 1885, foundations multiplied with a growing rhythm, even outside India and France: in Tunisia, 1885; China, 1886; Sri Lanka, 1886; England, 1887; Switzerland, 1888; Belgium, 1889; Canada 1892, the United States in 1903; and other countries. At the death of the foundress in 1904, the congregation had eighty-six houses. The development continued under the leadership of Mother Mary of the Redemption, 1905-1917, faithful collaborator of the foundress, and under succeeding general administrations down to our own day.

The Franciscan Missionaries of Mary first came to the United States in 1903 to serve the needs of immigrants from Canada. In subsequent foundations they served immigrants from Italy and Portugal and later took up work with Blacks, Native Americans and Hispanics. Today the Franciscan Missionaries of Mary Provincial House is located in New York City in the Bronx. Sisters sponsor and serve in two child care agencies in the Archdiocese of New York; in St. Francis Hospital, Roslyn, Long Island and in the Franciscan Children's Hospital in Brighton, Massachusetts. They serve in a variety of ministries in the

---

in order to respond to the needs of evangelization. Translator's note—One of the unique characteristics of their global mission is the creation of multi-cultural communities throughout the world wide network of provinces.

dioceses of San Francisco, Las Cruces, St. Louis, Chicago, Savannah, Providence and Fall River.

"The activity of the institute is manifold and adapted to local circumstances, always searching to preserve the basic principle of uniting the contemplative life in daily adoration of the Blessed Sacrament with missionary activity in all its forms, collaborating in a special way with the development of women in missionary countries."[37]

d) *The Franciscan Sisters of Rochester (1877)*

The Rochester Franciscans were founded in 1877 by Mother Alfred Moes, who had come to the United States from Luxembourg in 1851 with her older sister, who became Sister Barbara. The two sisters had the intention of joining a religious teaching congregation. Led by the Holy Spirit, the two sisters first joined the School Sisters of Notre Dame and the Marianites of the Holy Cross before they petitioned Father Pamfilo da Magliano, OFM of Allegany, New York to receive them as Third Order Franciscans. In 1856, Mother Alfred and three other sisters began the Sisters of St. Francis of Joliet, Illinois. Through the intervention of Bishop Thomas Foley of Chicago, Mother Alfred completed her term as superior general in 1876. When Mother Alfred traveled to Minnesota to open schools there, Bishop Foley separated the Joliet congregation from the sisters working in Minnesota. Twenty-four sisters chose to remain with Mother Alfred and, with the approval of Bishop Grace of St. Paul, formed the nucleus of the Sisters of St. Francis of the Congregation of Our Lady of Lourdes. Mother Alfred's spirit and zeal attracted many young women, and the community opened schools in Minnesota, Ohio, Wisconsin, and Kentucky. The new community, like the community at Joliet, experienced rapid growth and the congregation received papal approbation in 1912.

A devastating tornado in the city of Rochester, Minnesota in 1883 showed Mother Alfred that a hospital was needed but she also foresaw that the city would become a mecca of healing. The story is told by Dr. W. W. Mayo, recorded in the *Northwest Chronicle,* for December 2, 1916:

---

[37]E. Frascadore, *Francescane missionarie di Maria,* in DIP, IV, col. 348.

...the Mother Superior of the little convent sent for Doctor Mayo. She told him she had a vision of the future. It had come upon her in a waking dream, but so vividly and with such force that she had to reveal it. Her vision was of a great hospital in Rochester.... To that hospital, she had been told in her vision, would come patients from all parts of the world. And she had seen, in her fancy, the name Mayo respected the world over for surgical achievements. "But I am nearly sixty years old," said Dr. Mayo. "How can I achieve such fame? How can I build such a hospital? How would the world know it if we did?" "You have sons," answered the Mother Superior. "They will be great surgeons, wonderful surgeons. The world will find a path to your door."[38]

Thus, in 1889, the sisters built St. Marys Hospital which later grew to become the Mayo Clinic and the congregation extended its ministry to health care. Through several expansions, St. Marys has grown from a twenty-seven bed facility to the largest privately owned hospital in one unit in the United States. A school of nursing was added in 1906, and St. Marys became an educational facility for health care professionals.

The Rochester sisters were always dedicated to the education of young women, and out of the Winona Seminary (1894) grew the College of St. Teresa (1912) which prepared women to take positions of leadership in parishes, schools and hospitals. The college drew students from across the United States and other countries until it closed in 1989.

Through the impact of the teachings of the Second Vatican Council, many religious congregations adapted their lives and their apostolates to the needs of the contemporary world. Changes in governance, renewal in spirituality, liturgical life and prayer brought the Franciscan Sisters of Rochester into contact with people from a variety of cultures extending from the barrios of Bogota to the

---

[38]Carlan Kraman, O.S.F., *Odessey in Faith*, Rochester, Minnesota, 1990, p. 171.

hills of Kentucky. With increased collaboration with the laity, the sisters are involved in care of the elderly, the education of children and adults, advocacy for the poor, distribution of food and clothing to those in need, and offering of shelter to the homeless. The congregation now includes associate members, lay men and women, and clergy who share Franciscan values and commitment and wish to "journey together" in a public and formal way called "cojourning." The sisters and cojourners are working in twenty-seven states and eight other countries.[39]

e) *The Franciscan Missionaries of the Infant Jesus (1879)*
This congregation dedicated itself from the beginning to "the education of girls, especially poor girls and orphans." The congregation began at Aquila in 1873 when

> Barbara Micarelli, with her sister Carmela and Catherine Vicentini, started a small community following the religious life, inspired by Franciscan spirituality and dedicated to catechetical educa-tion, care-providing activity for little children and charitable-social work for the poor, the elderly and the sick. The group was directed by Father Eusebio da Pratola (+1885), a Friar Minor of the Observance. The day of the foundation is consid-ered December 25, 1879 when Barbara Micarelli received the Franciscan habit and made her pro-fession at Rome in the hands of the minister gen-eral of the Friars Minor, Father Bernadino da Portogruaro, OFM. Barbara Micarelli took the name in religion of Maria Giuseppa di Gesù Bambino.[40]

The institute grew rapidly, even if in the earliest years there were some notable differences and even difficulties in interpretation of the Franciscan charism between the foundress and the Commissary of the Friars Minor appointed "to give spiritual direction to the institute." The congregation "carries on its educational and care-providing activities in Italy, Libya, Belgium, Germany and the United

---

[39]These countries include Bolivia, Colombia, El Salvador, Japan, Peru, Singapore, South Africa, and Thailand.

[40]G. Rocca, *Francescane missionarie di Gesù Bambino*, in DIP, IV, col. 341.

States. As the foundress had wished, the congregation prefers to be involved with the care of orphans and the poor. In mission territories, the institute...works in Latin America, in Peru, Argentina, Bolivia, Columbia, and in the Philippines."[41] In 1986 the congregation numbered 925 professed members.

f) *The Capuchin Sisters of the Holy Family (1885)*

On May 11, 1885 the Capuchin Father Luis Amigo y Ferrer gave Constitutions to a group of Secular Tertiaries who for some years had been living the common life at the Marian sanctuary of Mantiele in Spain. With the approval of the Archbishop of Valencia, given at the same time, the institute of the Capuchin Sisters of the Holy Family was established. This institute from that very year dedicated itself to the care of those stricken with cholera in the city of Masamagrell. The congregation grew rapidly because it exemplified the female branch of the Congregation of Capuchin Tertiary Friars of the Sorrowful Mother founded by the same Fr. Luis Amigo in 1889 for the care of those in prison, and for the rehabilitation of minors. The institute received final approval on March 6, 1902 from Pope Leo XIII who personally received many requests from bishops of Spain.

From its beginning the Congregation of the Capuchin Sisters of the Holy Family followed the Rule of the Third Order Regular, as did the male branch. The particular purpose of the institute was the reeducation of young girls living together in a model of the family life. The sisters also offered their assistance in hospitals, orphanages and homes for the elderly.

Presently the congregation besides being in various countries of Europe, is found in Argentina, Brazil, Columbia, Costa Rica, Ecuador, Guatemala, Panama, Venezuela, the Philippines and Zaire. In 1986 the congregation numbered 1,461 professed sisters.[42]

g) *The Franciscan Sisters of the Heart of Jesus (Franciscan Sisters of Malta 1886)*

This congregation of Franciscan sisters from the

---

[41]From the *Annuario Cattolico d'Italia*, 1984-1985, ed. Italiana, Roma, 1984, p. 832.

[42]See Mariano d'Altari, *Cappuccine della Sacra Famiglia*, in DIP, II, col. 201-202.

archipelago of Malta, started because of the work of a founder and a foundress. The first initiative came from the diocesan priest Giuseppe Diacono who in 1880 established at Victoria on the island of Gozo in Malta, an association of elderly ladies called the "Twelve Stars of the Sacred Heart." These ladies ministered to the poor and abandoned youth in the city. The first superior, Virginia de Brincat, in religion known as Sister Margaret of the Sacred Heart, is considered the co-foundress of the institute. Together with the Bishop of Gozo, Bishop Pietro Pace, she wished to give the institute a much wider horizon, in contrast with the intent of Fr. Diacono who wished to limit the activity of the congregation simply to the island of Gozo. Bishop Pace, who became Archbishop of Valletta in 1889, promoted the foundations of the Franciscan sisters on the island of Malta and outside beginning at Corfu, in order to help a local community of Maltese who lived there. Fr. Diacono, summoned to other places in the diocese, removed himself from the direction of the work he had begun. The institute received approval of the diocese in 1886, the Papal Decree of Praise in 1937 and final approval in 1946. In 1903, the congregation was aggregated to the Friars Minor.

Under the direction of the enterprising co-foundress and with the support of the bishops of Gozo, the congregation had remarkable growth even in other countries; in Sicily in 1921 and in Eritrea in 1925. Later the congregation spread to England, Pakistan, the United States, Brazil and Australia. "The special purpose of the Franciscan Sisters of Malta is the Christian apostolate through instruction, christian and civil education of the youth and also the exercise of charity towards the sick. The activity of the Franciscan sisters is carried on in primary and secondary schools, in day care centers, boarding schools, in orphanages, hospices, hospitals, rest homes and other works of this kind."[43] In 1986 the institute numbered 604 professed sisters.

---

[43]See P. Calliari, *Francescane del Cuor di Gesù*, in DIP, IV, col. 281.

CHAPTER XII

FURTHER DEVELOPMENTS IN THE TWENTIETH CENTURY

1. Evolution of legislation: the Constitution *Conditae a Christo*

At the beginning of our own century an important Constitution *Conditae a Christo* was published by Pope Leo XIII on December 8, 1900. This was the first papal document to give juridical status to the custom which at first had been timidly and then more widely introduced into the Church during the nineteenth century. According to the generally accepted procedure, new congregations of simple vows were established with the sole approval of the local ordinary, the bishop.[1] The Constitution *Conditae a Christo* divided religious institutes—in fact recognizing them as such—into diocesan and pontifical. The institute was diocesan if it had received only the approval of the bishop of the diocese; it was pontifical "if it had already received assurance from the Holy See that their Constitutions would be examined,"[2] or had received acknowledgement of its canonical existence through "the *Decree of Praise* or an approval of the constitutions."[3]

The Constitution *Conditae a Christo* also contained counsels and regulations to be observed in the process of approving new institutes. It also set forth the details of the bishops' involvement in the admission of candidates, the

---

[1]See the Constitution *Conditae a Christo*, in Pietro Cardinal Gaspari, *Codicis Juris Canonici Fontes*, vol. III, Romae, 1925, pp. 562-566.

[2]Juan B. Ferreres, *Las religiosas según la disciplina del nuevo Codigo de derecho canónico*, 1920, p. 28.

[3]R. Lemoine, *Le droit des religieux, op. cit.*, p. 294. The *Conditae a Christo* is divided into two chapters: "alterum de Sodalitatibus quae Sedis Apostolicae commendationem vel approbationem nondum sunt assecutae, alterum de ceteris, quarum Sedes Apostolica vel leges recognovit vel institutum commendavit aut approbavit." *Ibid.*, p. 563.

financial administration, and the election of general superiors both male and female. "The publication of this bull," observes Boudinhon,

> marks an important step in the development of legislation concerning religious congregations of simple vows. It would be more exact to say that *Conditae a Christo* represented the official codification of legislation which until that point had been fluid and in process of formation. Of course, there already were many institutes which lived out in community the evangelical counsels, and these institutes were subject to laws and constitutions. However, there existed no official text of laws formulated to determine the position of all religious families of simple vows with respect to the Holy See and the bishops.[4]

In 1901 the *Normae*, or Regulations were published to complete the Constitution *Conditae a Christo*. These Regulations are practically a collection of norms habitually followed by the Holy See in the approval of Constitutions of new religious institutes. With these norms, the Apostolic See now not only recognized approvals of new congregations made by local ordinaries, but took these approvals as the norm. "It is by means of such norms," Ferreres notes with precision, "...that one sees clearly that the Holy See no longer wanted to approve an institute of simple vows until the life of this institute had been lived for some years as an experiment, as it were, with the approval of the local ordinary alone."[5]

On July 16, 1906 Pope Saint Pius X published the motu proprio *Dei Providentis* in which he decreed that the request of a *nihil obstat* from the Holy See was to precede the establishment of a new religious family.[6] It was in fact a limitation on the freedom with which diocesan bishops

---

[4]Msgr. Boudinhon, *Les Congrégations à voeux simples*, in *Le Canoniste contemporain*, n. 294, ann. 1902, p. 352. See Lemoin, *op. cit.*, p. 284, note 3.

[5]Ferreres, *Las religiosas*, *op. cit.*, p. 28.

[6]See the motu proprio *Dei Providentis*, in Gasparri, *Codicis Canonici Fontes*, *op. cit.*, pp. 674-676.

up to this time had approved new congregations. The *nihil obstat* was of course given after determined requirements concerning the new foundations had been furnished and ascertained.[7] Nevertheless this was a simple authorization; it could not be interpreted as approval of the foundation. The approval of the foundation continued to be the judgement and responsibility of the ordinary.

Not quite two years later the Congregation for Religious was established in the reorganization of the Roman Curia accomplished by Pius X in the Constitution *Sapienti Consilio* of June 29, 1908.[8] This congregation began to follow more closely and directly the rise of new congregations. Letters and instructions sent out during this period, almost as if in preparation for the Code of Canon Law of 1917, accented the similarity of the congregations to religious orders of an earlier time. This similarity would be completely clear with the promulgation of the Code. This Code "officially recognized for the first time the same rights and title to the professed of simple vows as to the professed of solemn vows."[9]

---

[7]The motu proprio decreed that to receive the license for establishing a congregation of simple vows in his diocese, the bishop should present to the Council of Bishops and Regulars a "libellum supplicem" in which the bishop states: "quis qualisque sit novae sodalitatis auctor, et qualis causa ad eam instituendam ducatur; quibus verbis conceptum sit sodalitatis condendae nomen seu titulus: quae sit forma, color, materia, partes habitus a novitiis et professis gestandi; quot et quaenam sibi opera sodalitas assumptura sit; quibus opibus tuitio eiusdem contineatur; an similia in diocesi sint instituta, et quibus illa operibus insistant." *Ibid.*, p. 675.

[8]See *Sapienti Consilio*, in Gaspari, *Codicis Juris Canonici Fontes*, *op. cit.*, pp. 726-736. In this reorganization eleven "Sacred Congregations" were established, three "Tribunals" and five "Offices." For further information concerning the history and the name of the departments of the Holy See in charge of religious congregations and orders, see Lemoine, *op. cit.*, p. 297, note 3. Briefly we note: Pope Sixtus V in 1587 instituted the congregation concerned with consulting with religious men and women. Under the pontificate of Clement VIII, 1592-1605, this entity was united to the Congregation of Bishops and took the title of "Sacred Congregation of Bishops and Regulars." Innocent X, in 1652, restored the "Sacred Congregation concerned with the status of Regulars." In 1847 the "Sacred Congregation of Bishops and Regulars" was re-established. This status continued until the time of *Sapienti Consilio* which re-established the new autonomous congregation, "De religiosis."

[9]Lemoine, *op. cit.*, p. 298. "Cannon 488, 1," the author notes, "welcomes religious congregations to the title of religious orders and declared them 'Religious.'" *Ibid.*

2. Some congregations at the beginning of this century

a) *The resurgence of the Franciscan Tertiary Sisters of Blessed Angelina.*

In a special way we remember the rebirth of the Congregation of Blessed Angelina of Montegiove, which was, as you may remember, dissolved by Pope Pius II in 1461 by the bull *Ut tollatur discursus.*[10]

The monastery of Blessed Angelina in Foligno had accepted the cloister completely in 1615, and lived its cloistered life through the eighteenth and nineteenth centuries. It limited its "external" activity to the education of some young girls who were welcomed into the monastery where they remained continually for a three year period of studies.

In the second half of the nineteenth century the sisters, striving to avoid eviction from their monastery, gave highest priority to their work in education. Their monastery had been seized as property of the state in consequence of the revolutionary laws of 1860-1866. In 1879 the nuns asked for and were granted "dispensation from the cloister" as they intended, that with this dispensation the monastery would be able to welcome "a number of students not greater than half the number of the choir sisters. Later on, the nuns received permission to welcome twenty students, irrespective of the number of the choir nuns. The students were culturally better cared for...; the teachers living in the cloister were allowed to go outside the cloister for feastdays."[11] In 1886, with the blessing of the far-sighted Father Bernadine of Portogruaro, Minister General of the Friars Minor, and with the permission of Church authorities, the Monastery opened a school outside the monastery and the nuns went there to teach. At the end of that same year the nuns presented a request to Pope Leo XIII "to give themselves as Tertiaries more completely to the welfare of the youth." At first "a mitigation of the cloister for three years" was granted. In 1901 the "papal cloister" was declared to be "episcopal," and finally in 1903, the nuns

obtained complete dispensation from the cloister

---

[10]See above, p. 115.

[11]Filannino, *Il monastero di Sant'Anna, op. cit.*, p. 235.

and permission to change their habit.... From that time on the monastery changed its appearance. Although retaining some features of the monastic spirit, which had in three centuries' time left its mark upon the religious, they now sought to enflesh in their time the original spirit, making a different but no less valid contribution to the Church and society through the education of youth.[12]

Soon some sisters left the venerable monastery of Saint Ann to establish "communities in Assisi, Anzio, Moricone, Rome, Amelia and Viterbo, thus giving rebirth to the 'Congregation' which had been shattered in the fifteenth century."[13]

The renewed institute received final approval of their Constitutions in 1923, thus becoming an institute of Pontifical Right.

b) *Franciscan Sisters of Christ the King, Venice (1907)*

Because of a unique relationship with earlier congregations of Franciscan sisters we speak here about this congregation. The present institute had its beginnings in 1878 when two religious sisters from the Franciscan Congregation of the "Tertiaries of Saint Joseph," "that had been dissolved in 1866-67 by the civil laws of suppression decreed by the House of Savoy,"[14] decided to re-establish their institute. These two sisters were Paola Ferrari, who took the name in religion Sister Mary Chiara of the Sacred Heart, and Luigia Penso, in religion known as Sister Maria Luigia of Jesus. This effort was successful and the new institute obtained diocesan approval from the Cardinal Patriarch of Venice in 1907. In their turn, the Tertiary Franciscan Sisters of Saint Joseph, suppressed in 1866, had been a revitalization of a community of Franciscan Tertiaries which began in 1459 at San Francesco della Vigna in Venice through the efforts of two Tertiaries Maria Benedetta Carignano and Angelica Canal. This foundation had been approved by Pope Sixtus IV in 1471. For centuries these Tertiaries dedicated themselves to the

---

[12]*Ibid.*, pp. 236-237.

[13]*Ibid.*, p. 257.

[14]G. Rocca, *Francescane di Cristo Re, di Venezia*, in DIP, IV, col. 278.

apostolate of education and instruction of children and young girls and the assistance of elderly women. In 1810 these sisters were scattered following the Napoleonic suppression. The new institute, begun in 1878, took the name the "Franciscan Sisters of the Assumption and Saint Joseph" and followed the Rule of the Third Order Regular of Leo X, as had the two institutes which preceded it. The name of the institute was changed to its present name in 1928 by the decree of Cardinal La Fontaine, Patriarch of Venice. The institute received the Papal Decree of Praise in 1937 and final approval of their Constitutions in 1949. The purpose of the congregation today is described as furthering "the coming of the kingdom of Christ in its members and the brothers and sisters through the proclamation of the gospel, and the animation and formation of Christian life, especially in the Eucharist, apostolic-charitable service with preference for the poor and the humble, for children, the young, the sick and the elderly."[15] Today the activity of the institute is carried on in Italy, Brazil and Africa. In 1986 the congregation numbered 431 professed sisters.

c) *The Daughters of Mercy of the Franciscan Third Order (1919)*

This congregation was begun in Blato, Yugoslavia in 1919, through the efforts of Sister Mary of Jesus Crucified, who was known in the world as Mary Petkovic. Like most other congregations of Franciscan sisters elsewhere, the origins of this institute are closely connected with the needs of the time and the place. In the diocese of Dubrovnik in 1906 there was a community called the "Handmaids of Charity," a congregation of sisters from Brescia dedicated to the education of young women. Unfortunately, this congregation had to leave the country because of events associated with World War I, 1914-1918. The Bishop of Dubrovnik, Josef Marcelic, proposed to the Franciscan Tertiary Mary Petkovic, his penitent, that she continue carrying on the work of the Handmaids of Charity. The acceptance of this proposal meant the beginning of a new congregation. Mary Petkovic showed herself at once to be a dynamic and effective directress,

---

[15] *Francescani in Italia, Annuario, op. cit.,* p. 252.

and the institute experienced rapid expansion. In 1936 the first sisters left for South America. Mother Mary of Jesus, who governed the congregation until 1961, went to visit her daughters in South America in 1940. Again because of World War II, 1939-1945, the superior general was not able to return to Yugoslavia until twelve years later. In the meantime, encouraged by her dynamic leadership, the congregation expanded its activity to include work in colleges, orphanages, and hospitals in Argentina, Paraguay, Chile, Peru and Uruguay. Unable to have their own institutions in Yugoslavia because of government regulations, the sisters there worked in State hospitals, homes for the elderly and in various parochial ministries. In 1952 the foundress transferred the General House to Rome. In 1974 the congregation numbered more than five hundred professed sisters divided into three "regions" and spread throughout the countries of Latin America.[16]

3. The Rule of Pius XI (1927)

The new Code of Canon Law, published in 1917, required the revision of Rules and Constitutions of religious orders and congregations with adaptation to the decrees and directives of the new legislation.

In the congregations of Franciscan sisters that came into existence amid the different events of the eighteenth and nineteenth centuries, those matters that pertained to the Rule and Constitutions were rooted in the widest of differences. Those congregations which at their beginning had recourse to the Holy See to seek direction concerning the Rule, received, as direction and response, the Rule of Leo X of 1521. The majority of the congregations, however, had arisen in a diocesan setting and most often had received the approval of Constitutions and Statutes from episcopal authority. Many of these congregations considered their own Constitutions as fundamental law without having made any recourse to a Rule, strictly so called. The Rule of Leo X itself had now become "less suitable and in some points contrary to the new Code." A new edition of the Rule, which would be a Rule for all religious Franciscans was the desire of many people.

---

[16]See G. Rocca, *Figlie della Misericordia del Terz'ordine regolare di san Francesco*, in DIP, III, col. 164f.

It so happened that the minister general of the Capuchin Friars Minor, Father Giuseppe Antonio da Persiceto, 1920-1926, took the initiative in 1922 to prepare a new text of the Rule for about sixty Tertiary congregations of sisters and nuns aggregated to his order. The Sacred Congregation of Religious, as it was then called, reviewed the project and in 1924 replied that the Congregation agreed "the Rule of Leo X ought to be replaced by another.... But this Rule ought not be one that concerned sisters only but also male religious, as did the Rule of Leo X."[17] The Congregation also gave some practical direction for amending the proposed draft and invited the collaboration of the other ministers general.

> In the audience of April 13, 1926 (this notation can be read on the title page of the booklet containing the text of the new Rule) the Holy Father approved the new text of the Rule of the Franciscan Regular Tertiaries, edited by mutual agreement with the four generals of the four branches.
>
> The pope held back the proposed text in order to place it in a new bull which he intended to promulgate during the year commemorating the seven hundredth anniversary of the death of Saint Francis. The pope also kept some historical notes presented to him.[18]

In May of 1926 Cardinal Camillo Laurenti, Prefect of the Sacred Congregation of Religious, authorized the minister general of the Third Order Regular, Fr. Arnaldo Rigo, to examine this new text for discussion and approval of the new Constitutions of the order at the general chapter. The chapter wished to dedicate itself to this task in July of that same year.

The Rule was promulgated on October 4, 1927 at the close of the anniversary year of Saint Francis and inserted in the Apostolic Constitution *Rerum Conditio.*[19]

---

[17]Archivio SCRIS, Busta R-73, Regola TOR 1927.

[18]*Ibid.* These "historical points" concerning the "former Rule of the Third Order Regular" were autographed by Fr. Raniero Luconi, TOR (+1951). He never in his lifetime knew that these points were directly considered by the pope.

[19]See this Constitution in *Acta Apostolicae Sedis* XIXX (1927), pp.

The Rule was divided into eight chapters instead of the ten chapters of the Leo X Rule, but it follows substantially the same outline and directives.

As was explicitly said in the above mentioned Apostolic Constitution, this Rule took the place of the Rule of Leo X and any other official document which might have been considered as basic legislation. The Rule was given to all the congregations of the Third Order Regular of Saint Francis, male and female. Thus, that fundamental uniformity of legislation desired by the Code of Canon Law was accomplished.

The pope characterized this Rule as "deeply imbued with the Franciscan spirit, *franciscali spiritu plenius inbuta*." However, as Esser noted much later in his commentary, many congregations received the Rule of 1927 when their religious life had already become stabilized, and for this reason they made no great effort to conform their customs and lifestyle to the spirit of the new Rule.[20]

4. Sorrowful events

Among the sorrowful events of this century are the two World Wars, the Civil War in Spain and the fall of countries in eastern Europe under communist governments which brought suffering to many congregations of Franciscan sisters.

At the beginning of the twentieth century there were laws in France which harassed religious orders and congregations. Many institutes felt themselves forced to send their own candidates outside the country, even to other congregations of like spirituality to obtain their religious formation. Some communities had to leave the country and some, almost perforce, began a missionary apostolate which later was proven providential.

361-367. The original copy, with affixed seals, is preserved in the Archives of SCRIS. *Ibid.*

[20]"There is no question at the present time that congregations inserted the New Rule as an introduction to their Constitutions, but it held a very hidden and rose-thorned position. Their life, previously regulated, continued to follow its established way. Neither rules nor customs were adopted or formed to conform to the spirit of the New Rule." Cajetan Esser, *Life and Rule.* A commentary on the Rule of the Third Order Regular of Saint Francis, translated by Sister Honora, O.S.F. and edited by Marion A. Habig, O.F.M., Franciscan Herald Press, Chicago, Illinois, 1967, Preface, p. ix.

Still more seriously difficult became the conditions of life in Spain during the Spanish Civil War, 1936-1939. This war produced a great number of martyrs for the faith. An anti-clerical and anti-religious policy had been institutionalized in the Constitution of 1931. Subsequent legislative activity proscribed all religious symbols in schools and forbade religious men and women to dedicate themselves to teaching. The so-called "laws of religious confessions and associations" which followed rendered life almost impossible for religious orders.[21]

Soon persecution passed from the area of legislation to that of physical violence against persons and things and with the passing of time, this turned into a veritable "hunt for priests, religious and sisters" who "were frequently assassinated."[22] According to the official catalog published by the "Office of Information and Statistics for the Church in Spain" in 1954, among the victims of the persecution were 4,317 diocesan priests; 2,489 religious men; 283 religious women and 249 seminarians.[23] It is enough for us to remember here that as of 1985 there were 106 separate processes for canonization of saints before the Congregation for the Causes of Saints, involving 1,206 persons, victims of the Spanish persecution.[24] Religious Institutes of women have published articles and volumes on their martyrs "and almost all have been the result of an accurate research of data reported with exactness and objectivity."[25]

The national territories of eastern Europe, following the events of World War II, found themselves under communist rule. Ideological influences soon made their presence felt through new laws and in many countries, especially in Czechoslovakia, Romania and Hungary. In addition, Franciscan sisters were forced to abandon their community life, to break off official contacts with outside authorities of their congregations and to live the religious life

---

[21]See Justo Fernandes, Alonzo, *Spagna, Martiri della guera di—*, in *Bibliotheca Sanctorum*, Prima Appendice, 1987, col. 1297.

[22]*Ibid.*, col. 1302.

[23]See A. Montero Moreno, *Historia de la persecución, religiosa en España, 1936-1939*, Madrid, 1961, p. 760.

[24]See Fernandes, Alonso, *op. cit.*, col. 1306.

[25]*Ibid.*, col. 1308. See there a bibliography.

privately or secretly. Their situations until 1988 were very difficult.

Nevertheless, when all things are considered, the twentieth century for most of the congregations of Franciscan sisters was a period of constant expansion, not only into various countries but also into mission lands. Almost all institutes reached their highest membership during the years 1950-1965. Everyone now realizes that after that date a noticeable decline in the area of vocations to the religious life was experienced for many reasons rather than for any one reason. New methodologies and more intense and careful formative activity among Christian youth gives good hope for the future. *Sic Deus adiuvet!*

5. Towards a new Rule

Following World War II and the consequent rapid change in outlook and conduct that pervaded the whole of society, a desire for renewal based upon a return to the sources and a deeper awareness of one's own charism was felt in religious orders almost everywhere even before Vatican II. The documents of the Second Vatican Council, especially the Constitution *Lumen Gentium* and the decree *Perfectae Caritatis*, seemed to welcome such desires and in fact, they traced out a practical path to follow.

In this new atmosphere, in male and female congregations who followed the Rule of the Third Order Regular of Saint Francis promulgated by Pius XI in 1927, there arose in different quarters a kind of dissatisfaction with the text as if in it the principles of Franciscan spirituality had not been well presented, or at least had not been presented in terms that were clear and in harmony with the aspirations of new candidates. So there began some initiatives in Tertiary congregations in preparation for a new document which in time and with wider participation became drafts for a Rule.

In 1965, twenty-five congregations of Franciscan sisters in France and Belgium came together for a study-project on the Rule addressed uniquely to the sisters and had the title of *Rule of Life of the Franciscan sisters*. This document comprised twelve chapters, was published in 1972 and was widely distributed. It was known under the name of the *"French Project."*

At this same period, in 1967, the "Franciscan Cooperative" of Holland edited its own text composed of six chapters. It too was approved and adopted by the assembled capitulars of nineteen Dutch congregations of Franciscan sisters. The work of this group was called the "Dutch Rule."

A third document was proposed by the German congregations; it had eight chapters and was known as the "German Rule." More than a Rule, it was, at the same time a teaching instrument, and later it was withdrawn at the International Franciscan Meeting in Assisi in 1979.

Finally, the Fourth Interobediential Congress of the Third Order Regular gathered in Madrid in 1974; this Congress prepared a draft entitled: "An Understanding of the Franciscan Penitential Life." Divided into six chapters, it was called the "Madrid Document."

In retrospect today, we can say that the sole common negative component in these efforts was the limitation of involvement, a lack of serious effort to seek common agreement and the aim at drafting a single document which would serve all the male and female congregations who followed the one Rule of the Third Order Regular of Saint Francis. Each group went on its own way without knowing what the others were doing. Where there was such a rush in divergent ways, there was neither the will nor the strength to correct this divergence. Much later this fact would result in many difficulties. Every project thus proved to be independent and at times based on different if not contrasting principles. Only the hard work and patience of the international organizations established after the international assembly in Assisi in 1979 succeeded in ironing out differences and fostering the beginnings of convergence.

The Assisi Assemblies 1976, 1979

Among the various projects for a new Rule that appeared at this time, the French Project quickly gained ascendancy. The promoters of this project announced the first *International Assembly for Franciscan Sisters* at Assisi in October of 1976. These were days of reflection and study. Representatives of the male Third Order Regular noted two fundamental weaknesses in the French Project: (1) It was intended solely for Franciscan sisters, excluding friars. This was contrary to the constant tradition in the movement of the Third Order both Secular as well as Regular from the time of Saint Francis, to the present Rule which was one and only one Rule for the brothers and sisters; (2) the French Project seemed to ignore penitential spirituality which had always been characteristic of the Third Order as has been rediscovered in the Meetings of Franciscan Studies on the "Penitential Movement."

The International Meeting at Assisi closed without a clearly defined over-all plan. The organizing body promised to communicate the various projects dealing with the Rule so that there could be further study, in preparation for a new meeting within two or three years.

A second *International Franciscan Meeting* was announced for October 1979, again in Assisi. In the meantime, representatives of the male Third Order Regular repeatedly made known their desire for collaboration, emphasizing the major interest of the order for a single project which would preserve a single Rule for the friars and the sisters.

The *International Meeting* at Assisi in October 1979 represented a moment of disagreement, and then of final convergence of the various currents of thought existent among the members of the Third Order. All those present for this meeting clearly saw that the line of approach to the problems, until then employed, did not satisfy the expectations of many. At the end of this meeting, which had voted for the adoption of the French project as a working draft for a new Rule, important resolutions were approved for the continuation of the work. One resolution invited "the collaboration and integration of the male congregations in the studying and drafting of the Rule." Another resolution was to increase the number from two to four of "guides for the international Franciscan aspirations." These first two "guides" were from the Order of Friars Minor and the Capuchin Friars Minor and they had assisted the French Project from its beginning. Two more "guides," one from the Conventual Friars and one from the male Third Order Regular were added.

In this same meeting two international bodies were established whose duty from that time on would be to oversee and promote all the work relating to the drafting of the Rule. These two entities were the *International Franciscan Bureau* (BFI), comprising six female and six male ministers general of the congregations of the Third Order Regular, and the *International Franciscan Commission* (CFI) which was composed of nine members. The BFI would have the task of supervision and have supreme responsibility for the entire Rule project. The CFI would have the task of organizing the work practically and establishing the methodology for completing a final document that would involve all the male and female congregations of the Third Order Regular. The "guides" of the four Franciscan families took part in both the BFI and the CFI as counselors and experts, but they did not have the right to vote.

The Meeting at Grottaferrata, March 8-10, 1980

All these resolutions were fully implemented in the important meeting held at Grottaferrata in Rome. Present for this meeting for the first time were all the members of the BFI and the CFI and the four "guides."[26]

In this meeting the goals and the methodology for the

---

[26]The International Franciscan Bureau (BFI) comprised: Sister Elizabeth Delor, Superior General of the Franciscan Sisters of the Kingdom of Jesus Christ, President; Sister Giovanna Achille, Superior General of the Franciscan Alcantarines; Sister Alma Dufault, Superior General of the Franciscan Missionaries of Mary; Sister Eliska Petschnerova, Superior General of the Franciscan Teaching Sisters; Sister Christine Wittmers, Superior General of the Franciscan Daughters of the Sacred Hearts of Jesus and Mary; Father Luis Cuesta y Nozal, Minister General of the Tertiary Capuchins of the Sorrowful Mother, representing the male congregations.

The CFI had the following members: Sister Carmen Ciria, Franciscan Sisters of the Holy Spirit; Sister Roberta Cusak, Executive Director of the Franciscan Federation of Sisters and Brothers of the United States of America; Sister Louise Dendooven, Franciscan Missionaries of Mary, Coordinator; Sister Maria Andrea Frech, Sisters of Saint Francis of Montpellier, Treasurer; Sister Ethelburga Hacker from the Secretariat of the German Franciscan Sisters; Sister Bernadette Nourdin, Sisters of Saint Francis of Assisi of Lyons, Secretary; Sister Romulda Trinchera, President of the Franciscan Movement of Religious Sisters, from the Franciscan Missionaries of the Immaculate Hearts; Sister Augusta Visentin, Franciscan Missionaries of the Sacred Heart; Brother Columban Keller, Missionary Brothers of Saint Francis, representing the male Congregations. The four "periti" were: Fr. Bernadin Beck, O.F.M., Fr. Fidele Lenaerts, O.F.M. Cap., Fr. Candido Lorenzoni, O.F.M. Conv. and Fr. Raffaele Pazzelli, TOR. All these members worked out of their respective tasks from the Grottaferrata Meeting of 1980 to the General Assembly at Rome in March of 1982 without any substitution or change of personnel.

future work were clearly identified and in accordance with the directives of the 1979 Meeting in Assisi:

a) One single Rule should be drafted, and it should be common for the friars and sisters of the Third Order Regular;

b) The text should contain those basic principles of Franciscan spirituality to which the various congregations of friars and sisters had variously been inspired so that every congregation would be able to recognize itself in the Rule. It was agreed that these fundamental values should be presented as four: poverty, minority, penance-conversion, and contemplation.

c) The basic text should remain the one approved in the Assisi Meeting, but it should be amended and integrated so as to correspond to the demands of the new situation, i.e. friars and sisters working together towards a common Rule.

d) A Work Group should be established with the task of editing the new document under the careful directives of the CFI. It would be assisted by four male Franciscan experts who were immediately appointed: Fra. Jean-François Godet, O.F.M., Fr. Francesco S. Pancheri, O.F.M., Conv., Fr. Jaime Zudaire, O.F.M. Cap., and Fra. Bartolomeo Pastor-Oliver, T.O.R.[27]

e) All male and female congregations which follow the present Rule of the Third Order Regular should be notified concerning the work accomplished up to that time. They should receive complete documentation and should be invited to present observations and proposals for the new text on the congregation level.

It was clear that to reach this common view it would be necessary that there be, if not "compromise" at least a mutual understanding among the main currents of thought within the Third Order Regular, represented then by the French Project and the Madrid Document.

Beginning with the historical fact of the variety of origins and special character of many congregations, some congregations even arising from non-Franciscan initiatives, a single restricted point of view could not be

---

[27]Following the meeting at Reute in September 1980, this group of periti were no longer present. Only Fr. Jean-François Godet remained to guide the Work Group as animator.

imposed on all congregations. Thus the promoters of the French Project had to admit and to understand the reality and value of the "Penitential" tradition in the heart of some congregations, especially those of earlier origin in a line of continuity with the penitents who followed Francis of Assisi. On the other hand, the defenders of the "Penitential" tradition, had to admit that many modern congregations, and today these are among the most numerous, had their beginnings completely outside "Penitential" spirituality and more under the influence of the Friars Minor and the Poor Clares. Therefore, these congregations could not be constrained to accept penitential spirituality as the sole constituent element of a new draft of the Rule.

This "bi-lateral" understanding was the sole means able to preserve the unity and singularity of one common Rule for the entire family of the Third Order Regular. This unity and singularity was considered by all as a goal and a precious good of highest importance.

In the meeting of the CFI which followed at Assisi on June 11-12, 1980, the structure and tasks of the "Work Group" were outlined and established in detail. The Work Group was made up of ten members coming from different continents and representing the different "demands" within the Third Order.[28]

The specific task of the Work Group was thus outlined: beginning with the basic outline, the text approved at the Assisi Meeting of 1979, the Group was to draw up a new draft of the text in the light of the observations and proposals coming from the congregations. In the meantime, the congregations had been studying the basic text with the purpose of including in it some spiritual contributions or essential points gleaned from the Madrid Document and the Dutch Rule according to the plan adopted at the

---

[28]This Work Group comprised: Sister Margaret Carney, Sisters of Saint Francis, Pittsburgh, Pa.; Sister Isabella Ciruzzi, Franciscan Missionaries of Assisi; Sister Elena Echavarren, the Capuchin Tertiary Sisters, Saragozza, Spain; Br. Paulus Hahn, O.S.F., from Bad Bergzabern, Germany; Fr. Thaddeus Horgan, Society of the Atonement, Washington, D.C.; Sister Ignatia Bombay, India; Sister Marianne Jungbluth, Eupen, Belgium; Sister Marie Benoit, Luchernet, Toulouse, France; Sister Maria Luiza Piva, Santa Catarina, Brazil; Sister Honoria Montalgo, Pasto, Columbia. All the members of the Work Group were present at Reute except Br. Paulus Hahn.

Grottaferrata Meeting. Every article of the new text, in order to be approved, needed to receive a qualified majority, that is an approval of two thirds for the first and second ballot. The text had to be redrafted between the first and second ballot when this kind of majority was lacking. For the third voting a simple majority, one half plus one, was required. In this case, however, the alternative form of the article would also be presented to the CFI for the final decision.

The Reute Draft, 1980 and the Brussels Draft, 1981

The Work Group was in session at Reute, Germany from September 1-10, 1980. Even though they had to struggle through a series of difficulties of various kinds, they completed the preparation of a new draft which at that stage was called "the Reute Draft." The CFI and the BFI met on the days of September 11-13 to examine this draft and decided to send it to all the congregations for further study with the request that further proposals and modifications be submitted. These proposals and observations were to be motivated and specific, and they were to be submitted to the office of the CFI before April 15, 1981.

In the meantime the two bodies placed in charge of the project for the new Rule continued their international meetings for the purpose of giving order to the forth-coming work, to co-ordinate the perspectives and proposals that were expected from the congregations and to resolve the practical questions which arose from time to time. The BFI met in Rome on November 8-9, 1980. The CFI met on December 12, 1980 at Alassio, Savona and again on February 26-27 at Montpellier in France. The principal objective of the BFI from that time on was to prepare adequately for the approaching General Assembly of the Congregations of the Third Order Regular. The suggestions from all the congregations were reduced to concrete and exact resolutions. Among them, it is worth noting here, was a resolution which established a joint trust to take care of the expenses connected with the coming General Assembly, travel and lodging, for those male and female General Superiors having restricted financial resources. Another resolution re-affirmed the equality of the vote for both large and small congregations. The role and procedures for the Work Group were established for the next meeting; at that time the Work Group would have "to write the Reute draft anew by taking into consideration the observations and proposals received from the congregations so as to achieve a draft of text that would be inspirational in character, brief and concrete and faithful to the gospel vision of Francis."

The Work Group met in Brussels, Belgium from May 10-20, 1981. The congregations which sent in observations and proposals numbered 205. Strengthened by the shared experience at Reute, the members of the Work Group proceeded with their work in good fashion, faithfully following the program lines set up for them by the CFI. This body met at Brussels on May 21-22 and examined the new text attentively, and found that this draft was truly imbued with a living spirit. It seemed rich and complete, and supported by an internal logic which was clear and coherent. Here indeed was well founded hope that all the congregations would be at home with this project, and that the discussion and approval of the text at the approaching General Assembly would not present any serious problems.

It was decided to send the new text, the Brussels Draft, as soon as possible to every congregation. Thus the General Counselors and the entire congregation, if so desired, might study it and discuss it so that the male and female ministers general might bring it to the coming General Assembly with final "desiderata"—desired suggestions—along with the approval of the entire congregation.

Towards the General Assembly

The meetings of the BFI and the CFI, after Brussels, had as their principal goal the preparations for the General Assembly. First of all, it was confirmed that the prime purpose of the assembly would be to present and discuss the Brussels draft and arrive at a final draft approved by the Assembly. The drawing up of regulations for the work of the Assembly was discussed. This document had been edited in such a way that the Assembly would be able to evaluate its usefulness and objectivity. That is, it was respectful of the freedom of the Assembly in its decisions, but had characteristic features of rigorous efficiency because the Assembly was to be so large. It was decided to have plenary sessions plus small group meetings each day which would facilitate the interchange of ideas. For the first days of the Assembly, it was planned to have a sufficiently long time for the presentation of the basic values which permeated the text and for the presentation of each one of the chapters so that the entire Assembly might arrive at a spiritual deepening of its knowledge of the Rule before passing on to discussion, the making of amendments and the voting. With respect to the system adopted for the voting in the Assembly, three points were suggested:

a) An indicative vote, a vote showing more or less satisfaction would be taken after the presentation of each chapter; if necessary, this indicative vote would be brought for proposals of amendment in the small groups;

b) A vote showing orientation or direction would be taken on the basic draft and on the proposed amendments. Each vote showing orientation which had two thirds of the votes for approval would be considered final.

c) A deliberative vote finally would be used for each article, each chapter for those parts of the text which had not achieved a two thirds vote in the vote of orientation.

The General Assembly officially opened on the morning of March 1, 1982 at "Domus Pacis" in Rome and closed on March 10.

It was certainly the largest and most important General Assembly of male and female Tertiary congregations ever held in history. Present were 192 male and female ministers general, or their delegates. Including the Work Group, the "guides," the outside observers, the translators, the members of the secretarial staff and other offices, the number of the participants was more than 260, coming from thirty-seven countries and five continents. In its preparatory phases, planning and execution, the Assembly was completely in the hands of the men and women professing the Rule of the Third Order Regular.

The ten days of discussion, meetings and prayer in common quickly matured a process begun some time previously, bringing the participants to a much more profound and shared understanding of what it means to belong to the Third Order Regular. Little by little, as historical and doctrinal points were clarified and illustrated, the awareness grew that in the very great variety of the origins of the Tertiary congregations,there was a treasury of common and basic values which seriously demanded the preservation of *unity*—the Rule, and also allowed the continuance of a precious *pluralism*—the Constitutions. Once having arrived at this conviction, as a vital and essential point, progress became rather easy with occasions of real attention and sensitivity to the exigencies of particular traditions.

The complete *Acts* of the General Assembly were published. Separately were published also the principal presentations (suggestions, motions, etc.) which formed the object of the considerations and discussions leading to the improvement and final approval of the text of the Rule.

This material, which can be easily examined, and the quasi unanimous approval of each article and chapter, are convincing proof of the high degree of unity—in thought and intention—reached by the male and female congregations of the Third Order Regular of Saint Francis.

The text of the Rule, approved by the Assembly, was

The Cardinal Prefect of this same Congregation, Edward Pironio, announced to the BFI and to other interested persons, on April 30, 1983, the "solemn Pontifical confirmation" of the new Rule with the following communication:

SACRED CONGREGATION FOR RELIGIOUS
AND SECULAR INSTITUTES

Prot. n. Sp. R. 463/79   *Rome, April 30, 1983*

In the audience the Holy Father gave me on December 17th, last year, I allowed myself to present him with the text of the *Rule and Life of the Brothers and Sisters of the Third Order Regular of Saint Francis*, approved by this Sacred Congregation with a few modifications, asking him to kindly ratify it by a solemn Pontifical document, dated December 8th. The Holy Father acceded kindly to my request.

I am glad to inform you that H. E. Monsignor Martinez Somalo Eduoard, Substitute for the Secretary of State, by the letter prot. n. 104-237, dated April 21st, has transmitted here the Brief

Franciscanum vitae propositum, by which the Holy Father confirms the text of the *Rule*, a copy of which is sent to your Paternity together with an exemplar of the *Rule*.

Rejoicing with the whole Franciscan family at this token of kindness on the part of the Holy Father, I heartily wish that this solemn confirmation be a new stimulus for a life of generosity in the religious consecration in imitation of the holy Patriarch Francis of Assisi.

I am pleased, on this occasion, to express to you my respect and religious wishes in Christ and His Holy Mother.

Edward Cardinal Pironio,
Prefect

The new Rule of the Third Order Regular thus carries papal approval dated December 8, 1982.

6. The International Franciscan Conference, CFI 1985

At the end of the General Assembly of 1982 that discussed and approved the final draft of the new Rule, the proposal was made to establish an international body which would permanently group together the institutes which follow this Rule and be solicitous of their interests.

Having closely examined and discussed the possible goals and the working of this future organization, the unity of mind reached in this Assembly was such that the proposal was embraced almost unanimously.

To implement this project, now that the Assembly was to close, an International Franciscan Body, the OFI, was elected. Full authority was granted to this organization to provide those things that were necessary to its realization: the choice of an *ad hoc* committee to prepare Statutes which would regulate the life and activity of this entity; supervision in the drafting of these statutes, and lastly the convocation of the next General Assembly which would have the obligation of discussing and approving these statutes. The four "guides" were asked to continue their work as "periti and counselors," as they had in the past. The OFI would be responsible for reaching all the goals until the election, if it should take place in the new Assembly, of the directing body of the new organization.

The General Assembly of 1982 was concluded and a short time later an *ad hoc* committee for the preparation of the OFI Statutes was formed. This committee comprised seven members chosen from the most qualified in the area of jurisprudence and also representing the various geographic areas. The Statutes, prepared during two years of intensive work by this committee, with periodic revisions made in conjunction with the OFI, were sent to all the male and female congregations which follow the Rule of the Third Order Regular, almost four hundred congregations, for corrections, suggestions and proposals. The *ad hoc* committee, after receiving replies from the congregations, held a joint meeting at Manage, Belgium. The committee worked out the restructuring of the Statutes according to the indications received from the congregations and submitted the new draft for the evaluation of the OFI. The OFI, together with the four "periti" examined the

Assembly was held in Assisi on the premises of the "Citadella Cristiana" on October 19-20, 1985. Those participating, as in the preceding Assembly, were almost exclusively the male and female ministers general of the congregations following the Rule of the Third Order Regular.

The discussion and approval of the Statutes was only one part of the Assembly's work. The fundamental goal of the meeting was presented as that

> of fostering communion regarding the Rule and life of the friars and sisters of the institutes of the Third Order Regular of Saint Francis according to the three principle directives of the Rule:
> —to follow faithfully in the footsteps of Our Lord Jesus Christ (Rule, 8, 25)
> —to bear witness to the gospel with word and action (Rule 9, 29)
> —to announce peace in word and in heart (Rule 9, 30).[29]

---

[29]*Regolamento dell'Assemblea Generale*, 19-26 ottobre 1985. 1. *Obiettivi del'assemblea generale, a.*

The main part of the work consisted in making a deeper study of the status of Franciscan presence on the five continents in view of the process of change in contemporary society. Four well-known representatives of world Franciscan scholarship guided the Assembly in careful consideration of the positive aspects and desirability of Franciscan presence in the Church.

Deeply felt experiences were presented and replies were given and argued, as Franciscans, concerning the new needs of the people. It was seen that such experience would have to touch directly the "spirit and life" of about two hundred thousand Franciscan men and women religious living the consecrated life.[30] Indirectly, there are millions more men and women with whom these friars and sisters have contact.

The Statutes of the "International Conference of the Institutes of the Friars and Sisters of the Third Order Regular of Saint Francis" were discussed article by article and approved with the amendments deemed useful. This process of approval really marked the birth of the new body whose goals are thus described in the Statutes:

a) To foster within each institute and among the institutes of the same Third Order Regular throughout the world a true communion inspired by Franciscan life and spirituality, according to the contents of the Rule and its fundamental values based on the gospel and in accord with the teaching of the Church;

b) To create and foster solidarity among the member institutes through the following means:

—exchange of help in spiritual and material matters;

—collaboration in the apostolate;

—reciprocity of information and communication;

—particular attention to the institutes with fewer members or more isolated from others, to help/collaborate in the formation of members;

—the creation and support of Franciscan associations and other national and regional bodies, especially in those cases where these means have been requested;

c) To collaborate with the First and Second Orders and with the Secular Franciscan Order;

---

[30]In the more careful estimate, there are that many friars, sisters, and nuns of the Third Order Regular of Saint Francis.

d) To encourage and make known research concerning the spirituality and history of Franciscanism;

e) To represent the institutes of the Third Order Regular in the Church, in the Franciscan family and in the world;

f) To support and promote initiatives in defense of the universal rights of human persons such as freedom, justice and peace, the ecology, etc.[31]

The Franciscan International Conference has a "Permanent International Council" (CIP), composed of seven members: President, Secretary General and five counselors.[32] "The President, Vice President and the Secretary General constitute the executive committee of the Permanent Council,"[33] and normally reside at the office of Franciscan International Conference which is in Rome.

7. The activity of the Franciscan International Conference, 1986-1988

After the establishment of the Franciscan International Conference by the General Assembly of 1985, the
Conference by the General Assembly of 1985, the

San Paolo alla Regola, n. 6. The present address of the Franciscan International Conference is Piazza di Risorgimento n. 14, 00192 Roma.

The principal activities of the Conference itself, communicated through the activities conducted by the Permanent Council during the first three years of its existence can be summarized as follows:

a) A commission on "Spirit and Life" was formed with

---

[31]Conferenza francescana internazionale. Statuti, 5 *Obiettivi: 5.1.-5.6.*

[32]The first Permanent International Council, elected in the same Assembly of 1985, comprised: the President, Christine Wittmers (Germany), Superior General of the Franciscan Daughters of the Sacred Hearts of Jesus and Mary; Counselors: Br. Matthew McCormack (Ireland), Superior General of the Brothers of the Third Order Regular of Penance of Saint Francis of Assisi; Sister Yvonne D'Sousa (India), Superior General of the Missionary Sisters of Ajmer; Sister M. Teresa della Pietra (Italy), Superior General of the Franciscan Missionaries of the Sacred Heart; Sister Amanda Franco Gomez de Carmargo (Brazil), Superior General of the Franciscan Sisters of the Heart of Mary; and Sister M. Teresa Gargnon (Canada), Superior General of the Sisters of Saint Francis of Lyons; the Secretary General was Sister Alma Dufault, former Superior General of the Franciscan Missionaries of Mary.

[33]Conferenza francescana internazionale, Statuti. *9.2. Competenze, 9.2.2.*

nine members from different countries. This commission has as its purpose searching out the most suitable ways to help the member institutes of the Third Order Regular. Among other things, the commission has identified materials for study for personal and community use dealing with the spirituality of the Third Order Regular.

b) The commission publishes a bulletin three times a year called TAU-INFO which informs member institutes of the Conference about the activities of the Permanent Council and the more important events concerning the Third Order Regular institutes throughout the world. This bulletin also carries important notices concerning other branches of the Franciscan family and is published in seven languages.

c) Members of the Permanent Council have participated in various meetings of the National Federations, such as CEFEPAL (Brazil), MOREFRA (Italy), INFAG (Germany) and the Franciscan Federation (USA), and have promoted cooperation with the other branches of the Franciscan family.

d) The President of the Permanent Council has occasionally participated in meetings of the Conference of the Ministers General of the four male Franciscan families together with the Minister General of the Secular Franciscan Order.

e) The Permanent Council collaborated to achieve the status of "Non-government Organization" with the United Nations.

f) The Permanent Council has begun contacts on the international level with the Secular Franciscan Order.

8. Corollary: Aggregation

Through the centuries the majority of the congregations of Franciscan sisters have experienced a special relationship, called "aggregation," with one of the male Franciscan Orders.

The extent and form of this aggregation may be different from institute to institute, and also different according to the centuries involved and the stage of development of each institute. So here we state the most general aspects.

Today "aggregation" is defined as "a juridic act by which a religious order admits a congregation of religious to participation in its own liturgical laws and indulgences. The religious congregation intends in some fashion to adopt some norms which will be of inspiration to its religious spirit."[34] But in the past, "aggregation" was not always limited to a simple participation in spiritual benefits of indulgences. Sometimes it implied a kind of jurisdiction.

Aggregation could occur at the time of the first constitution or the birth of the congregation, and also, after the congregation had been established. In the first case, the order could more easily inspire the spiritual orientation and the legislation of the new congregation which afterwards remained under the aegis of the same order. When aggregation took place after the congregation had already been established, it served to reinforce those elements of spiritual affinity already present and to share privileges and indulgences. "It is a matter," says Macca, "of a maturation process which brings a very definite characterization to the initial appearance, at least partially, of the beginning."

The ancient juridical practice could vary from institute to institute and could also require visual connections, such as a habit "which was substantially of the same color and form as the habit worn by the members of the First Order." Some congregations of Franciscan sisters began their existence not only aggregated but "subject to the order." This implied a kind of jurisdiction exercised by the Friars Minor even as far as the choice of major superiors was concerned.

Today the affiliation admitted by the Code of Canon Law is essentially, if not exclusively, concerned with the spiritual aspects "always preserving the canonical autonomy of the aggregated institute."[36] "According to the outlook of the Church following Vatican II, new relationships with the Order of Friars Minor are concerned with the

---

[34]See V. Macca, *Aggregazione*, in DIP, I, col. 150. Also see L. Fanfani, *Il diritto delle religiose*, Rovigo, 1950, pp. 14-55.

[35]See Macca, *loc. cit.*, col. 151.

[36]Canon 580 of the *Code of Canon Law*.

special aggregation of spiritual communion, apostolic collaboration and freely sought consultation."[37]

"At present," wrote Father Iriate in 1983, "the Franciscans have seven congregations under their direction and eleven male and 270 female congregations affiliated with them; the Conventuals have four male and thirty-three female affiliated congregations; the Capuchins, nine male and eighty-nine female; and the regular Tertiaries, two male and thirty-two female."[38]

[37]G. Rocca, *Francescane missionarie de Gesù Bambino*, in DIP, IV, col. 341

[38]Iriate, Lazaro, O.F.M. Cap., *Franciscan History*, Franciscan Herald Press, Chicago, 1983, p. 522.

CHAPTER XIII

THE SPIRITUALITY OF FRANCISCAN SISTERS

The "Rule and Life of the Brothers and Sisters of the Third Order Regular of Saint Francis" was approved by Pope John Paul II and intended for the entire movement of the Third Order Regular, male and female. Besides representing and expressing the basic unity of this Franciscan family, the Rule shows its essential elements of spirituality. It follows from this that the spirituality of Franciscan sisters will be fundamentally that of the Third Order Regular.[1]

categorical response, we believe it is useful to give some distinctions and some enlightenment on the question.

"In the sphere of Franciscan spirituality one can identify three main currents that all refer to Saint Francis, but each is distinguished by its own orientation and particular expression,"[2] this is to say, each one distinguishes itself by the emphasis it puts on one or the other of the various elements of Franciscan spirituality. And this emphasis becomes a characterization. The three currents are practically identified with the three Orders of Saint Francis.

Starting from a different point of view, one is able to affirm with greater detail that each of the three Franciscan Orders, besides receiving "the dominant ideas of Franciscan Spirituality" which are "the common

---

[1]We say *fundamentally* because a Rule by its nature, does not have the obligation of containing all the spirtuality of a religious order which follows that Rule. The spirituality will instead be completely expressed in the Constitutions which are proper to each order or religious congregation.

[2]Lino Temperini, *La spiritualità penitenziale nelle Fonti Francescane*, in ANALECTA TOR XIV (1980), p. 522.

patrimony, has its own set of spiritual elements that characterize each one in the sphere of Franciscan tradition."[3] Whether this is sufficient for us to speak of a distinct spirituality is a question for discussion. It is certain, however, that there does exist a spiritual characteristic proper to each of the three Franciscan Orders. We call it a spirituality. To be able to identify that spirituality of the Third Order, it is first of all necessary to be clear about the nature of this order. Today we know with certainty that the Third Order is the continuation, with new contributions, of the penitential movement which existed before the time of Saint Francis; a movement which was known to Saint Francis; a movement which he followed. "In 1206, Francis before Bishop Guido renounced his father Peter Bernadone, changed his clothing to that worn by the penitents (*exivi de saeculo*) and officially entered the penitential state."[4] In that penitential movement there were some constant elements of spirituality which formed its charism. The Third Order of Saint Francis: "thus takes its life from the convergence of two spiritual streams: the one, the gospel witness of Francis, the other, the penitential movement."[5] We can thus assert that the elements of penitential spirituality were made an integral part of the spiritual endowment belonging to the Saint of Assisi: he assimilated these elements into his own charism. In the Third Order which had its beginning with Saint Francis, there are some new elements which were not present in the earlier penitential movement;[6] there are also elements coming from penitential spirituality. This double category of these elements establishes the standard that characterizes the Third Order of Saint Francis.

[3]L. Temperini, *La tradizione spirituale*, in R. Pazzelli-L. Temperini, *La tradizione storica e spirituale del nostro movimento*, ed. CSI-TOR, Roma, 1980, p. 18

[4]L. Temperini, *Il Terzo ordine regolare di San Francesco nel ambito del francescanesimo*, pro manuscripto, p. 1.

[5]*Ibid.*, p. 4.

[6]Saint Bonaventure almost certainly alludes to these elements when, describing the Order of Penance of Saint Francis, he wrote: "Set on fire by the fervor of his preaching, a great number of people bound themselves by new laws of penance according to the rule which they received from the man of God." LM, IV, n. 6, in *The Life of St. Francis*, translated by Ewert Cousins, p. 210.

1. The main components of penitential spirituality

Perhaps few other religious orders today can benefit, as can the Third Order, from so many high level studies done in the last twenty years that bring to light both spiritual and historical aspects of the Third Order. For reasons readily recognizable, a group of scholarly Franciscans under the initiative of Father Léon Bédrune, O.F.M., representing the four families,[7] towards the end of the 1960's, wanted to get into the middle of an investigation that had begun decades earlier in the scientific field. The area of this investigation was the "famous Franciscan movement which included even married people,"[8] "the Penitential movement." This investigation was begun especially because a new opinion had been proposed by the assertions of scholars, including persons outside Franciscanism, concerning the "penitential origins" of Francis of Assisi.[9] Furthermore, the Second Vatican Council had urged religious institutes to "return to the sources," that is, to return to their true beginnings in the

the directives received from him. Later on, towards the end of the thirteenth century, this "penitential movement" began to call itself or was called "the Third Order of Saint Francis."

The group of ardent scholars engaged in the project increased in number and has continued to the present time to promote Study Meetings, in different cities of Italy, and has published the Acts of these Meetings in several volumes.[10]

---

[7]That is, the Friars Minor, the Conventuals, the Capuchins and the Regular Tertiaries.

[8]Léon Bédrune, O.F.M., *Présentation*, in *L'Ordine della Penitenza, op. cit.*, p. 5.

[9]See Meersseman, *Dossier, op. cit.*, p. 1 and following.

[10]1. *L'Ordine della Penitenz a di san Francesco d'Assisi nel secolo XIII. Atti del primo Convegno di Studi Francescani* (held in Assisi, July 3-5, 1972). Edited by O. Schmucki, Istituto Storico dei Cappuccini, Roma, 1973, Republished in 1988.

2. *I Frati Penitenti di san Francesco nella società del Due e Trecento*, Acts of the second Meeting for Franciscan Studies held in Rome, October 12-14, 1976. Edited by Mariano d'Alatri, Istituto Storico dei Cappuccini, Roma, 1977.

3. *Il Movimento Francescano della Penitenza nella società medioevale*,

Limiting our considerations here to the theme in which we are interested, we note that the above mentioned studies furnish full evidence that "Penance" as it developed in the penitential-Franciscan charism is composed of and explained by the two principal characteristic elements:

—"*continuous conversion*" in the biblical sense of "metanoia," that is, a redirecting of oneself toward God, as a constant tending toward Him which implies leaving behind instinctual life which centers on self, and the undertaking of a life in which God is the center of activity and aspiration;

—*active and effective charity*, on behalf of the brothers and sisters in Christ, an active charity extended to those who have greater need of it, a dedicating of oneself in many ways to the "works of mercy," both spiritual and corporal.

2. Explanation of these concepts

Since the two elements mentioned above are so essential to the make-up of this movement as to constitute its characteristics, it seems fitting and necessary to insist again in detail on their meaning, both theoretical and practical, so that each of our readers may have a clear and complete understanding of them.

a) *The life of penance*

We note first of all, that the term "penance" does not primarily have here the common meaning which has been retained in modern languages, but the biblical meaning of penance.

It is well known that in modern languages the word "penance" most often means actions of external mortification, such as fasting, abstinence from a particular kind of

---

Acts of the third Meeting for Franciscan Studies held at Padua, September 25-27, 1979. Edited by Mariano D'Alatri, Istituto Storico dei Cappuccini, Roma, 1980.

4. *Prime manifestazioni di vita comunitaria, maschile e femminile, nel movimento francescano della Penitenza (1215-1447)*, Acts of the fourth Meeting for Franciscan Studies, held in Assisi, June 30 to July 2, 1981. Edited by R. Pazzelli-L. Temperini, International Historical Commission of the T.O.R., Roma, 1982 and in the ANALECTA TOR, XV (1982).

5. *La Supra Montem di Niccolò IV (1289): genesi e diffussione di una Regola*. Acts of the fifth Meeting for Franciscan Studies held in Ascoli Piceno, October 26-27, 1987. Edited by R. Pazzelli-L. Temperini and the ANALECTA TOR, Rome, 1988.

food or from other pleasurable things and even causing bodily pain by some physical means such as a hair shirt or the "discipline."[11]

This is not the principal meaning of the word *penance* in the biblical context or meaning. It is only a secondary or derived meaning. The first meaning of *penance* in the biblical sense is conversion of the heart, return to God, change of outlook, that is, a resolution for the future to follow the will of God.

Penance, in this sense, corresponds to the biblical meaning of the word "metanoia," which was in its turn translated into the Latin "conversio." Thus the three words: *metanoia, penance* and *conversion* in this context have the same meaning and are interchangeable.[12]

"So Franciscan penance," writes Lino Temperini,

indicates above all an interior psychological-spiritual attitude that turns the primary interests of the soul and the impulse of the heart

"Penance" expresses, therefore, a type of relationship with the Lord, a way of seeing the world as a turning toward God-Love, a particular way of achieving evangelical perfection. These are spiritual moments of a more intense conversion to God by means of conformity to Christ who is the only way to draw near to the Father. (See John 14:6.)

Penance is like a fulcrum on which rests the entire organism of the supernatural life, it is a concept that confers a characteristic tonality and a special dynamism to the development of the spirit. It shapes and draws to itself the

---

[11]By the term the "discipline" in the context of bodily mortification is understood a traditional "implement of penance ordinarily consisting in a complex of cords or chains, small or large, plain or ending with little pellets or bars of hard substances (wood or metal), used to chastise the body with scourging." A. Lanz, *Disicplina*, in *Enciclopedia Cattolica*, IV, col. 1743.

[12]For the biblical and Franciscan meaning of "penance," see further details in R. Pazzelli, *Saint Francis and the Third Order*, op. cit., pp. 1-4.

principles and means of Christian perfection, nourishing a continuous turning toward God who is seen as love and sought out of love.

This profound orientation, that arises from a definite decision to seek God, guarantees the basic idea of the Primacy of the Spirit: it animates progress in the spiritual life and stimulates its dynamism, it constantly keeps awake enthusiasm, nourishes commitment and influences all the moments of existence that involve the body, the psyche, the mind, and the will. Consequently, the penitential life does not originate in the fear of divine punishment, nor is it motivated by the will to expiate faults or even principally to obtain eternal blessedness, but by its attraction towards God who is presented as the highest Good and the mystery of love.

The external forms of penance, fasts, sacrifices, mortifications, prayer, vigils, are none other than partial and secondary expressions of an intimate conversion of the heart which implies the supremacy of the spirit, tending toward God, and the consequent avoidance of every form of evil.

Following the penitential spirituality, the Friars and Sisters of the Third Order of Saint Francis, called for centuries "the Franciscan Order of Penance," have their own style of life, their own way of evaluating things, or of reacting to happy or sorrowful events, and of defining their human life. They have their own way of putting themselves before the eternal, of specifying their hopes. In other words, they have their own view of earthly things which they look upon with admiration and detachment; they are optimistic and happy in the Lord, generously involved in giving testimony to the love that God has for His creatures; they are available to their brothers and sisters, full of faith in Providence.

From this style of spiritual life, centered on penance, flow all the elements of sanctification as so many corollaries that orbit around the vital and impelling idea: an unceasing conversion to the living God (Acts 14,14).[13]

b) *The life of active charity*

From the above statements there is enough evidence to show that charity and availability to the brothers and sisters are corollaries or natural consequences of an interior conversion deeply lived. A life of active charity is the life of penance achieved . "Remain in my love" (John 15:9). Scripture says clearly: "Whoever does not love the brother or sister whom he can see, cannot love God whom he has not seen" (1 John 4:20)."Penance that is born of a more intense love of God," Temperini continues,

> projects itself in daily reality and embraces all the necessities of our brothers and sisters, be they spiritual or material.
>
> In the spirit of Saint Francis, the brothers and sisters of penance have renewed that fraternal love which characterized the first Christians.

emarginated, the illiterate in missionary countries, the afflicted or those suffering in body or spirit have always been the ones beloved by the Friars and Sisters of the Third Order of Saint Francis.

> Together with the penitential spirituality, charitable service (of the works of mercy) is to be considered a characteristic of the life of the Tertiary Regulars. A life full of God, in a continuous state of conversion to Him, cannot help but overflow in active love for those in need. The concrete sign of conversion in Saint Francis was his embrace of the leper, his attention to the poor, the humble, the suffering, to men without God, and to those thirsting for truth and peace.[14]

---

[13]L. Temperini, *La tradizione spirituale*, in R. Pazzelli-L. Temperini, *La tradizione storica e spirituale del nostro movimento*, CSI-TOR, Roma, 1980, pp. 22-23.

[14]*Ibid.*, p. 24.

3. The voice of history

a) *The life of penance*

Here we would like to take a look—a bird's eye view, of course—at those centuries that went before Francis of Assisi and those centuries which followed his life to show that the primary element, "conversion," is clearly present from the beginning of the penitential movement. Before the fourth century in the East there were the forerunners of that way of life which would later be called the penitential movement. They were called *apotaktikoi*, a word which Cassian translated into Latin as "abrenuntiantes," those who renounce the "world." In the West these people were called "conversi": they were those who had decided upon a conversion, a more or less radical breaking with the kind of life experienced in the past, called "the world," and the making of a commitment, often public, to live "penance," a new kind of life in which God is the center of one's existence. This life of penance began by entering in a practical way into one of the many forms of the life of penance which had developed in many different ways according to circumstances from the time of the fourth century and later.

The very concept of "conversion" tells us that the purpose of such a decision was to make God the reference point and the aim of one's own life: a highly spiritual goal.

Theologically, *conversion* was considered a gift of God and also a response on the part of a human being in the presence of divine initiative. This idea was clearly presented as early as Dionysius of Alexandria (+264 AD) and we again find the idea unchanged in a spiritual treatise of the twelfth century, the *Book of Penance* by the Anonymous Benedictine of the Twelfth Century. "When there is the return to God (*poenitentia*), there is also pardon. The grace of conversion (*poenitentia*) comes to the sinner from God, from whom also comes pardon. Thus each time God grants the grace of conversion, He also gives pardon."[15]

In the seventh century, Saint Isidore of Seville, Bishop of that city from 601 to 636, speaking of penance and the meaning of "conversion of the heart," emphasizes and

---

[15]See Pazzelli, *Saint Francis and the Third Order*, *op. cit.*, p. 37.

explains the interior dimension which should make of penance a Christian "way of life." Saint Isidore clearly teaches that penance is not only an act or a rite; nor is it a temporary internal disposition. It is and should remain a constant disposition of the religious spirit, a permanent consecration to a new style of life, interior as well as exterior, but most of all interior. "One could say," writes Bartolomeo Pastor Oliver, who has the merit of having brought to light this text,

> that Saint Isidore presents a complete psychology and a pastoral outline of conversion. The noblest aspect of this is the penitent's intention to uproot from the soul that type of complacency which could invade it after repentance.... He, therefore, insists upon those constructive and mystical aspects of perfect sorrow which focus one's entire interior attention upon the contemplation of God and sighs with desire for eternal life in Him.[16]

the penitential life.

This element of deep interiority, neglected or perhaps even forgotten in the movement itself, forgotten in the Order of Penance at the time of Saint Francis, was "rediscovered" and lived and taught by Saint Francis insistently and in great detail to his penitents.[17]

b) *The works of mercy or active charity*

The other essential element of the charism of penance is active charity. It grows, in a systematic way very slowly through the centuries, at least according to our present knowledge of penitential documentation. It follows the development of society in its practical manifestations. In this growth, there were always in the past as there are now in the present, those who suffer or have need of assistance: it is indeed to these practical needs of mankind that

---

[16]Pazzelli, *op. cit.*, p. 18; indicating reference to original article Bartolmé Pastor Oliver, TOR, *Consideraciones historico-espirituales sobre algunas expresiones de Penitencia voluntaria y de "conversio"-"abrenuntiatio" monástica hasta el siglo XIII*, Vienna, 1981, manuscript, p. 52.

[17]On this question see the detailed treatment we have given in *St. Francis and the Third Order*, *op. cit.*, pp. 65, 120-122.

the penitential movement has always sought to bring succor by following the teachings of the great masters of the ages.

The most complete text concerning penitential teaching on this subject which has come down to us is from the tenth century. But this is not to say that it is the most ancient. It comes to us from Ratherius, Bishop of Verona, a remarkable personality of the high middle ages who lived exactly in that most tortured century in the two thousand year history of the Church which is rightly called the "dark century." Ratherius lived from 887 to 974. A monk of the Abbey of Lobbes, a disciple of the great teacher Ilduin, Ratherius was elected Bishop of Verona in 926. A strong personality with ideas of reform, he was not capable of compromises and he was impatient for the realization of his plans. Soon he lost favor with Hugh of Provenza, the first king of Italy. Hugh imprisoned Ratherius in a tower in Pavia. There Ratherius composed his most important work, the *Praeloquiorum libri sex*. In this work he gives spiritual counsel to people of every state in life, and among them the penitents.

It will be helpful to read again his words written a thousand years ago: "Are you a penitent or do you desire to become one? Remember above all the rule of penance given by the Baptizer of the Lord: 'Produce fruits worthy of penance.' The penitent must put this into practice with generosity if he desires to obtain the mercy of the Lord." Ratherius, thereupon, gave the spiritual motive for each of the corporal and spiritual works of mercy to which the penitent should dedicate himself.[18] Thus, practically for Ratherius, "to do penance" means "to perform worthy fruits of penance," that is, perform the works of charity for one's neighbor.

Ratherius' teaching regarding perseverance in the "life of penance" is interesting and significant:

> The way of penance and perseverance in it is a difficult thing. Who can pretend to remain there by his strength alone? Invoke, then, divine help every day or rather every moment; whether in silence or in whatsoever thing you do, ask for it

[18]See Pazzelli, *op. cit.*, p. 170, note 99.

seriously of the Lord: O God, create in me a pure heart! And if You see that because of bad habits of the past it is difficult for you to remain in such a life, I beseech you, do not abandon it.

Later on, continuing with the same line of thought, Ratherius says: "It is difficult to carry a large stone uphill; it is easier to go down hill with it. Equally so, no one can be perfect from the beginning.... Attach yourself to Christ and exclaim: 'Draw me after thee' (Cant. 1:4)."

Ratherius of Verona, who died a thousand years ago, bears witness that the two elements of the penitential life, perseverance in the way of penance or continuous conversion and the works of active charity, were already considered essential in his day.

4. The two elements in the Rules

These two elements, the life of penance and the works of active charity, will form the cornerstones of the life and spirituality of the penitents and the spirituality of those

propositi, was edited in 1221 as is well known, through the collaboration of Saint Francis with Cardinal Ugolino. In n. 21 it speaks of the *religious man* who will instruct the brothers and sisters at their monthly meetings. The document says: he must "exhort and strengthen them to persevere in their penance and to put into practice the works of mercy."[19]

This admonition will be repeated almost literally in the Rule of Nicholas IV in 1289, where it says: "They shall take care to have a religious man...who will exhort them with zeal, encourage and persuade them to live a life of penance and to put into practice the works of mercy."[20]

This text of the Rule of Nicholas IV remained legally in force also for those female associations of Franciscan inspiration whose sisters began to live a community life and more correctly the religious life, at least until 1521

---

[19]"Eos moneat et confortet ad poenitentiae perseverantiam et opera misericordiae facienda." cf. Meersseman, Dossier, p. 103.

[20]"Qui eos ad poenitentiam et misericordiae opera exercenda hortetur sollicite, moneat et inducat." See *Seraphicae legislationis textus originales*; 1897, p. 89.

when Pope Leo X desired to give these new entities their own Rule, one more suitable for the religious life. Even the Rule of Leo X preserved those essential elements repeating almost the same expressions: "They are to have a religious man who on certain days shall proclaim the Word of God and lead them to penance and the practice of virtue."[21]

All this has been confirmed by an eminent Franciscan scholar: "These two elements, continuous penance and mercy or active charity, represent and summarize, it seems to us, the whole specific purpose of the Order of Penitents, establishing its reason for existence in the ecclesial community."[22]

These elements establishing the charism of the Third Order have remained intact through the centuries and have been automatically inserted into the many congregations of Franciscan sisters which have arisen from the time of the fifteenth century to the present. All these congregations, at times without knowing it, have been marked by the presence of the two essential elements of the charism and spirituality of the penitents who followed Saint Francis, those elements of continuous or on-going conversion and mercy or active charity, to meet both the spiritual and material needs of our neighbor, especially the most needy or abandoned, following the spirit of the Saint of Assisi. We see down through the centuries the manner of practically meeting these needs has been as vast and varied as the horizon under which this activity develops. But the substance is always the same, based on Christian charity which knows how to respond to the needs of our brothers and sisters.

The new Rule of 1982 includes the same realities, though in different terminologies: "Led by the Lord, let them begin a life of penance." (Art.6); "They wish to live this evangelical conversion of life in a spirit of prayer, poverty and humility." (Art. 2); "The brothers and sisters are called to heal the wounded, to bind up those who are bruised, and to reclaim the erring" (Art. 30).

---

[21]"Habeat virum religiosum qui illis verbum Dei certis diebus proponat et eos ad poenitentiam et virtutes inducat": *ibid.*, pp. 287-297. Bordoni, *Archivium*, p. 382.

[22]Atanasio Matanic, *I penitenti francescane dal 1221 (memoriale) al 1289 (Regola bollata) principalmente attraverso i loro Statuti e le Regole*, in *L'Ordine della Penitenza, op. cit.*, p. 56.

The way of putting this into practice is subject to change but the principles remain the same.

5. Corollary. *How penance became the characteristic of the "Brothers and Sisters of the Penance"*

If you would like to look into the historical question of how, when and why penance-conversion, as we have just described it with its constituent elements, became the principal characteristic of the Brothers and Sisters of Penance, that is of the Third Order of Saint Francis, the clarifications and precise details of the latest historical studies furnish an adequate and satisfying response.

We begin with the four principal elements which all agree go back to the constitutive nucleus of Franciscanism to which some other elements can be added: poverty, minority, penance-conversion, and prayer-contemplation.

As we have already noted, today it is beyond all dispute that the beginnings of Francis' conversion were penitential. It is likewise equally certain that right after the begin-

nity by Innocent III, there must have been verified a change of emphasis in the rapidly growing group regarding the characteristics by which the group presented itself to the people. In the primitive preaching before going to Rome, to those who asked them "where do you come from?" they "confessed with simplicity that they were penitents from Assisi."[23] Soon (we do not know exactly when) they began to call themselves "Friars Minor." Burchard of Ursberg, as early as 1210, referred to the *Penitentes de Assisio* as *Pauperes Minores*.[24] James de Vitry, in his letter from Genova in October 1216, clearly states that the "Pauperes de Assisio" were commonly called *Frati minori* and the followers of Saint Clare the *Sorelle minore*.[25]

The Rule of 1221 says: "and whoever is the greater among them should become like the younger."[26] Schmucki notes that "this passage bears all the signs of relative

---

[23]See 3 Comp. 37, OMN, p. 925; cf. AnP 19, Isabelle, *Workbook for Franciscan Studies*, p. 102.

[24]See Cf. Lemmens, *Testimonia minora*, p. 17; OMN, p. 1605.

[25]*Testimonia minora*, p. 79; OMN, p. 1608.

[26]RNB, *Francis and Clare*, p. 114.

antiquity. Most probably it was added very early to enrich the biblical and disciplinary elements of the Proto-Rule."[27] From Celano's remark in the *Vita prima* it seems that Francis was struck by the expression "they are to be minors" as soon as it was suggested and wanted it to become the actual name of his fraternity.[28]

Although Francis' understanding of "minors" is doubtlessly the evangelical one,[29] it cannot be denied that the social-political situation in Assisi, the home of the first friars had some influence on Francis, causing him to decide that his followers should be called and really be "minores" by choice. Even without any association with the *minori* of the city, Francis knew the *maggiori* and *minori* competed for control and were in constant conflict with the *one another*. The novelty was quite evident: even those who were "maggiori" in the world voluntarily became "minori" like Francis, wanting to compete with no one. "Minority" will also be the characteristic of the spirituality of the Friars Minor.

Another element characteristic of the new fraternity immediately developed—poverty—chosen for the love of God and "to follow in the footsteps of His Son."[30] From the moment he heard the gospel passage on the "mission of the apostles," which practically marked the beginning of the fraternity of itinerant preachers, Francis understood that the *vita evangelica* included life in poverty. Not that Francis had not practiced poverty since the first days of his conversion (the decision made at San Damiano and the formal renunciation of his patrimony before Bishop Guido) but now poverty became an essential element of his evangelical vocation.[31] The gospel passage showed Francis *how* and *why* he should practice poverty from

[27]Schmucki, O., *Linee fundamentali della "Forma vitae" nell'esperienza di san Francesco*, in *Lettura biblico-teologica delle Fonti Francescane*, by G. Cardaropoli-J.M. Conti, Ed., Antonianum, Roma, 1979, p. 211.

[28]"For he wrote in the rule, 'and let them be lesser brothers,' and when these words were spoken, indeed, in that same hour, he said: 'I wish that this fraternity should be called the Order of Friars Minor.'" 1 *Cel.* 38, OMN, p. 260.

[29]It is evident that the expression of the Rule of 1221 is a paraphrase of Mt. 20:25-26 and Lk. 22:26.

[30]Cf. *Letter to the entire Order*, v. 51, *Francis and Clare*, p. 61.

[31]D.V. Lapsanski, *Evangelical Perfection, an historical examination of*

then on. This very same desire to accept and put into practice the invitation and the challenge of the gospel text is equally evident in the story of the conversion of Bernard of Quintavalle, his first companion. Heeding the advice of Francis, Bernard "hastened therefore to sell all his goods and gave the money to the poor, though not to his relatives; and laying hold on the title to the way of perfection, he carried out the counsel of the holy gospel: 'If thou will be perfect, go, sell what thou hast, and give to the poor, and thou shalt have treasure in heaven: and come, follow me.'"[32]

Then follows the important remark that "his conversion to God was a model to all others who would come after him: they should sell their patrimony and distribute the money to the poor."[33]

Even the short allegorical work, the *Sacrum Commercium*,[34] considered as "the testimony of the spirituality that the Franciscan community was developing right after the death of St. Francis"[35] tells us that poverty was

the prologue on, in fact, "it affirms categorically that poverty is the most important among the various virtues that prepare the heart of man to receive God."[36]

---

the concept in the early Franciscan sources. The Franciscan Institute, St. Bonaventure University, N.Y., 1977, p. 100.

[32]1 Cel. 24, OMN, p. 248.

[33]See 1 Cel. 24, OMN, p. 249.

[34]*Sacrum Commercium Sancti Francisci cum domina Paupertatae,* Florence-Quaracchi, 1929. By an unknown author and uncertain date of origin; many scholars propose accepting 1227 as the year of its composition. Concerning this work, C. Esser noted that, "unfortunately, this precious record, which bears such eloquent witness to the spirituality of the order, still in its infancy, later underwent certain misinterpretations which earned it the mistrust of historians, mainly in regard to the time of its origin. Today, this work may be seen as a very faithful interpretation of the mind and intention of St. Francis. As such it must be carefully considered next to the sources of the early life of the order already familiar to us. In certain critical points it can even correct them." *Origins of the Franciscan Order,* Franciscan Herald Press, Chicago, 1977, p. 8.

[35]Lapsanski, *Evangelical Perfection,* pp. 77-78.

[36]Lapsanski, p. 78. Poverty, in the meaning of the anonymous author of the *Sacrum Commercium,* requires as its first constructive element "freely renouncing earthly goods." The second element is the inclination toward spiritual goods and the third "the desire for eternal goods."

These two elements—minority and sublime poverty—also became the two basic points for the spirituality of the Second Order, the Poor Clares; to these elements was added, mostly because of the ecclesiastical disciplines in force at that time, the total exclusion from the world, with a strict cloister and without any external apostolic activity; in this way the order was also characterized by the contemplative life.

Consequently, it was "penance" that remained the primary characteristic of only the Order of the Brothers and Sisters of Penance.

For centuries these characteristics and particular traits of the three Franciscan Orders have been practically forgotten. In our own time they have gradually been rediscovered, explained again and placed in a proper perspective so that there might be fuller understanding of Franciscan spirituality. It is fitting and proper that each order have its own features well defined.

These are reflections on that unique, mysterious light that was the man and Saint, Francis of Assisi, as Raoul Manselli, well-known lover of all that is Franciscan, loves to repeat again and again.

PONTIFICAL DOCUMENTS[1]

Date	Document	Pope
1226, January 30	*Ut vivendi normam*, l	Honorius III
1234, November 21	*Ut cum maiori*, l	Gregory IX
1253, August 26	*Excelsi dextera*, b	Innocent IV
1254, November 21	*Etsi animarum*, b	Innocent IV
1295, July 11	*Cupientes cultum*, l	Boniface VIII
1298	*Periculoso ac dete stabili*, d	Boniface VIII
1304, February 11	*Dum levamus*, b	Benedict XI
1317, December 30	*Sancta Romana*, b	John XXII
1318, January 23	*Gloriosam ecclesiam*, b	John XXII
1319, February 23	*Etsi Apostolicae Sedis*, b	John XXII
1320, April 8	*Dudum dilectis*, l	John XXII
1323, November 18	*Altissimo in divinis*, l	John XXII
1403, January 14	*Provenit ex vestrae devotionis*, b	Boniface IX
1413, August 26	*Personas vacantes*, b	John XXIII
1428, August 19	*Sacrae religionis*, b	Martin V
1428, December 9	*Licet inter coetera*, b	Martin V
1430, June 19	*Ex Apostolicae Sedis*, b	Martin V
1430, July 27	*Pervigilis more*, l	Martin V
1431, November 15	*Ad apostolicae dignitatis*, b	Eugene IV
1436, March 2	*Ad ea ex Apsotolicae Sedis*, b	Eugene IV
1436, March 2	*Aeternae beatitudinis*, b	Eugene IV

---

[1]b=bull; br=brief; c=constitution; d=decree; l=letter; m=moto proprio.

1440, May 2	*Apostolicae Sedis providentia*, b	Eugene IV
1447, February 5	*Ordinis tui*, b	Eugene IV
1447, April 1	*Vestrae devotionis*, b	Nicholas V
1447, July 20	*Pastoralis officii*, b	Nicholas V
1449, September 18	*Romanus pontifex*, b	Nicholas V
1458, December 29	*Speciali gratia et favore*, b	Pius II
1461, December 3	*Ut tollatur discursus*, b	Pius II
1465, September 14	*Devotionis et sinceritatis*, b	Paul II
1468, May 26	*Excitat arcanum*, b	Paul II
1471, December 15	*Romani pontificis*, b	Sixtus IV
1473, November 17	*Decet Apostolicam*	
...	...per ..., b	Sixtus IV
1477, October 16	*Ex apostolicae servitutis*, b	Sixtus IV
1480, November 24	*Ad Christi Vicarii*, b	Sixtus IV
1482, September 24	*Exponi nobis fecistis*, b	Sixtus IV
1482, December 16	*Quanto contentiones*, l	Sixtus IV
1483, September 15	*Intelleximus quod longo*, l	Sixtus IV
1507, October 15	*Exponi nobis fecistis*, b	Julius II
1508, February 8	*Romani pontificis*, b	Julius II
1509, January 7	*Exponi nobis fecistis*, b	Julius II
1517, August 31	*Ea quae per Sedem Apostolicam*, b	Leo X
1521, January 20	*Inter coetera nostri regiminis*, b	Leo X

1527, March 10	*Ad uberes frustuc*, b	Clement VII
1553, October 11	*Cum sicut accepimus*, l	Julius III
1566, May 29	*Circa pastoralis*, c	Pius V
1567, April 16	*Superioribus mensibus*, b	Pius V
1568, July 3	*Ea est officii nostri ratio*, b	Pius V
1570, January 24	*Decori ac honestati*, b	Pius V
1572, December 30	*Deo sacris virginibus*, b	Gregory XIII
1586, March 29	*Romani pontificis providentia*, b	Sixtus V
1631, January 13	*Pastoralis romani pontificis*, b	Urban VIII
1749, April 30	*Quamvis justo*, b	Benedict XIV
1900, December 8	*Conditae a Christo*, c	Leo XIII
1906, July 16	*Dei Providentis*, m	Pius X
1908, June 29	*Sapienti consilio*, c	Pius X
1927, October 4	*Rerum condicio*, c	Pius XI
1982, December 8	*Franciscanum vitae propositum*, br	John Paul II

BIBLIOGRAPHY

ALESSANDRINI, A, *Angelina da Montegiove*, in *Dizionario Biografico degli Italiani*, III, Roma 1984.

ANDREOZZI, G. *San Rocco in Montefalco, La "Porziuncola" del Terz'ordine regolare*, in "Analecta TOR," IV (1945-1947), pp. 208-221.

BARRUEL, *Storia del clero in tempo della Rivoluzione francese*, translated from the French by Giulio Alvisini, Roma 1974.

BARSOTTI, S., *Un fiore serafico. Il Beato Giovanni Cini*, Quaracchi 1906.

BARTOLI, M., *Francescanesimo e mondo femminile nel XIII secolo.* in *Francesco, il Francescanesimo e la cultura della nuova Europa*, Istituto della Enciclopedia Italiana, Roma 1986, pp. 167-180.

BARTOLI, LANGELI A., *I Penitenti a Spoleto nel Duecento*, in *L'Ordine della Penitenza*, pp. 303-330.

BASTIEN, P., *Directoire à l'usage des Congregations a voeux simples d'après les plus recent documents du Saint Siège*, Roma, 1911.

BEGGIAO, D., *La visita Pastorale di Clement VIII (1582-1600)*, Roma, 1978.

BIHL, M., OFM, *De Tertio Ordini Sancti Francisci in Provincia Germaniae Superioris sive Argentinensis syntagma*, in AFH 14 (1921), pp. 138-198; 442-460.

BIZZARI, A., *Collectanea in usum Secretariae Sacrae Congregationis Episcoporum et Regularium*, Romae, 1863.

BOAGA, E., *Aspetti e problemi degli Ordini e Congregazioni religiose nei secoli XVII e XVIII*, in *Problemi di Storia della Chiesa nei secoli XVII-XVIII*, Dehoniane, Napoli 1982, pp. 91-135.

BOAGA, E., *La soppressione innocenziana dei piccoli conventi in Italia*, Roma 1971.

BONI, A., *Gli Istituti religiosi e la loro potestà di governo (c. 607/c.596)*, Ed. Antonianum, Roma, 1989.

CICALESE, A., *Note e appunti sui monasteri di Napoli tra il Cinquecento e l'Ottocento*, in *Campania sacra*, 1972.

COLAGIOVANNI, EMILIO, *Religiose italiane. Ricerca sociografica*, Roma, USMI, 1976.

CREYTENS, R., *La riforma dei monasteri femminili dopo i decreti tridentini*, in *Il Concilio di Trento e la riforma tridentina*, Atti del Convegno storico internazionale (Trento 2-6 settembre 1963), Roma 1965, pp 45-84.

DAL PINO, F. A., *I Frati Servi di S. Maria dalle origini all'approvazione (1233ca-1304)* Louvain 1972.

DE GUBERNATIS, D., *Orbis Seraphicus, Historia de tribus Ordinibus a seraphico Patriarca Sancto Francisco institutis*, Romae-Lugduni 1682-1685.

DEL RE, N., *Chiara da Montefalco, santa*, in *Bibliotheca Sanctorum*, III, coll. 1217-1222.

FANFANI, L., *Il diritto delle religiose conforme al codice di diritto canonico*, Torino 1922.

FANTOZZI MICALI O., ROSELLI, P., *Le soppressioni dei conventi a Firenze. Riuso e trasformazione dal secolo XVIII in poi*, Firenze 1980.

FERNANDEZ, A. J., *Spagna, Martiri della guerra di___*, *Bibliotheca Sanctorum*, Prima Appendice, 1987, coll. 1291-

Napoli 1920.

FERRERES, J. B., *Las Religiosas segùn la disciplina del nuevo Còdigo de derecho canonico. 1920*.

FILANNINO, A., *Il monastero di Sant'Anna nell'età moderna e contemporanea*, in *La Beata Angelina*, pp. 221-315.

Francescani in Italia Annuario, coordinatore Umberto Sciamé, Movimento francescano, 1986.

FRASCADORE, E., *Elisabetta d'Ungheria, santa*, in DIP, *III*, *coll. 1114-1115-*

FRASCADORE, E., *Elisabettine, Suore*, in DIP, III, coll. 1114-1115.

FRASCADORE, E., *Francescane, Suore*, in DIP, IV, coll. 182-216

FRASCADORE, E.-ODOARDI, G., *Francescane, monache*, in DIP, IV, coll. 174-182.

FRIEDBERG, AEMILIUS, *Corpus Juris Canonici*, Lipsiensis secunda, pars secunda, *Decretalium Collectiones*, Graz 1959.

GALUZZI, ALESSANDRO, *La vita religiosa in Italia dopo il concilio di Trento*, in *Problemi di storia della Chiesa nei secoli XV-XVI*, Dehoniani, Napoli 1979, pp. 201-222.

GAMBARI, E., *Congregazione religiosa*, in DIP, II, coll. 1560-1568.

GAMBARI, Æ., *Institutorum Saecularium et Congregationum Religiosarum evolutio comparata*, in "Commentarium pro Religiosis et Missionariis" 29 (1950), pp. 224-280.

GASPARRI, PETRUS CARD., *Codicis Juris Canonici Fontes*, vol. III, Romae 1925.

GHILARDI G, *Difesa delle corporazioni religiose*, Torino 1864.

HULST (VAN), C., *Penitenti recollettine, in Limburgo*, in DIP, VI, coll. 1371-1381.

INI, A. M., *Nuovi documenti sugli Spirituali di Toscana*, in AFH 66 (1973), pp. 305-377.

IRIATE, L., *Franciscan History*, Franciscan Herald Press, Chicago 1983.

IVANCIC, S., *Cronologium seu Historica Monumenta Tertii Ordinis Regularis de Poenitentia S. Francisci*, Editio Assisiensis, cura R. Pazzelli, anno 1957 exarata.

JACOBILLI, L., *Vita della Beata Angelina da Corbara, contessa di Civitella, institutrice delle monache claustrali del Terz'ordine di san Francesco e fondatrice in Foligno del monastero di Sant'Anna primo delli sedici che ella eresse in diverse province*, Foligno, Altieri 1627.

JEDIN, H., *Storia della Chiesa*, vol. VI, *Riforma e Controriforma* vol. VII, *La Chiesa nell'epoca dell'assolutismo e dell' illuminismo*, Jaca Book, Milano 1975.

JEMOLO, A. C., *Scritti vari di storia religiosa e civile*, Milano 1965.

LA PUMA, *Evoluzione del diritto dei religiosi da Pio IX a Pio XI*, in *Acta congressus iuridici internationalis 4*, Roma 1937.

LARACCA, I. M., *Il patrimonio degli Ordini religiosi in Italia. Soppressione e incameramento dei loro beni (1848-1873)* Roma 1936.

LECLERCQ, J., *Clausura in Oriente e occidente*, in DIP, II, coll. 1166-1174.

LEDÓCHOWSKA, T., *Conservatorio*, in DIP, II, coll. 1627-1629.

LEFLON, J., *La crisi rivoluzionaria (1789-1815)*, in vol. XX/1 di *Storia della Chiesa* di A. Fliche-V. Martin, Torino 0000.

LEMAITRE, H., *Statuts des Religieuses du Tiers Ordre Franciscain dites Soeurs Grises Hospitalières (1483)* in AFH 4 (1911), PP. 713-731.

LEMOINE, R., *Le droit des Religieux. Du Concile de Trent aux Instituts séculiers*, Bruges 1956.

LESAGE, G., *L'accession des congregations à l'état religieux canonique*, Ottawa 1952.

LORTZ, J., *Storia della Chiesa considerata in prospettiva di storia delle idee*, vol. II, *Evo moderno*, Paoline, Milano 1973.

MAGNINO, R., *Alle origini della crisi contemporanea. Illuminismo e Rivoluzione*, Raggio, Roma 1946.

MAINKA, R., *I movimenti per la Chiesa povera nel XII secolo*, in AA. VV., *La povertà religiosa*, Clarentianum, Roma 1975, pp. 141-155.

MANSELLI R Santità

Marchitelli, E., *Le Suore Francescane Alcantarine ieri e oggi*, Marietti, Torino 1981.

MARIANO D'ALATRI, *Leggenda della Beata Angelina da Montegiove. Genesi di una biografia*, in *La Beata Angelina*, pp. 33-46.

MATANIĆ, A., *Il "Defensorium Tertii Ordinis beati Francisci" di san Giovanni da Capestrano*, in *Il movimento francescano*, pp. 47-57.

MATANIĆ, A., *San Giovanni da Capestrano e la vita comunitaria dei Penitenti francescani*, in *Prime manifestazioni*, pp. 81-90.

MENESTÒ, E., *I processi per la canonizzazione di Chiara da Montefalco a proposito della documentazione trecentesca ritrovata*, Montefalco 1983.

MENESTÒ, E., *Le Penitenti Lucrezie*, in *La Beata Angelina*, pp. 357-419.

MENS, ALCANTARA, *Beghine e Begardi, Beghinaggi*, in DIP, I, coll. 1165-1180.

MENS, ALCANTARA, *Beghine e Begardi*, in EC, II, coll. 1143-1148.

MONJAUX, N., *Les Religieuses franciscaines*, Paris 1897.

MONTICONE, A., L'applicazione del concilio di Trento a Roma. I "riformatori" e l'Oratorio (1566-1572), in "Rivista di storia della Chiesa in Italia," VIII (1954), pp. 23-48.

MUZZARELLI, F., Tractatus canonicus de Congregationibus iuris dioecesani, Romae 1943.

MUZZITELLI, G., *Raccolta di alcuni recenti decreti riguardanti gli ordini religiosi*, Roma 1916.

NESSI, S., *Santa Chiara da Montefalco e il Francescanesimo*, in "Miscellanea Francescana" 69 (1969), pp. 369-408.

PASCHINI, P., *I monasteri femminili in Italia nel Cinquecento*, in *Problemi di vita religiosa in Italia nel Cinquecento*. Atti del Convegno di Storia della Chiesa in Italia (Bologna, 2-6 Settembre 1958), Padova 1960, pp. 31-60.

PASZTOR, E., *Elisabetta d'Ungheria, langravia di Turingia, santa*, in *Bibliotheca Sanctorum*, IV, coll. 1110-1121.

PAZZELLI, R., The Rule and Life of the Brothers and Sisters of the Third Order Regular of Saint Francis, a Commentary, translated from the Italian by Nancy Celaski, O.S.F., IFC, Rome 1991.

PAZZELLI, R., *St. Francis and the Third Order*, Franciscan Herald Press, Chicago 1989.

PAZZELLI, R., *Il Terz'ordiine regolare di San Francesco attraverso i secoli*, Roma 1958.

PAZZELLI, R., *La personalità di Giovannni XXII e la Bolla "Altissimo in divinis" del 18 novembre 1323*, in *Prime manifestazioni*, pp. 39-65.

PAZZELLI, R., *San Francesco e il Terz'ordine. Il movimento penitenziale pre-francescano e francescano*, Messagero, Padova 1983.

PAZZELLI, R., E TEMPERINI, L., *La tradizione storica e spirituale del nostro movimento*, CSI-TOR, Roma 1980.

PÉANO, P., *The Franciscan Sisters, origins, history and constant values, from Le Religiose Francescane, Origini, storia e valori costanti revised and completed by Jean de Schampheleer, O.F.M. and Jean-François Godet*, Movimento francescano, Roma 1983. Unpublished manuscript translated from the Italian by Aidan Mullaney, T.O.R., Steubenville 1991.

PÉANO, P., *Manifestations de la vie en commun parmi les Tertiaires franciscains de la France méridionale*, in *Prime manifestazioni, pp. 113-131.*

PIERGILI, B., *Vita della B. Chiara detta della Croce da Montefalco*, Foligno 1663.

PRÉCLIN, E.-JARRY, E., *Le lotte politiche e dottrinali nei secoli XVII e XVIII (1648-1789)*, in vol XIX Fliche-Martin, Torino 1976.

RINIERI, I., *Il Congresso di Vienna e la Santa Sede (1813-1815)*, Roma 1904.

ROSA, M., *Per la storia della vita religiosa della Chiesa in Italia tra il Cinquecento e il Seicento*, Studi recenti e questioni di metodo.

RUSSO, CARLA, *I monasteri femminili di clausura a Napoli nel secolo XVII*, Napoli 1970.

SCIROCCO, A., *Governo e Paese nel Mezzogiorno nella crisi dell'Unificazione*, Milano 1963.

SENSI, M., *Documenti per la Beata Angelina da Montegiove in* "Picenum Seraphicum" XI (1974), pp. 315-404.

SENSI, M., *Il movimento francescano della Penitenza a Foligno*, in *Il movimento francescano*, pp. 399-445.

SICARD, I., *La riforma de los religiosos intendada por Clemente VIII (1592-1605)*, Bogota 1954.

TEMPERINI, L., *La spiritualità penitenziale nelle Fonti Francescane*, in "Analecta TOR" XIV (1980), pl. 543-588.

TORRES, J., *Approvazione delle Religioni*, in DIP, I, coll. 765-773.

VERNET, F., *Béghards, béguines hétérodoxes, I. Histoire, II. Doctrines*, in DTC, II/1, coll. 578-535.

WADDING, L., *Annales Minorum*, ad Claras Aquas (Quaracchi), 1932ss.

WILLAERT, L., *La restaurazione cattolica dopo il concilio di Trento*, (1563-1648), in vol. XVIII di *Storia della Chiesa* di A. Fliche, - V. Martin, SAIE, Torino 1976.

INDEX OF PERSONS AND PLACES[1]

Aachen (Aquisgrana), 123
Aalst (Limbourg), 88
Achille, G., 186
Alassio (SV), 189
Alessandra of Montegiove,
    (mother of Blessed
    Angelina), 64
Alessandrini, A., 65, 68, 221
Alexander IV, Pope, 12-14
Alvisini, G., 137, 147
Amedeus of Silva, b., *ofmc*,
    91-92
Amelia, 177
Amigò y Ferrer, Luis, 171
Ancona, *mon.* of Santa Maria,
    84
Andrea of Fingisone, *min.*, 35
Andrea Franceschini, *tor*, of
    Milan, 79
Andrea of Perugia, *min.*, 34
Andreozzi, G., *tor*, 16, 36, 221
Andrew II, King of Hungary,
    (father of St. Elizabeth), 18
Angela of Foligno, *St.*, *pen.*, 23,
    35
Angela Maria del Giglio,
    (Sister), 129
Angela Merici, *St.*, 118
Angelina of Montegiove, *b.*, *tor*,
    xiii, 46, 63, 64, 67, 68,
    70-77, 80, 82, 83, 88, 90,
    176
Anonymus Benedictus of the
    XII Century, 207

Anthony (*Bis.* of Todi), 76
Anthony of Padua, *St.*, *min.*, 24
Antonio of Tablada, *tor*, 105
Antonio of Massa Marittima,
    min., 69
Anzio, 177
Aquila, see L'Aquila
Arenas, (Avila), 164
Arras, 56, 59, 121
Ascoli Piceno, 129, 203;
    mon. of Santa Margarita, 66,
    76, 84
Assisi, 3, 66, 69, 79, 129, 130,
    177, 184, 185, 187, 188,
    194, 201, 203, 211, 212,
    213; *conv.* of San Damiano,
    213; *mon.* of San Quirico,
    66, 76, 84
Augusta, city of, 54
Augustine, *St.*, *Rule of*, 9, 13,
    14, 24, 25, 29, 30, 32, 33,
    34, 109
Augustine of Stroncone, *min.*,
    83

Bachmann, Mother Mary
    Francis, 151-153
Bale, 44
Bardou, Joseph, 167
Barruel, 137, 147, 221
Barsotti, B., 47, 221
Bartoli, M., 7, 221
Bartoli Langeli, A., 23-25, 29,
    221

[1]Numbers indicate the pages where the subject is treated in some detail. Abbreviations used, *ab.*=abbey; *b.*=blessed; *cap.*=Friar Minor Capuchin; *card.*=cardinal; *conv.*=convent; *emp.*=emperor; *min.*=Friar Minor (until 1517); *mon.*=monastery; *obs.*=Friar Minor of the Observance; *ofmc*=Friar Minor Conventual; *op*=Dominican; *pen.*=penitent or belonging to the Order of Penance; *rec.*=Recollect; *St.*=Saint; *tof*=Third Order Franciscan; *tor*=Third Order Regular; *bis.*=bishop; *vic.*=vicar.

Bartolomeo Baro, *pen.*, 16
Bartolomeo de Benamatis of
    Perugia, *tor, 75, 79, 80*
Basel, 50
Basil, *St.*, Rule of, 109
Bastien, P., 221
Battista of Montefalcone, *min.*,
    91
Beauharnais, Josephine
    (spouse of Napoleon
    Bonaparte), 139
Beck, B., *ofm*, 186
Bédrune, Leon, *ofm*, 202
Beghard (s), 7, 30, 42-44, 47,
    48, 50
Beggiao, D., 221
Beguine, 7, 9-11, 25-27, 40,
    41-44, 47-50, 54, 108, 111
Benedict of Norcia, *St.*, Rule of,

Benedict XIV, Pope, 122, 128;
    Quamvis iusto, 122, 128
Benozzo, Gozzoli, *art.*, 36
Berengario of Sant'Africano,
    (*vic.* of the *Bis.* of Spoletto),
    31, 35-37
Berger, Mother Mary Odilia,
    164-165
Bergues, *St.* Winoc, 56
Bernardine of Portogruaro,
    ofm, 176
Bernard of Quintavalle,
    min., 214
Bernardone, Peter, (father of
    St. Francis), 201
Besançon, 50
Bevagna, 35
Bihl, M., *ofm*, 25, 55, 221
Bindo, called Binolo (grand-
    father of *b.* Angelina), 64

Binolo, see Bindo
Bittrich, Haus, 39
Bittrich, Enrico, 39
Bizzarri, A., 142, 221
Blato (Yugoslavia), 178
Boaga, E., 119, 120, 126, 127,
    221
Bolzano-Bozen, 131
Bonaparte, Napoleon, *emp.*,
    133, 138, 139, 140, 141,
    147
Bonaventure of Bagnoregio,
    St., min., 201
Boni, A., *ofm*, 9, 221
Boniface VIII, Pope, 12, 38, 39,
    83; *Cuientes cultum,* 38;
    Periculoso ac detestabili, 29,
    41, 99, 100, 109
Boniface IX, Pope, 66; *Provenit*

Bordoni, F., *tor,* 59, 79, 85, 96,
    107, 211
Borgo a Mozzano, 123
Borromee of Nancy, 119
Boudinhon (*Msgr.*), 174
Burchard of Ursberg, 212
Brescia, 178
Bressanone, 130-132
Brettinesi, 12
Brincat, de, Virginia, see
    Virginia of Brincat
Brothers of Penance of Jesus,
    12, 13, 15
Brothers of the Free Spirit, 43
Brussels, 88, 189, 190

Caesarius of Aries, *St.*, 40
Cairo, 156
Calais, 61
Caldaro-Kaltern, 131
Calliari, P., 172

Cambrai, 56, 59, 88
Canal, Angelica, *tof,* 177
Capistrano, John, *St.,* 75, 81
Cardaropoli, G., *ofm,* 213
Carignano, Mary Bernadette, *tof,* 177
Carmelites, 11, 12, 15
Carney, Margaret (Sister), x, xii, 188
Carniglia (*Msgr.*), 111
Caroline Augusta, (Empress of Austria), 136
Cassian, G., 207
Castellammare of Stabia, 162, 163
Cavallari, A., (*Card.* Archbishop of Venice), 177
Cecca of Burgaro (Sister), 67
Cecilia of San Giovanni in Todi (Sister), 76
Celano, see Thomas of Celano
Chappotin, (de) Helene (Mother Mary of the Passion), 16
Charles III di Durazzo, (King of Naples), 64
Cicalese, A., 221
Ciria, C., 186
Ciruzzi, I., 18
Civitella del Tronto, 65
Clare of Assisi, *St.,* xi, 1, 24, 32-34, 36, 40, 81, 212; Rule of, 1, 2, 32, 55, 81, 82, 94, 99, 109, 110
Clare of Montefalco, *St.,* 30-37
Clare of Rimini, *pen.,* 36
Clare (Sister) of Santa Margherita in Ascoli, 76
Clarians, 78, 79, 80, 85, 87
Clement V, Pope, 47-49
Clement VII, Pope, 105-106; *Ad uberes fructus,* 105-106
Clement VIII, Pope, 175

Clement IX, Pope, 118
Clement Wencelaus, see Wencelaus, C.
Coimbatore, 167
Colagiovanni, E., 221
Colloredo, Girolamo, (*Bis.* of Salisburg), 135
Colmar, 44
Cologne, 88, 123
Colonna, Giacomo, (James), *card.,* 24, 31, 35
Colonna, Peter, *card.,* 31
Compostella, 73, 105
Consalvi, Ercole, *card.,* 140
Conrad of Marburg, 18-20
Conrad of Tubigen, (*Bis.* of Toul), 25
Conti, M., *ofm,* 213
Conventuals, 1, 80, 85, 86, 104, 130, 202
Corfù, 172
Cremona, 105
Creytens, R., 109-112, 114, 115, 222
Crohin, Jean, *min.,* 60
Cuesta y Nozal, L., 186
Cusack, Roberta (Sister), 186

Dal Pino, F.A., 11-15, 222
d'Alatri, Mariano *cap.,* 61, 62, 64, 65, 171, 202, 203, 224
Dames, English, 121-123, 128
Daughters of the Blessed Virgin, 119
Daughters of the Cross, 119
Daughters of the Presentation, 119
Degenhard, (*Bis.* of Augusta), 54
De Gubernatis, D., *ofm,* 70, 103-105, 222
della Pietra, M.T., 196

Delor, E., 186
Del Re, N., 30, 222
Dendooven, Louise, *fmm*, 186
Diacono, Joseph, 172
Diderot, D., 136
Dilligen, 7, 54
Diogenes, see Dionysius
Dionysius of Alexandria, 207
di Paolo, Elena, of Spoleto,
    pen., 24
Discalced Friars, 115
Dixmude, 56
Douceline of Digne, *b.*, 13
D'Souza, Y., 196
Dubrovnik, 178
Dufault, Alma, *fmm*, 186, 196
Dunkirk, 58
Durante, (*musician*), 126
Duren, 124

Fanfani, L., 198, 222
Fantozzi, Micali O. Roselli, 222
Ferentino (France), 156;
    mon. of St. Clare of Charity,
    156
Fernandes, Alonzo J., 182, 222
Ferrandina, A., 222
Ferrari, Paula, 177
Ferreres, J.B., 173, 174, 222
Fiandina of Corbara (grand-
    mother of *b.* Angeline), 64
Filannino, A., 82-84, 89, 91,
    101, 102, 176, 222
Fliche-Martin, 121, 224, 226
Florence, 14, 16, 105, 151;
    house of "La Fantina," 151;
    mon. of Sant'Onofrio (St.
    Hubert's), 66, 76, 84
Foligno, 30, 63, 65, 67, 70, 77,

Egger, Adriano, 132
Eisenach, 18, 19
Elena di Paolo of Spoleto, *pen.*,
    24
Elias (prophet), 11
Elizabeth of Hungary (or
    Thuringia), *St., pen.*, xii,
    18-21, 53, 123
Elsear de Dombes, *tor*, 28
Emilio Alfieri of Asti, *min.*, 65
Esser, Cajaetan, *ofm*, 181, 214
Eugene IV, Pope, 72, 74-77,
    81-83; *Ad apostalicae digni-*
    tatis, 73; *Ad ea ex*
    Apostolicae Sedis, 75;
    Aeternae beatitudinis, 75;
    Apostolicae Sedis providen-
    tia, 77; *Ordinis tui*, 81, 82,
    102
Eusebio of Pratola, *ofm*, 170

Ann, 66-68, 70, 71, 74-77,
    83, 92, 102, 113, 177
Forno, M., 122, 123
Frances Frémont de Chantal,
    St., 118
Frances, (Sister) of
    Saint'Onofrio (*St.* Hubert) in
    Florence, 76
Francesco Spineti, see Spineti,
    F.
Franciscan Sisters:
    Capuchin Sisters of the
        Holy Family, 171
    Daughters of Mercy of the
        Franciscan Third Order,
        178-179
    Daughters of St. Francis of
        Assisi, 123
    Elizabethans of Aachen, 53,
        123
    Franciscan Elizabethans,

also called Bigi, 53
Franciscan Elizabethans of
Padua, 53, 144-145
Franciscan Missionary
Sisters of Giglio of Assisi,
129-130
Franciscan Missionary
Sisters of the Immaculate
Heart of Mary, 155-157
Franciscan Missionary
Sisters of the Infant Jesus,
170-171
Franciscan Missionaries of
Mary, 166-168
Franciscan Missionaries of
Our Lady, 61-62
Franciscan Sisters of
Allegany, N.Y., 154-155
Franciscan Sisters of St.
Peter of Alcantara,
161-164
Franciscan Sisters of Christ
the King, Venice, 177-178
Franciscan Sisters of
Dilligen, 7, 54
Franciscan Sisters of the
Heart of Jesus (Franciscan
Sisters of Malta, 1889),
171-172
Franciscan Sisters of the
Immaculate Conception of
Sebenic, 124
Franciscan Sisters of
Kaufbeuren, 54-55
Franciscan Sisters of St.
Mary of the Assumption
and St. Joseph, 177-178
Franciscan Sisters of Mary,
164-166
Franciscan Sisters of
Oldenburg, Indiana, 149,
150

Franciscan Sisters of St.
Francis of Philadelphia,
151-153
Franciscan Sisters of
Rochester, 168-170
Franciscan Sisters of the
Sorrowful Mother, 117
Franciscan Teaching Sisters
of Christ the King,
157-158
Franciscan Teaching Sisters
of Hallein, 135-136
Franciscan Tertiary Sisters
of Blessed Angelina,
176-177
Franciscan Tertiary Sisters
of Bressanone, 130-132
Franciscan Tertiary Sisters
of St. Joseph, 160, 177
Grey or Hospital Sisters, 53,
55-62, 116, 119, 142
Penitent Recollect Sisters (of
Limburg), 116-117, 121,
137, 142
Poor Daughters of the Holy
Stigmata of St. Francis,
150-151, 160
School Sisters of St. Francis
of Amsteten, 136
School Sisters of St. Francis
of Christ the King,
157-158
School Sisters of St. Francis
of Vienna, 136
Francis of Assisi, St., xi, 1, 5,
8, 16-21, 23-25, 35-38, 40,
44-46, 49, 65, 81, 86, 88,
95, 107, 109, 115, 156,
180, 185, 188, 190, 193,
200-202, 206-208, 210-215
Francis, (Bis. of Spoleto), 24

231

Francis of Damiano, *min.*, (brother of St. Clare of Montefalco), 35, 36

Francis de Sales, 118

Franco Gomez of Camargo, A., 196

Frascadore, E., *ofm*, 27-28, 53, 95, 97, 114, 157, 168, 222

Fraticelli, the, 43, 45, 47, 76

Frech, M.A., 186

Frederick, II, *emp.*, 19

Friedberg, Ae., 41, 47, 222

Furnes, 56

Galasso of Naples, *min.*, 70

Galuzzi, A., 223

Gambari, E., 112, 121, 125, 128, 129, 223

Gand, 116

Gasparri, F., *card.*, 173-175, 223

Gatti, M., 25

Genova, 212

Gerald (*Bis.* of Basilea), 50

Gerard (*Bis.* of Spoleto), 24, 32, 34

Gherard of Villamagna, *pen.*, 16

Ghilardi, G., 223

Giacomo, see Jacques

Giambonnini, the, 12

Giordano, (*card. Bis.* of Albano), 69

Giovanna, see Joan

Giovanni, see John

Girault, Severin, *tor, b.*, 138

Godet, J.F., *ofm*, 187

Gozo, 172

Graz, 124, 157

Gregory XIII, Pope, 114;

Deo sacris virginibus, 114

Gregory IX, Pope, 11, 17, 18, 20; *Ut cum maiori*, (Nov. 21, 1234), 17

Gregory XI, Pope, 59

Grosseto, 12

Grottaferrata, 186-189

Guglielmo, see William

Guido II (*Bis.* of Assisi), 201, 213

Hackelmeier, Sister Teresa, 149

Hacker, E., 186

Hahn, P., 188

Hallein, 135-136

Hermans, A.M., 112, 119, 120, 125

Hermits of St. Augustine, 12,

Honorius III, Pope, 9, 11, 19; *Ut vivendi norman*, 11

Hororius IV, Pope, 15

Horgan, T., 188

Hoss, Anna-Crescenzia, *tor, b.*, 55

Houschoot, 58

Hubert of Casale (Ubertino), *min.*, 31

Hueber, Maria, 130, 131

Hugh of Digne, *min.*, 12-13

Hugh of Provenza (King of Italy), 209

Humiliati, the, 6-7

Hulst van C., 117, 142, 223

Hyères, 13

Idungo of Prufenig, 40

Ignatia (Sister), 188

Iduin, 209

Imola, 105

Ingolstadt, 26
Ini, A.M., 48, 223
Innocent, III, Pope, 212
Innocent, IV, Pope, 11, 13, 14, 86; *Etsi animarum,* 14; *Excelsi dextera,* 14
Innocent, VIII, Pope, 33
Innocent X, Pope, 175
Innsbruck, 132
Iriarte, L., *cap.,* 92, 116, 199, 223
Isidore of Seville, *St., bis.,* 207, 208
Ivanic, S., *tor,* 39, 223
Ivette de Huy, see Yvette

Jacobilli, L., 63, 65, 223
Jacopa, (mother of St. Clare of Montefalco, 36
Jacques of Vitri, *card.,* 9, 212
Jacques (Giacomo) of Gonzo, *min.,* 35
Jacques (Giacomo) of Montegiove (father of *b.* Angeline), 64
Jedin, H., 223
Jemolo, A.C., 223
Jerusalem, 11
Joan Frances (sister of St. Clare of Montefalco), 30, 36
John XXII, Pope, 43, 47, 48, 50; *Altissimo in divinis,* 45; *Dudem dilectis,* 50; *Etsi Apostolicae Sedis,* 48, 50; *Gloriosam ecclesiam,* 43; *Sancta Romana,* 43, 45, 48, 49, 74, 76, 77
John XXIII, (Pisan Pope), 55, 58; *Personas vacantes,* 55, 56
John Capistrano, see Capistrano

John Paul II, Pope, 3, 200; *Franciscanun vitae propositum,* (Rule of 1982), 2-3, 193
John of Amelio, (*Bis.* of Spoleto), 35
John of Mibuccio, *min.,* 35
John of Parma, *min.,* 13
John of Termis, (spouse of Blessed Angeline), 64
Joseph II, (*Emp.* of Austris), 134
Joseph Anthony of Persiceto, *cap.,* 180
Julius II, Pope, 97, 104; *Exponi nobis fecistis,* 1507, 103-105; *Exponi nobis fecistis,* 1509, 97, 104; *Romani pontificis providentia,* 97, 104

Kaufbeuren, 55
Keller, C., 186
Kirchmayr, R., 55
Kirnigl, Isidore, *ofm.,* 131
Kodric, M.S., 158

Lacordaire, H., 141
Ladislaus, (King of Naples), 64, 65
La Fontaine, P. (*Card.* Archbishop of Venice), 178
Lambert of Liege, 8
Lamennais, U., 141
Langeli, A. Bartoli, see Bartoli Langeli, A.
Lanz, A., 204
Lapsanski, D.V., 213, 214
La Puma, 223
L'Aquila, 190; *mon.* of St. Elizabeth, 74, 84
Laracca, I.M., 159, 160, 223

Lateran IV, Council, 9, 11, 12, 29, 34
Lateran V, Council, 94, 107
Laurenti, Camilo, *card.*, 180
Leclercq, J., 40, 41, 223
Ledòchowska, T., 126, 224
Ledré, Ch., 137
Leflon, J., 224
Lemaitre, H., 56, 58, 60, 224
Lemmens, L. *ofm*, 212
Lemoine, R., 139, 142, 146-148, 173-175, 224
Lenaerts, F., *cap.*, 186
Leo X, Pope, 2, 93, 94, 96-98, 107, 116, 124, 131, 135, 143, 156, 157, 178, 179, 180, 181, 211; *Et quae per sedem apostolicam*, 107; *Inter coetera nostri regiminis*, 171, 173, 176; *Conditae a Christo*, 149, 173, 174
Lesage, G., 224
Limbourg, reform of, 116-117, 121, 137
Lobbes, *ab.*, 209
London, 147
Lorenzoni, C. *ofmc*, 186
Lortz, J., 133, 134-139, 141, 158, 159, 224
Louis of Angiò, King of Sicily, 64
Louis IV, Landgrave of Thuringia, (spouse of St. Elizabeth of Hungary), 18, 19
Louis (Ludovico) of Casoria, *ofm*, 53
Louise of Marillac, *St.*, 118
Louvain, 10
Lucca, 123, 135

Luchernet, N.B., 188
Luconi, R., *tor*, 180
Ludivico, see Louis
Luther, Martin, 98
Luxembourg, 124, 168
Lyons, Second Council of, 12, 13, 15, 29

Macca, V., 198
Magdalenes, the, 119
Madrid, 184, 187, 188
Magnino, B., 133, 224
Magonza, 18, 19
Mainka, R., 8, 224
Maistre (De) G., 141
Malines, 114
Manage, 194
Manselli, R., 215, 224
Mantiele, 171
Marcelic, Joseph (Bis. of Ragusa, Dubrovnik), 178
Marchant, Pierre, 116
Marcheselli, Giuseppe (Joseph) A. *ofmc*, 129
Marchitelli, E., 163, 164, 224
Margaret of Cortona, *St. pen.*, 23, 35
Margaret Porete, beguine, 44
Margaret of the Sacred Heart, (Sister) (Virginia of Brincat), 172
Margaret, (Sister) of St. Ann's in Foligno, 76
Margaret, (Sister) of San Quirico in Assisi, 76
Margil, Anthony of Jesus, *obs.*, 117
Mary Clare of the Sacred Heart, (Sister) (Paula Ferrari) 177

Mary of Jesus Crucified, (Sister) (Mary Petkovic), 178
Mary Joseph of the Child Jesus, (Sister) (Barbara Micarelli), 170
Mary Louise of Jesus, (Sister) (Louise Penso), 177
Mary of the Passion, (Sister), 167
Mary of the Redemption, (Sister), 167
Maribor (Yugoslavia), 157
Marsciano (Perugia), 64, 67
Marseille, 13, 14
Martines, Somalo E., (Substitute Secretary of State), 192
Martin V, Pope, 58, 63, 68, 69, 72, 73, 76, 83, 114; *Ex Apostolicae Sedis*, 58, 71; *Licet inter coetera*, 68-70, 72; *Pervigilis more*, 69, 70; *Sacrae religionis*, 63, 67, 70, 75
Masamagrell, 171
Matanic, A., 75, 211, 224
Mattea, (Sister), *pen.*, 24
McCormack, M., 196
Meersseman, G.G., *op.*, 202, 210
Menestò, E., 31, 35, 78, 224
Mens, A., *cap.*, 7, 9, 10, 224
Micarelli, Barbara, 170-171
Micarelli, Carmela, 170
Moes, Mother Alfred, 168-169
Momigliano, A., 94
Moncla, S., 61
Monjaux, N., 83, 225
Montalembert, C., 141
Montalgo, H., 188
Montefalco (Perugia), 24, 30-32, 34-36, 75; St. Francis Church, 36
Montegabbione, (TR), 64
Monteluco of Spoleto, 25
Montero Moreno, A., 182
Monticone, A., 225
Monpellier, 13, 189
Moricone, (RM), 177
Munich, (Bavaria), 26, 39
Muzzarelli, F., 225
Muzzitelli, G., 225

Nantes, 167
Napoleon, See Bonaparte
Naples, 64, 126, 134, 162
Neerinck (de) Jeanne (Sister Johanna of Jesus), 116, 117
Nessi, S., 24, 29, 30, 34, 33, 36, 37, 225
Neumann, John St., C.SS.R., 151-153
Nicholas IV, Pope, 1, 15, 28, 34, 35, 48, 73, 80, 95; Rule of, 1, 2, 7, 25, 27-30, 46, 53, 54, 56, 65, 66, 73, 82, 94, 143-145, 210;
Nicholas V, Pope, 59, 75, 78, 79, 87; *Pastoralis officit*, 75, 78, 79, 87; *Romanus Pontifex*, 79; *Vestrae devotionis*, 59
Nieuport, 56
Noro, Agnes, (Mother), 144
Nourdin, B., 186

Oblates of the Immaculate Conception, 129
Observants, 59, 81-86, 91, 92, 100, 102, 104, 106, 117, 123, 170
Odoardi, G., *ofmc*, 3, 129
Oliger, L., *ofm*, 36

O'Neil, Sister Mary Teresa, 154-155
Onofrio (Hubert) of Montavio, *tor,* 72, 74, 75
Ootacamund (India), 167
Orsella, Monaldi, (Sister), 71
Orsini, Napoleon, *card.,* 31, 35
Otranto, 19

Pace, Pietro (Archbishop of La Valletta), 172
Padua, 144, 145, 203; house of "*B.* Angelina," 74, 144; civilian hospital, 144
Palac, B.N., 158
Palazzini, P., *card.,* 98
Pancheri, F.S., *ofmc,* 187
Papi, L., 137
Paris, 14, 44, 118, 164

187, 208
Pasztor, E., 225
Paul II, Pope, 59, 85; *Devotionis et sinceritatis,* 59; *Excitat arcanum,* 85
Pavia, 209
Pazzelli, R., *tor,* x-xiii, xv, xvi, 6, 8, 16, 17, 23, 27, 28, 43, 45, 46, 63, 69, 79, 80, 86, 87, 98, 107, 186, 201, 203, 204, 207-209, 225
Péano, P., *ofm,* xi, 3, 17, 22, 23, 27, 47, 50, 55, 57, 59, 60, 66, 85-87, 91, 106, 108, 115, 116, 135, 136, 143, 225, 226
Penso, Louise, 177
Pepoli, Gioacchino, 159
Pergolesi, G.B., (musician), 126
Perugia, 9, 30, 73, 74, 83, 90;

Church of St. Severus, 90; *mon.* of St. Agnes, 90; *mon.* of St. Anthony, 74, 84, 90
Petagna, Francis S. (*Bis.* of Castellammare de Stabia), 163
Peter of Alcantara, *St., ofm,* 163, 164
Peter Bernardone, see Bernardone
Peter of Naples, 84, 91
Peter of Simone (*vic.* of the *Bis.* of Spoleto, 32
Petkovic, Mary, 178
Pfurner, Regina, 131
Piergili, B., 32, 226
Pironio, Edward, *card.,* 192, 193
Pius II, Pope, 59, 83, 176;

176
Pius V, *St.,* Pope, 41, 98, 99-102, 112, 114, 147; *Circa pastorallis officii,* 99, 101, 102, 109-111, 114, 119, 128; *Decori et honestati,* 112, 113; *Ea est officii nostri ratio,* 106; *Superioribus mensibus,* 106
Pius VII, Pope, 130, 139, 140
Pius IX, Pope, 152
Pius X, Pope, 122, 174, 175; *Dei providentis,* 174; *Sapienti consilio,* 175
Pius XI, Pope, 2, 138, 179, 180; Rule of, 2, 97, 132, 179, 183; *Rerum condicio,* 180
Piva, M.L., 188
Plougeron, B., 137
Poor Catholics, the, 7

Poperinghe, 56
Préclin, E.-Jarry, 226
Pressencé, E., 137
Pretschnerova, E., 186
Primadizzi, Jacques (Giacomo), *min.*, 81
Pucher, Margaret, 157
Purgaj, M. Lidvira, 157

Radermecher, Apollonia, 53, 123
Ragusa, (Dubrovnik), see Dubrovnik
Raniero, *card.*, 14
Ratherius of Verona, *bis.*, 209, 210
Ravenna, 19
Recollects, the, 115-117
Reute, 187-190
Riccardo (official of Basel), 50
Riccardo, Annibaldi, *card.*, 12
Riedler, Henry, 39
Rigo, Arnold, *tor*, 180
Rinieri, I., 140, 226
Rieti, *mon.* of St. Clare (Sta. Chiara), 84
Reformed, the, 116, 117, 123, 131
Rinieri, I., 140
Rio di Pusteria-Muhbach, 131
Robespierre, Maximillian, 138
Robert of Arbrissel, 8
Rocca, G., 54, 55, 117, 118, 124, 145, 151, 163, 164, 170, 177, 179, 199
Rolando (*Bis.* of Spoleto), 24
Rome, 156, 157, 160, 167, 177, 179, 186, 189, 191, 192, 196, 212; church of *Sts.* Celsus and Julianus, 73
Rosa, M., 226

Rose of Viterbo, *St., pen.*, 23
Rousseau, J.J., 136
Rudiger, *min.* (confessor of *St.* Elizabeth of Hungary), 18
Rudolfo, Pio of Capri, *card.*, 97
Russo, C., 226
Russo, Mary Louise, 162, 163

Sailer, G.M., 141
Saint-Omer, 56, 58, 59, 61, 121, 122; house of St. John, 61; convent of *St.* Catherine of Sion, 58; convent of *St.* Margaret, 58, 59; hospital of Our Lady of the Sun, 59, 61
Salamanca, 98
Salizburg, 135, 136
San Juan del Rio (Querétaro, Mexico), 117
Saric, K.C., 158
Scarlatti, A., (musician), 126
Schmucki, O., *cap.*, 202, 212, 213
Sciamé, U.G., *ofm*, 156
Scirocco, A., 162, 226
Sebenik, 124
Sensi, M., 63, 65-68, 70, 72, 74, 75, 77-80, 82, 226
Servants of the Mother of Christ of Marseille, 14
Servants of Mary, 13-15, 23
Sicard, I., 226
Sixtus IV, Pope, 32, 86, 87, 89, 91, 92, 96, 103, 104, 107, 108, 110, 114, 177; *Ad Christi vicardi*, 89, 96; *Decet apostolicam Sedem*, 86; *Ex apostolicae servitutis*, 88; *Exponi nobis fecistis*, 89, 90; *Intelleximus quod longo*, 91; *Pridem per alias*, 87; *Quanto contentiones*, 88; *Romani*

pontificis, 86, 87
Sixtus V, Pope, 107, 175;
    Romani pontificis
    providentia, 106-107
Soyer, Capistrano, *ofm*, 131
Spoleto, 24, 29, 31, 32, 33, 35
Spineti, Francis, *tor*, 80
Spira, 26
Spirituals, the, 35, 43, 45, 80
Stephen of Giacomo da Como,
    tor, 71, 72
Stoetlin, Jacques, *min.*, 60
St. Germain, treaty of, 130
Strasburg, 25, 44, 149

Theodora (sister of St. Clare of
    Montefalco), 36
Temperini, L., *tor*, 29, 200-204,
    206, 226

Urban IV, Pope, 1
Urban V, Pope, 76
Urban VI, Pope, 66
Urban VIII, Pope, 117, 122;
    Pastoralis Romani Pontificis,
    122

Valencia, 171
Vendome, *card.*, 118
Vendramini, Elizabeth, 53, 144
Venice, 111, 113, 144, 177,
    178; St. Francis *della Vigna*,
    77
Verdiana of Castel Fiorentino,
    pen., 16
Vernet, F., 42, 44, 47, 226
Verona, 209
Vettori, M., 131

Tiepolo, Ambassador of
    Venice), 111
Todd, Mary Jane, (Sister Mary
    Joseph), 154
Todi, 66, 75, 76, 78; *mon.* of
    St. John, 66, 78
Tolone, 13
Torres, J., 128, 226
Toulouse, 28
Tournai, 56, 88
Trent, 132; Council of, 5, 41,
    53, 54, 81-83, 92, 93, 96,
    98-101, 107-110, 112, 115
Trinchera, R., 186
Trinci, Paoluccio, *min.*, 65, 67
Troiani, Mary Catherine, *b.*,
    156, 157

Ugolino of the Counts of
    Segni, *card.*, (Pope Gregory
    IX), 216

Congress of, 139, 140
Vienne, Council of, 43, 44, 48,
    49
Vincent de Paul, St., 118
Vinci, (muscian), 126
Virginia of Brincat (Sister)
    (Sister Margaret of the
    Sacred Heart), 172
Visentine, A., 186
Viterbo, 177; *mon.* of St.
    Agnes, 66, 84
Voltaire, F.M., 136

Wadding, L., *rec.*, 65, 90, 99,
    226
Waldensians, 7
Ward, Mary, 121-123
Wartburg, 18, 19
Wencelaus, Clement (*Bis.* of
    Augusta), 54
Wetter, E.M.I.

238

Willaert, L., 121, 226
William (Guglielmo) of Casale, *min.*, 70, 71
William (Guglielmo) of Malavalle, *St.*, 12
Wisbecq Brugelette), 59
Wittmers, Ch., 186, 196
Worms, 26

Ypres, 56
Yvette of Huy, *b.*, 8

Zanetto of Udine, *min.*, 88
Zechner, Mary Therese, 135
Zudaire, J., *cap.*, 187